The Pharmacist's Guide to Compensation for Medication Therapy Management Services

Notices

The Pharmacist's Guide to Compensation for Medication Therapy Management Services

Edited by

Michael D. Hogue, PharmD
Assistant Professor, Pharmacy Practice
Director, Experiential Program
McWhorter School of Pharmacy
Samford University
Birmingham, Alabama

and

Benjamin M. Bluml, BPharm, MS
Vice President, Research
American Pharmacists Association Foundation
Washington, D.C.

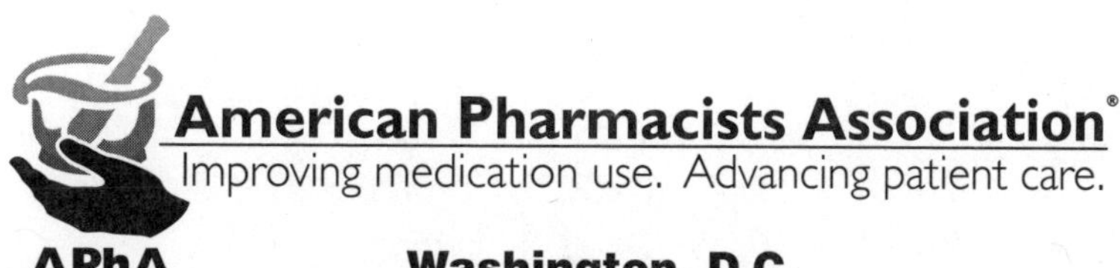

Washington, D.C.

Acquiring Editor: Sandra J. Cannon
Editor and Project Manager: Nancy Tarleton Landis
Proofreader: Kathleen K. Wolter
Indexer: Suzanne Peake
Book Design and Layout: Michele Danoff, Graphics by Design
Cover Design: Mariam Safi, APhA Creative Services

APhA was founded in 1852 as the American Pharmaceutical Association.

Published by the American Pharmacists Association
1100 15th Street, NW, Suite 400
Washington, DC 20005-1707
www.pharmacist.com

To comment on this book via e-mail, send your message to the publisher at aphabooks@aphanet.org.

Library of Congress Cataloging-in-Publication Data

The pharmacist's guide to compensation for medication therapy management services / edited by Michael D. Hogue and Benjamin M. Bluml.
p. ; cm.
Includes bibliographical references and index.
ISBN 978-1-58212-096-6 (alk. paper)
1. Pharmacy--Practice. 2. Insurance, Pharmaceutical services. 3. Pharmaceutical services. 4. Pharmaceutical services--Code numbers. I. Hogue, Michael D. II. Bluml, Benjamin M. III. American Pharmacists Association.
[DNLM: 1. Insurance, Pharmaceutical Services--economics--United States. 2. Medication Therapy Management--economics--United States. 3. Medication Therapy Management--organization & administration--United States. W 265 AA1 P536 2009]
RS100.P428 2009
615'.1068--dc22

2008036851

How to Order This Book

Online: www.pharmacist.com
By phone: 800-878-0729 (770-280-0085 from outside the United States)
VISA®, MasterCard®, and American Express® cards accepted

To all of the pharmacists who have dedicated
their professional lives to ensuring
appropriate medication use—payment or not—
just because it is what we do!

Contents

Section III

Resources

Preface

When *The Pharmacist's Guide to Compensation for Patient-Care Services* was published in 2002, payment for the nondispensing services of pharmacists was still largely a dream. Sporadic reports of pharmacists' being compensated directly by patients or occasionally by private insurance carriers were being published, and the profession was working hard to make the case that there was value in pharmacist engagement in ensuring appropriate medication use. Now, at the publication of *The Pharmacist's Guide to Compensation for Medication Therapy Management Services,* payment for our services has become better defined. Medicare Part D plans are routinely compensating pharmacists for helping patients make the best use of their medications, and private insurers and employers are beginning to recognize that dispensed medications that are not taken or not used appropriately are costing far too much.

The three factors that perhaps have had the greatest influence in moving pharmacy to the point of opportunity for compensation have been events outside our profession. First, the Health Insurance Portability and Accountability Act of 1996 mandated the creation of a new provider identification system, to be used for billing any health care product or service, that would ensure patient confidentiality. A plan for assigning these new National Provider Identifier (NPI) numbers was subsequently established by the Centers for Medicare and Medicaid Services. Because pharmacists (individually) had already received recognition as providers of mass immunization services under Medicare, the door was open for pharmacists to receive NPIs. The availability of provider identification numbers has removed a significant barrier to pharmacists' ability to bill for professional services. NPI numbers are available for pharmacies as well as for pharmacists (see https://nppes.cms.hhs.gov/NPPES/NPIRegistryHome.do), but pharmacists providing face-to-face services are encouraged to use their individual NPI numbers.

Second, the passage of the Medicare Prescription Drug Improvement and Modernization Act of 2003 (MMA) created an unprecedented opportunity for pharmacists in the Medicare Part D prescription drug program. This act (discussed in Chapter 3) was the first federal law specifically authorizing payment of pharmacists for medication therapy management services (MTMS). Although its language is not perfect, the law was appropriately seized by pharmacy professional societies, and education to equip pharmacists to take advantage of this new opportunity began in earnest.

The third major factor was a direct result of the MMA: recognition by the American Medical Association (AMA) Current Procedural Terminology (CPT) advisory committee that MTMS provided by pharmacists deserved their own coding scheme for billing. Previously, pharmacists' only real success in billing for professional services had been with using CPT evaluation and management codes to bill "incident to" the services of a physician. The requirements for billing in this manner are quite stringent and typically can be met only by pharmacists working in ambulatory care centers and physicians' offices. Although many pharmacists in those settings continue to be compensated on the basis of incident-to coding, the newly established Category I CPT codes for pharmacist-provided MTMS (described in Chapter 6) allow any pharmacist, regardless of practice setting, to bill for MTMS as long as the documentation requirements for use of the codes are met. Most likely, Category I codes would not have been approved without the outstanding efforts of the Pharmacist Services Technical Advisory Coalition, representatives from all national pharmacist membership organizations who helped build the coding infrastructure to support payment for pharmacist services.

Not discussed in detail in this book but important in its overall context is the emergence of a handful of privately held companies that seek to market pharmacists' MTMS to health plans and employers. These companies may offer unique opportunities for pharmacists to form networks and thereby gain access they would not have had individually to patients who are candidates for MTMS. It will be interesting to see what impact these companies have on pharmacy and pharmacists both financially and professionally—and potentially on the health care industry more broadly. Contact information for companies existing at the time of publication is included in the resources at the end of this book.

Never before has a path to compensation been clearer. Many details of individual pharmacist payment have yet to be worked out by insurers, but pharmacists have gained undisputed regulatory, policy, and professional recognition of their role in medication therapy management. We still have work to do to gain complete recognition that places the pharmacist on equal footing with other patient care providers, but our profession is well on its way to achieving its preferred future! We hope you enjoy this text, and we welcome your feedback on its content.

Michael D. Hogue
Benjamin M. Bluml
August 2008

Contributors

Marialice S. Bennett, BPharm
Professor of Clinical Pharmacy
Pharmacy Practice and Administration
The Ohio State University College of Pharmacy
Columbus, Ohio

Susan K. Bishop, MA[a]
Director, Federal Regulatory Affairs
American Pharmacists Association
Washington, D.C.

Daniel E. Buffington, PharmD, MBA
Director
Clinical Pharmacology Services, Inc.
Tampa, Florida

John Feather, PhD
Executive Director and CEO
American Society of Consultant Pharmacists
Alexandria, Virginia

Jean-Venable "Kelly" Goode, PharmD, BCPS
Associate Professor, Department of Pharmacy
Director, Community Pharmacy Practice Program
Virginia Commonwealth University School of Pharmacy
Richmond, Virginia

Brian J. Isetts, PhD, BCPS
Associate Professor
Department of Pharmaceutical Care & Health Systems
University of Minnesota College of Pharmacy
Minneapolis, Minnesota

Patty A. Kumbera, BPharm
Chief Operating Officer
Outcomes Pharmaceutical Health Care
Des Moines, Iowa

[a]*At the time of this writing.*

Brian R. Lehman, BPharm, MBA
Director of Pharmacy Benefits
OSU Managed Health Care Systems, Inc.
Columbus, Ohio

Lucinda L. Maine, BPharm, PhD
Executive Vice President
American Association of Colleges of Pharmacy
Alexandria, Virginia

Brand A. Newland, PharmD
Vice President
Outcomes Pharmaceutical Health Care
Des Moines, Iowa

Melody H. Ryan, PharmD, BCPS, CGP
Associate Professor
Department of Pharmacy Practice and Science
University of Kentucky College of Pharmacy
Lexington, Kentucky

Alan R. Spies, BPharm, JD, MBA, PhD
Assistant Professor of Pharmacy Administration
Southwestern Oklahoma State University College of Pharmacy
Weatherford, Oklahoma

Bradley P. Tice, PharmD
Chief Clinical Officer
PharmMD Solutions, LLC
Nashville, Tennessee

Virgil Van Dusen, BPharm, JD
Bernhardt Professor of Pharmacy Administration
Southwestern Oklahoma State University College of Pharmacy
Weatherford, Oklahoma

Timothy E. Welty, PharmD, BCPS
Professor
Department of Pharmacy Practice
McWhorter School of Pharmacy
Samford University
Birmingham, Alabama

Susan C. Winckler, BPharm, Esq[a]
Vice President, Policy and Communications
Staff Counsel
American Pharmacists Association
Washington, D.C.

[a] *At the time of this writing.*

Section I

Medication Therapy Management: Medicare and Beyond

Editor: Benjamin M. Bluml

Chapter 1

Evolution of Payment for Pharmacists' Services

Michael D. Hogue and Benjamin M. Bluml

Gaining compensation for nondispensing patient care services is perhaps the single most discussed topic in the pharmacy profession and has been for nearly four decades. This struggle is largely born out of the time when the pharmacy benefit was "carved out" of the total health care benefit and pharmaceutical products began being paid for by unique entities designed to manage the drug benefit: pharmacy benefit management companies (PBMs). Beginning in the late 1970s and accelerating through the 1980s and 1990s, PBMs experienced tremendous growth as employers and employer groups used them to manage the spiraling costs of employees' prescription drugs. But it was well before this that the modern debate about the worth of a pharmacist's professional services began.

The Professional Fee

In 1967, William S. Apple wrote the following:

> *Stated in simplest terms, the professional fee is the difference in dollars and cents between what the patient is charged for the prescription and what the pharmacist actually paid for the drug dispensed.... Rent, heat, light, advertising, insurance, salaries, and all the other expenses incurred in providing the professional service obviously must be paid for from the dollars realized as the professional fee. Dollars for taxes and return on educational and capital investments likewise must come from the same source.*[1]

Today we would call Apple's "professional fee" a dispensing fee. Few would believe that our current debate over payment for disease management and medication therapy management services (MTMS) is related to the original debate over the professional fee, but history does have a way of repeating itself. Apple's thoughts on the professional fee spurred a host of subsequent articles that pushed the envelope of pharmacists' compensation beyond dispensing services, including this reference in 1968 to a very early system of reimbursement:

> *[consider the] ancient apothecary who made no charge for the drugs which he dispensed, but...obtained a goodly fee for the incantations... which he uttered in preparing and dispensing them.*[2]

It is also interesting to note that the 1852 professional Code of Ethics adopted at the organizational meeting of the American Pharmaceutical Association (APhA; now the American Pharmacists Association) read:

As labor should have its just reward, and as the skill, knowledge and responsibility required in the practice of pharmacy are great, the remuneration of the pharmaceutist's services should be proportional to these, rather than to the market value of the preparation rendered.[2]

Thus, the fight to obtain compensation for pharmacists' professional services actually goes back well over 150 years, to the founding of our oldest professional society.

Another statement from 1968 could easily have been written today:

I have listened to many complaints from pharmacists about the status of our profession. It may be comforting to the self-employed pharmacist to be told by his accountant that last year he enjoyed a five percent increase in prescription dollar volume and a one percent increase in net profit, or for the salaried pharmacist to receive a 10 percent increase in salary, but the real fact of the matter is that both are losing ground. In a constantly expanding demand for pharmaceutical services, the self-employed pharmacist is retaining a smaller share and the salaried pharmacist is being pressured to constantly increase his productivity.[3]

Here, Apple was describing the tension that causes pharmacists to seek professional recognition through payment for services and, at the same time, express frustration that the profession is lagging behind in practice advancements.

In 1990 Hepler and Strand[4] defined "pharmaceutical care," a concept that has been broadly accepted by the profession but less broadly implemented in practice. Schools and colleges of pharmacy have embraced the all-doctor-of-pharmacy curriculum, graduating highly trained clinicians who are often frustrated once in practice because they either do not have the time to provide patient care or cannot get paid for those services.

Finally, as of 2006, the pharmacy profession is being paid for the first time by a major national insurer—Medicare—through contracted organizations known as prescription drug plan sponsors, to provide MTMS.[5] Perhaps pharmacy's ship has finally come in.

Drug Benefit versus Medical Benefit

After decades of the pharmacy benefit and medical benefit of most major employers being separate, nonlinked entities, many employers are beginning to recognize that more efficient, cost-effective use of pharmaceuticals can lead to a significant reduction in medical benefit expenditures (e.g., for physician visits and hospital stays). Employers are looking for ways to reduce health care costs while at the same time providing a robust health benefit package to entice the very best workers. A number of studies that document the effect of pharmacist-provided disease management and medication therapy management have been published in recent years, providing sound justification for employers and insurers to pay pharmacists for their services.

Perhaps the most significant such study is commonly known as the Asheville project, in which two employers in Asheville, North Carolina, partnered with a group of pharmacists trained in diabetes care. The employers contracted with the pharmacists through the APhA Foundation to work with employees with diabetes to achieve better glycemic control. The Asheville project had three specific aims: (1) assess short-term outcomes after the first 7 to 9 months of pharmaceutical care services, (2) assess the importance of environment, patient characteristics, and health behavior in explaining differences in clinical, economic, and humanistic outcomes of pharmaceutical care services for patients with diabetes, and (3) assess the persistence of outcomes in the patients with diabetes after up to 5 full years of pharmaceutical care services.[6]

The Asheville project's economic outcomes are of particular interest. Overall, the mean insurance costs per patient decreased each year in the 5-year analysis, with a fifth-year mean savings over baseline of $6602 per patient. At the same time, mean total prescription costs increased significantly each year. The study investigators attributed 60% of this increase to improved persistence and compliance with diabetes medications. It is important to note that the patients received an incentive to keep their appointments with their pharmacist: the employer waived the patients' out-of-pocket copayments for their diabetes medications as long as the patients kept their pharmacist appointments.

At baseline, the mean number of sick days away from work for the study group was 12.6 per patient per year, but at the end of the study this had been reduced by more than half, to 6.2 days. One of the two employers participating in the study estimated the value of this increase in productivity at $18,000 per year.[7]

The Asheville project strengthened the case for payment for pharmacists' clinical services. It showed that pharmacists can increase compliance with drug therapies, which is likely to increase prescription drug expenditure for the patient. But it also showed that this increase will likely be offset by decreases in overall health care costs (defined as expenses for hospitalization, emergency department visits, and physician visits). Finally, it showed that pharmaceutical care interventions to improve health outcomes will lead to a reduction in absenteeism, with a corresponding increase in employee productivity.

In 2004, the APhA Foundation launched similar projects in cooperation with five more national employers. Many state pharmacy associations, chain pharmacy organizations, and practice-based research networks affiliated with schools and colleges of pharmacy have also replicated the Asheville project. Early reports indicate that these efforts are producing results comparable to those in the Asheville project.

Schumock and colleagues[8] reviewed articles published between 1996 and 2000 demonstrating the value of pharmacists' services; an update of this review is planned for 2009. Another group recently reviewed economic evaluations of clinical pharmacy interventions in the hospital setting.[9]

Cost Avoidance and Service Valuation

Cost avoidance models have been used for many years to support the use of clinical pharmacists in both inpatient and outpatient settings. Pharmacists have not pressed the issue of direct compensation for their services, particularly in hospitals. In many cases, pharmacists' services have resulted in substantial overall savings (e.g., through reducing procedure costs or length of stay). Now, however, with increasing pharmacist salaries and decreasing insurance reimbursement, compensation for professional services has become quite important to the health system.

In 1983, hospitals lost their ability to bill in the fee-for-service fashion that outpatient providers continue to use for billing. In that year, diagnosis-related groups (DRGs) were established by Medicare for inpatient billing purposes.[10] The fee schedule under this system is based on the admission diagnosis of the patient. Hospitals receive a set amount per day for the DRG under which the patient is being treated. Of course, if the patient's condition worsens and expanded services are necessary, accommodations are made and reimbursement is adjusted. The DRG payment amount is considered to cover all hospital services, including pharmaceuticals and pharmacist services. Hospital pharmacists have used this payment system to their advantage, primarily for the purpose of justifying positions as health systems began to tighten their budgets and look for opportunities to eliminate unnecessary expenditures.

A question that often arises, particularly from ambulatory care pharmacists working in health systems, is "How do I assign a value to the services I provide?" This is a very difficult question to answer directly, because a number of factors must be considered. First, one must take into account personnel costs for providing the service (i.e., the pharmacist's salary), including time to provide direct patient care, time to document the service, and time to coordinate and communicate with other health care providers involved in the patient's care. The institution must also include fringe benefits (i.e., employee health insurance, payroll taxes, and other benefit expenses) in the calculation of personnel costs. The institution or pharmacy's accountant can provide this amount as a percentage of the pharmacist's salary.

Second, one must determine whether a specific intervention (I) typically results in avoidance of a particular event (E), and then assign a net value to this event:

Cost of I – Cost of E = Net value

Net value is either positive (indicating a net expense) or negative (indicating a net savings).

For example, Bond and Raehl[11] analyzed the impact of pharmacist-provided anticoagulation management in 1109 U.S. hospitals on death rates, length of stay, Medicare charges, bleeding complications, and transfusions. The National Clinical Pharmacy Services database and Expanded Modified Medicare Provider Analysis and Review data from the Centers for Medicare and Medicaid Services (CMS) were used for data extraction.

The mean charge for the study population, 717,396 Medicare patients with a diagnosis indicating a need for anticoagulation, was $17,124 per patient. In hospitals in which there was no pharmacist-provided heparin management service, Medicare charges were $1145 (6.6%) higher than the mean. In hospitals in which there was no pharmacist-provided warfarin management service, charges were $370 (2.16%) higher than the mean. For these two services in the Medicare population, this represents $885,550,334 in excess expenditures, which the authors imply could have been avoided if the hospitals had had a pharmacist-run anticoagulation service.

This study is just one example of ways in which cost avoidance can be valued. The authors conducted a national analysis of pharmacists' anticoagulation services, but a pre/post study design within the same institution could be used for a similar analysis. The costs associated with adverse events during a given time period in the absence of a pharmacist service could be compared with costs when the service is provided. The results would help establish the value of pharmacist services and could be used along with other factors to determine the fee that should be paid to the institution's pharmacists for their services.

Third, one must consider nonpersonnel overhead expenditures in determining the fee for professional services. In the inpatient setting, this might include technology needed to evaluate interventions (i.e., capital expenditures for computers or hand-held devices), drug information resources, continuing education and credentialing costs, laboratory expenses, and the cost of teaching aids and patient education material.

Finally, any determination of the fee one should charge for professional services must include a profit margin in order to perpetuate the service. Profit margins in the service industry are difficult to calculate. Pharmacists may find it helpful to refer to the national Medicare reimbursement schedules for physicians, which are updated annually on the CMS Web site (www.cms.hhs.gov/center/physician.asp), to assess whether the fees they are establishing are in line with those being paid by a national payer to other health care professionals. Data reported by the Lewin Group (Resource B) may also be useful.

Medical Model Recognition

In the past, many insurers have denied pharmacists payment for their claims because there was no method for identifying pharmacists as providers or because there were no coding systems that clearly allowed pharmacists to bill for their services. Both of these issues have now been resolved.

As part of the Heath Insurance Portability and Accountability Act (HIPAA) of 2003, CMS was mandated to issue a standardized National Provider Identifier (NPI) number to all health care providers so that electronic transmission of claims could be as secure and protective of patient-specific information as possible. By 2007, all insurers in the health care industry (including major medical, dental, and pharmacy insurers) had to accept NPI numbers as the sole identification in claims transactions.

Both pharmacists as individual providers and pharmacies as provider entities are eligible to apply for and receive an NPI number. This number belongs to the provider for the duration of the provider's career and moves with the provider as the provider changes practice locations. All providers receive a 10-digit NPI, and numbers for different types of providers are indistinguishable to the casual observer. Information and forms for applying for an NPI are available at https://nppes.cms.hhs.gov/NPPES/Welcome.do.

A significant step in the evolution of payment for pharmacist's services was the announcement in July 2005 by the American Medical Association's Current Procedural Terminology (CPT) advisory board of the creation of a set of time-based billing codes for MTMS provided by pharmacists. These codes were initially published by AMA as Category III codes, or codes for emerging procedures or services. Effective with publication of the January 2008 CPT manual, the codes were elevated to Category I status, meaning that these are documented services being provided in health care with a proven need for codes. The codes and their appropriate use are discussed in detail in Chapter 6.

References

1. Apple WS. Do you know your professional fee? *J Am Pharm Assoc.* 1967;NS7(1): 25–7.

2. Myers MJ. Professional fee: renaissance or innovation? *J Am Pharm Assoc.* 1968;NS8(12):628–31.

3. Apple WS. Pharmacists as professionals. *J Am Pharm Assoc.* 1968;NS8(7):344–6.

4. Hepler CD, Strand LM. Opportunities and responsibilities in pharmaceutical care. *Am J Hosp Pharm.* 1990;47:533–43.

5. Voluntary Medicare Prescription Drug Benefit. 42 CFR Part 423.

6. Cranor CW, Christenson DB. The Asheville project: factors associated with outcomes of a community pharmacy diabetes care program. *J Am Pharm Assoc.* 2003;43:160–72.

7. Cranor CW, Bunting BA, Christensen DB. The Asheville project: long-term clinical and economic outcomes of a community pharmacy diabetes care program. *J Am Pharm Assoc.* 2003;43:173–85.

8. Schumock GT, Butler MG, Meek PD, et al. for the 2002 Task Force on Economic Evaluation of Clinical Pharmacy Services of the American College of Clinical Pharmacy. Evidence of the Economic Benefit of Clinical Pharmacy Services: 1996–2000. Pharmacotherapy. 2003;23:113–32. Available at: www.accp.com/position/pos029.pdf.

9. De Rijdt T, Willems L, Simoens S. Economic effects of clinical pharmacy interventions: a literature review. *Am J Health Syst Pharm.* 2008;65:1161–72. Available at: www.ashp.org/s_ashp/docs/files/advocacy/policy_alert/AJHP_Economic_Effects_6_15_08.pdf.

10. 42 CFR §405.1804.

11. Bond CA, Raehl CL. Pharmacist-provided anticoagulation management in United States hospitals: death rates, length of stay, Medicare charges, bleeding complications, and transfusions. *Pharmacotherapy.* 2004;24:953–63.

Chapter 2

The Pharmacy Practice Activity Classification: A Foundation for Defining Medication Therapy Management Services

Lucinda L. Maine

Why do pharmacists have to go to school for 6 years just to take drugs from big bottles and put them in little ones?" Such a question has been asked of pharmacists and pharmacy educators innumerable times in past years—and, unfortunately, is still asked too often today. Certainly some of the functions pharmacists perform are more visible than other functions to outside observers, but how might it be possible to detail all of the functions and tasks that collectively make up the work of pharmacists in all settings?

This, in essence, was the question that propelled 10 pharmacy organizations to embark on a project from 1996 through 1998 that resulted in the Pharmacy Practice Activity Classification (PPAC). This chapter will review the rationale behind the effort to create a comprehensive classification of all pharmacists' activities, briefly describe the project, and discuss how the PPAC has helped the profession to gain appreciation for the scope and complexity of pharmacy practice and to thereby advance the case for compensation for our services.

Origins of the PPAC

The origination of the PPAC has been described in detail elsewhere.[1,2] A brief summary here will provide background for appreciating how this project has served as a framework for efforts to gain compensation for pharmacists' services.

Pharmacy practice has evolved over centuries as practitioners worked to keep pace with the needs of society. In early practice, compounding activities predominated. As manufacturers took on more of the formulation and mass production functions, pharmacists' role changed. Over the past three decades, increasing numbers of pharmacists have offered a wide range of new services aimed at addressing individual patient needs for medication management, as well as a variety of population-based services. All of these services, from traditional compounding to progressive patient care management, are part of the practice of pharmacy. Until the late 1990s, however, no comprehensive listing or classification of pharmacy services was available.

Other disciplines maintain classifications of services for billing, quality assurance, and other purposes. Medicine uses Current Procedural Terminology (CPT) coding as the basis for communicating to payers what services have been rendered. The Centers for Medicare and Medicaid Services (CMS) uses its own set of codes, referred to as the Health Care Procedural Coding System. Nursing has a reference taxonomy for the myriad activities in nursing practice, the Nursing Interventions Classification.[3]

Persistent calls from pharmacists and others working to advance a system for documenting and billing pharmacists' "cognitive services" resulted in the Professional Pharmacy Services (PPS) codes developed by the National Council for Prescription Drug Programs. Despite the availability of the PPS codes and other coding systems related to pharmacists' dispensing activities, there was no classification system that comprehensively communicated all activities encompassed in the global practice of pharmacy.

The American Pharmaceutical Association (APhA; now the American Pharmacists Association), with support from the Merck Foundation, convened a small work group in early 1997. The group met on the campus of the University of Iowa, where the leaders of the nursing classification project are located. By learning more about the nursing taxonomy project and considering the similarities and differences in pharmacy's rationale for embarking on a classification project, the team worked to define what a comprehensive taxonomy of pharmacy practice activities might encompass and how it might logically be structured. This group identified, from within pharmacy and from other disciplines, a list of reference sources to draw upon (Table 2-1).

The work group strongly believed that one pharmacy organization alone could not embark on such a project and expect to gain consensus on a comprehensive taxonomy for the whole profession. All of the profession's organizations were invited to collaborate, and a consortium of 10 organizations (Table 2-2) jointly embarked upon the PPAC development project.

Organizational collaborators were asked to identify pharmacy leaders from a wide variety of sectors of the profession to contribute to both the primary construction and to rounds of review and modification of the classification system. Various versions of the taxonomy were produced and circulated widely for comment, and the final classification was approved by each participating organization in 1998.

PPAC Structure and Framework

The PPAC is a hierarchical classification system that encompasses pharmacists' interventions and activities in logical clusters at as many as five distinct levels. The highest order in the taxonomy is the domain level; four domains were identified. Within the domains are classes of

Table 2-1

Sources Used in Building the Pharmacy Practice Activity Classification

Scope of Pharmacy Practice Project Function/Responsibilities delineation, developed by the American Association of Colleges of Pharmacy, APhA, American Society of Health-System Pharmacists, and National Association of Boards of Pharmacy
Principles of Practice for Pharmaceutical Care, as defined by APhA in 1996
National Council for Prescription Drug Programs (NCPDP) Professional Pharmacy Services Codes
Cognitive services coding frameworks used in Medicaid programs (e.g., Washington, Wisconsin)
Pharmacy activity classifications used by the On-line Prospective Drug Utilization Review Project (Iowa) and the National Community Pharmacists Association

Table 2-2

Organizations Collaborating to Create the Pharmacy Practice Activity Classification

Academy of Managed Care Pharmacy
American Association of Colleges of Pharmacy
American College of Apothecaries
American College of Clinical Pharmacy
American Pharmacists Association
American Society of Consultant Pharmacists
American Society of Health-System Pharmacists
National Association of Boards of Pharmacy
National Association of Chain Drug Stores
National Community Pharmacists Association

activities, which may be further broken down into specific activities or interventions. Some but not all activities are further divided into tasks and finally into steps. Figure 2-1 shows an example of all five levels of the taxonomy in one of the four domains. For the complete PPAC, go to www.pharmacist.com/AM/Template.cfm?Section=Search1&Template=/CM/HTMLDisplay.cfm&ContentID=2619 or telephone APhA at 800-237-2742.

The four domains of the PPAC are Ensuring Appropriate Therapy and Outcomes, Dispensing Medications and Devices, Health Promotion and Disease Prevention, and Health Systems Management. Representatives of each organization worked to reach consensus on the structure, hierarchy, content at each level, and specific language used for each PPAC component, incorporating feedback from practitioners and others both inside and outside the profession.

Several key points are pertinent to this overview of the PPAC. First, not every activity included in the classification is in the unique purview of pharmacists. Given the centrality of medication use to quality health care and the shared responsibility for medication use of prescribers, pharmacists, and other care providers, many of the activities and tasks included can be, and in fact are, included in other professions' classifications of their discipline-specific responsibilities. It is also true that pharmacists may delegate some of the activities in the PPAC to others, and specifically to their technical personnel.

Another key point is that because the PPAC is a comprehensive classification of the activities of pharmacists across all settings, it should not be assumed that every pharmacist performs all of the activities, tasks, or steps as part of his or her practice. Informal efforts to validate the PPAC when it was completed showed that pharmacists working in one practice setting were engaged in activities in specific sections of the classification, while those working in other settings identified different activities from other sections of the PPAC to characterize their practice. This is not surprising, but it is germane to discussion of how the PPAC serves as a basis for differentiating services for which pharmacists should be compensated.

Figure 2-1

Hierarchical Delineation of Pharmacy Practice Activity Classification

Domain A. Ensuring Appropriate Therapy and Outcomes

- Class A.1. Ensuring Appropriate Pharmacotherapy
- The pharmacist uses professional knowledge and skills to form clinical judgments.
  - Activity A.1.1. Establish relationship with patient
    - *Task A.1.1.1. Introduce self to patient and explain services*
    - *Task A.1.1.2. Determine patient's primary spoken language and communications ability/limitations*
    - *Task A.1.1.3. Determine patient's educational level*
  - Activity A.1.2. Obtain information to create and maintain confidential patient record
    - *Task A.1.2.1. Obtain diagnostic patient information*
      - Step A.1.2.1.1. Interview the patient or patient's representative
      - Step A.1.2.1.2. Obtain patient consent as needed to access medical information
      - Step A.1.2.1.3. Obtain/review the medical history or patient record
      - Step A.1.2.1.4. Consult other providers
    - *Task A.1.2.2. Obtain laboratory information*
      - Step A.1.2.2.1. Order laboratory tests
      - Step A.1.2.2.2. Obtain/review laboratory test results
    - *Task A.1.2.3. Obtain physical assessment information*
      - Step A.1.2.3.1. Perform physical assessment(s)
      - Step A.1.2.3.2. Obtain/review physical assessments performed by the patient or other providers
    - *Task A.1.2.4. Create a complete medication record*
      - Step A.1.2.4.1. Obtain and document prescription medication history
      - Step A.1.2.4.2. Obtain and document nonprescription medication history
      - Step A.1.2.4.3. Obtain and document complementary and alternative therapy history
      - Step A.1.2.4.4. Obtain and document devices history
      - Step A.1.2.4.5. Obtain the patient's social, family, and nutritional history

Initial Steps toward Recognition of Pharmacy's Classification System

Achieving consensus within the profession on a detailed, hierarchical classification of the myriad activities included in the contemporary practice of pharmacy, including administrative and public health-related activities, was no small feat, yet the leaders of the PPAC project knew that this was merely the beginning. Earning recognition for the taxonomy outside the profession was essential to accomplishing the aims that stimulated its creation.

One external target deemed essential for earning the PPAC significant recognition was the National Library of Medicine (NLM). NLM, and especially the office responsible for maintaining and integrating systems of classification relevant to medical science and practice, known as the Unified Medical Language System,[4] worked systematically throughout the 1980s and 1990s to identify logical classifications of a variety of biomedical systems and services. Leaders of the PPAC project met with NLM staff members before the PPAC was finished to explore the characteristics of a pharmacy practice classification that could earn NLM recognition. A key consideration for NLM was that a single classification product would be produced that would have broad acceptance by the primary community or communities of interest. This validated the original work group's instinct that a professionwide approach was important for the end product to find valuable uses.

Another key aspect of a classification from the vantage point of NLM was that the hierarchical structure could be developed with a numeric coding system that was sufficiently flexible to have additions over time yet be reasonably permanent. This would allow for cross-classification of the PPAC with other taxonomies and classification systems. This criterion was achievable in the work plan for the PPAC.

After initial discussions with NLM staff, the PPAC work group completed its effort, meeting the consensus and enumeration requirements. In 1999, NLM granted recognition of the PPAC as the official classification system for pharmacy practice activities in the Unified Medical Language System.

Laying the Groundwork for Defining Medication Therapy Management Services

Although APhA had long advocated recognition of pharmacists' cognitive services, a significant new commitment to advancing this agenda was developing around the time the PPAC project came to an end. APhA convened several teams of experts to serve as Strategic and Tactical Analysis Teams (STATs) on issues identified as essential to progress in the profession. A STAT on Payment and Empowerment was among these.

As the election season in 1999–2000 was getting under way, a variety of candidates drew attention to the lack of coverage of prescription medications in Medicare, the national health insurance program for the elderly and disabled. Candidates noted the inequity of a system that resulted in the highest bills for medication being paid by the oldest, and in some cases least fortunate, Americans. Believing that pharmacy needed a plan for enhancing coverage of medications and pharmacists' services for this population, APhA assigned the development of a viable proposal to the STAT on Payment and Empowerment.

One of the many elements in developing the proposal was identifying from the PPAC those activities that only pharmacists should perform, as distinguished from activities in the classification that could be delegated to other personnel. A copy of the delineation of pharmacist and technician activities, the latter being those not requiring professional judgment and performed under the supervision of a licensed pharmacist, is available upon request from APhA.

A model prescription benefit plan would recognize and provide payment for distinct levels of pharmacy service activities. Basic activities are those associated with filling and refilling routine prescriptions or medication orders. Increasingly complex pharmacy activities needed because of medication or patient characteristics (e.g., medications with special administration requirements, patients with multiple chronic conditions, polypharmacy) should be distinguished from simpler medication-distribution functions in a well-designed plan.

The PPAC continued to serve as an important reference for APhA committees and staff in the years after it was completed. During that time the terminology began to change with respect to pharmacists' patient care services; eventually, the terms "cognitive services" and "pharmaceutical care services" were subsumed by the term "medication therapy management services" (MTMS). This term was parallel to other recognized terms such as "medical nutrition therapy management," which won recognition as a covered Medicare benefit in the 107th Congress.

PPAC and Consensus on Medication Therapy Management Services

The political process in the 108th Congress (2003–2004) for inclusion of prescription medications and MTMS in the Medicare benefit is described in Chapter 3. The language in the Medicare Prescription Drug Improvement and Modernization Act of 2003 mandating inclusion of MTMS for high-risk, high-cost patients was extremely vague. Work by pharmacy organizations had secured the inclusion of MTMS in the legislation, and those same organizations appropriately determined in early 2004 that they should try to reach consensus on a specific portfolio of services that Congress, CMS, prescription drug plan sponsors, and Medicare beneficiaries should expect pharmacists to deliver to defined patient populations.

The leaders of the effort to reach consensus on MTMS turned to the PPAC as their resource document, since it was the product of consensus on pharmacists' services. It seemed logical that the organizations that had worked together to build the PPAC might continue working together to develop consensus on MTMS. Draft documents were prepared in advance by APhA and APhA Foundation staff members. Then, in a daylong session, members and staff representatives of the 10 national organizations listed in Table 2-2 and the National Council of State Pharmacy Association Executives (now the National Alliance of State Pharmacy Associations) worked to refine assumptions and specific language, with the goal of achieving consensus on the professional activities encompassed in MTMS. Chapter 3 discusses the consensus definition in more detail.

Conclusion

The investment in developing a comprehensive taxonomy of services and activities performed or overseen by pharmacists has benefited the profession. The PPAC has proven itself to be a clear and detailed framework and springboard for important projects. Perhaps no other project will hold more promise for changing the profession than the development of consensus on how pharmacy defines MTMS.

The official definitions and descriptions of MTMS by CMS remained extremely vague in the final regulations and other resources released in early 2005 to guide the work of entities that would begin delivering the Medicare Part D benefit in 2006. CMS was collecting significantly more data from plans regarding MTMS offerings in 2008, but it has not provided firm requirements for plans in regard to MTMS.

To those who have worked diligently for many years to earn recognition for pharmacists' patient care services, no matter what they are called, the following sentence from the 2005 final regulations is a welcome prophecy: "Notwithstanding the lack of current MTMP [medication therapy management program] standards and performance measures, we believe that MTMP must evolve and become a cornerstone of the Medicare Prescription Drug Benefit."[5]

Pharmacy's leaders will continue to work individually and collectively to provide clarity on the scope of MTMS, the value of these services, and quality assurance mechanisms to ensure that they are delivered appropriately to individuals and populations at risk from the adverse consequences of prescribed medications.

References

1. Kaminsky NU, Basgall J. Taxonomy project moves pharmacy practice closer to a uniform language. *J Am Pharm Assoc.* 1997;NS37(6):629–31.

2. Pharmacy Practice Activity Classification. *J Am Pharm Assoc.* 1998;38(2):139–48.

3. McCloskey JC, Bulechek GM, eds. *NIC (Nursing Interventions Classification): Iowa Intervention Project.* 2nd ed. St. Louis: Mosby-Year Book; 1999.

4. Unified Medical Language System. Available at: www.nlm.nih.gov/research/umls/metaa1.html. Accessed 2005 Mar 28.

5. *Federal Register.* 2005;70(Jan 28):4281.

Chapter 3

Understanding the Medicare Modernization Act of 2003 and Regulations Covering Medication Therapy Management Services

Susan C. Winckler and Susan K. Bishop

Although medication therapy management services (MTMS) are necessary for patients of any age, the first major health care insurance program to mandate coverage for medication therapy management (MTM) programs was Medicare. Medicare is the federal health insurance program for individuals age 65 years and older, some individuals with disabilities under age 65, and individuals with end-stage renal disease (those with permanent kidney failure requiring dialysis or a transplant).[1] In 2006, the Medicare program expanded from Part A hospital insurance[2] and Part B medical insurance[3] to include Part D insurance for prescription drug expenses, including MTMS for Medicare beneficiaries and dual-eligible beneficiaries[4] (Medicare beneficiaries who are also eligible for full benefits through their state Medicaid program).

Rather than being administered directly by the government, the Medicare drug benefit under Part D is administered by risk-bearing private plans that contract with the government. Approved plans either provide Part D coverage only (stand-alone prescription drug plans [PDPs]) or are integrated, managed care plans offering all Medicare benefits (Medicare Advantage prescription drug plans [MA-PDs] under Part C Medicare Advantage, a managed care approach to Part A and Part B). PDPs and MA-PDs have some flexibility in designing their plans, but the MTM programs must meet certain requirements established by Congress and detailed in subsequent regulations by the Centers for Medicare and Medicaid Services (CMS).

The purpose of the MTM program under Medicare Part D is to provide services that will optimize therapeutic outcomes for targeted beneficiaries. The Medicare Prescription Drug Improvement and Modernization Act of 2003 (MMA) defines the MTM benefit as follows:

> *A medication therapy management program...is a program of drug therapy management that may be furnished by a pharmacist and that is designed to assure...that covered Part D drugs under the prescription drug plan are appropriately used [by targeted beneficiaries] to optimize therapeutic outcomes through improved medication use, and to reduce the risk of adverse events, including adverse drug interactions. Such a program may distinguish between services in ambulatory and institutional settings.*[5]

Eligibility for Medicare Coverage of MTMS

In consideration of funding limitations as Congress designed the new drug benefit, only certain beneficiaries are eligible for Medicare coverage of necessary MTMS.

This chapter was reviewed by Marcie Bough, Anne Burns, and Kristina Lunner of the American Pharmacists Association Government and Professional Affairs staff.

CMS has clarified that Part D beneficiaries who do not meet the criteria for "targeted beneficiaries" are responsible for the costs of necessary MTMS.[6] (As with other health care services, all patients have the option of accepting or refusing MTMS.)

Medicare Part D enrollees who are considered targeted beneficiaries under the statute include the following:

1. Patients who have multiple chronic diseases (e.g., diabetes, asthma, hypertension, hyperlipidemia, congestive heart failure),
2. Patients who are taking multiple covered Part D drugs, and
3. Patients who are identified as likely to incur annual costs for covered Part D drugs that exceed a level specified by the Secretary of the Department of Health and Human Services.

Under the CMS implementing regulations, PDPs and MA-PDs are allowed to determine the number of medications and the number and type of chronic diseases that qualify a plan enrollee as a targeted beneficiary. Thus, the plans have a part in identifying targeted beneficiaries.

The limitations established by CMS and the plans significantly narrow the population of beneficiaries eligible for Medicare coverage of MTMS. Often, patients with only one chronic disease could benefit from MTMS, particularly if the disease involves significant medication therapy. In 2006 the number of chronic conditions required by plans for eligibility varied from two to five, and many plans required patients to have specific conditions such as diabetes and congestive heart failure in order to qualify for the service.[7] According to CMS data, Part D MTM plan criteria for 2007 were comparable to those for 2006.[8] The required number of chronic conditions again ranged from two to five, and 89% of the plans required the beneficiary to have a specific chronic condition or conditions to qualify.

The requirement for multiple covered drugs is also a significant limiter. Plan definitions of "multiple" covered drugs in 2006 ranged from 2 medications to 24, with a median of 6.[7] In 2007 the number of required Part D medications again varied from 2 to 24.[8]

The drug expenditure threshold further focuses Medicare resources on patients who may most benefit from MTMS; analysts estimate that one in five Medicare beneficiaries has an annual drug expenditure of $5000 or more. CMS defined the level of annual costs to be used as a threshold for MTMS eligibility at $4000 for plan years 2006 and 2007, and it is anticipated that the threshold will remain at $4000 through 2009. Nearly all Medicare Part D plans have consistently followed that threshold since 2006.

Patients who do not meet the criteria for targeted beneficiaries have the opportunity to secure necessary MTMS at their own expense. Also, some Part D plans are offering MTMS to all beneficiaries even though Medicare support for these services is limited to the targeted population. In 2007, CMS allowed plans to submit requests to make changes to their programs in order to promote evolving MTM best practices.[8]

MTM Program Structure

The law requires the plans to develop their approach to MTMS in cooperation with licensed and practicing pharmacists and physicians and specifies that the MTM programs may include elements intended to

- Enhance enrollee understanding—through beneficiary education, counseling, and other means—that promotes the appropriate use of medications and reduces the risk of potential adverse events associated with medications,
- Increase enrollee adherence to prescription medication regimens (such as refill reminders, special packaging, and other compliance programs and other appropriate means), and
- Detect adverse events and patterns of overuse and underuse of prescription drugs.

Despite recommendations that CMS define a minimum package of MTMS that plans must provide, CMS decided against such an approach in the final regulations and in 2006 through 2008 guidance to plans. Although the regulation makes reference to the pharmacy profession's definition of MTM, CMS believes that "insufficient standards and performance measures exist to support further specification for MTM Program (MTMP) services and service level requirements." Plans have flexibility in determining the MTMS they offer.

CMS documented its belief that MTM will "evolve and become a cornerstone of the Medicare Prescription Drug Benefit" and indicated a commitment to work with pharmacy and other stakeholders to evaluate MTM programs and establish appropriate standards. CMS plans to identify best practices that can eventually be adopted as standards for MTM programs. Efforts to identify such best practices and measure providers against them are ongoing and are a component of PQA, Inc., a pharmacy quality alliance (www.pqaalliance.org). Established in 2006, the alliance plans to improve health care quality and patient safety by measuring performance at the pharmacy and pharmacist levels.

MTM Compensation

In setting payment structures for MTMS, the law requires plan sponsors to consider the resources used and time required to implement the MTM program. CMS did not designate a certain amount plans must pay pharmacists or other providers of MTM program services. CMS does not have statutory authority to set such rates, so fees for MTMS are established by the plans and the providers with whom they contract. The Lewin consulting group, commissioned by the American Pharmacists Association (APhA), conducted a survey of the costs involved in delivering MTM and published recommended unit payments for MTMS based on industry estimates.[9] The executive summary of that project is included as Resource B at the end of this book.

Plans must describe, as part of their application to participate in Part D, how they will consider the resources used and the time required to implement MTM in establishing their fees. Plans must, upon request, disclose to CMS the management and dispensing fees and the portion paid for MTMS to pharmacists and other providers. A significant portion of the cost is determined by the MTM provider—whether a pharmacist or other health care professional delivers the services. The MMA explicitly identifies pharmacists as MTM providers, but it also creates the opportunity for other qualified providers to participate. In the final implementing regulations, CMS articulated the belief that pharmacists will be providers of MTMS but emphasized that plans can also use other qualified health care professionals as providers of MTMS. According to a survey of plans by APhA, although a majority of plans do not include face-to-face interaction as part of their MTM programs, the plans that do so use pharmacists as the primary providers of those services.[7]

CMS considers MTM programs to be administrative activities similar to quality assurance, drug utilization review, or fraud, abuse, and waste control measures. Therefore, MTM program services do not involve direct beneficiary cost sharing, and Part D enrollees who qualify as targeted beneficiaries are not required to pay separate fees for these services. Program costs are, of course, reflected in the plan's premium rate.

To facilitate monitoring of MTM operations, plans must provide CMS with information about the procedures and performance of their MTM programs according to guidelines specified by CMS.

Defining MTMS

As described in this chapter, the parameters for MTM contained in the statute and regulations governing the Medicare program are quite broad. This breadth is consistent with the approach of other payers: payer policy should articulate the parameters for coverage for eligible services but does not define health care practice. The actual structure and definition of health care practice comes from the health care professions and their regulators, articulated in state practice acts and standards of practice.

Medicare's addition of coverage for prescription drugs and MTMS served as an impetus for the pharmacy profession to define MTMS and articulate criteria for MTM programs. The profession envisioned a comprehensive definition, one that would encompass MTM programs and services offered in all types of settings and situations.

The development of the profession's consensus definition was chronicled in the *Journal of the American Pharmacists Association*[10] by pharmacist Ben Bluml, an APhA Foundation staff member who helped shepherd the definition development process. APhA, as the only national professional association representing all pharmacists, committed to coordinating the efforts to define MTMS. A working group was convened to develop a draft document, and three essential concepts emerged:

1. MTM is a distinct service or group of services that can occur in conjunction with or independent of the provision of a drug product.
2. MTM encompasses a broad range of professional activities and responsibilities.
3. MTM programs should include a core set of considerations to provide value to key stakeholders in the health care delivery system.

These concepts and the draft definition were presented to 11 national organizations, with the goal of developing language that was acceptable to every organization. As acknowledged by Bluml, achieving consensus with such organizational diversity presented a daunting challenge, but it would add immeasurable strength to the final document. At the conclusion of the process, each organization approved the definition and program criteria (Figure 3-1), providing the profession's description of this important practice.

The definition distinguishes MTMS from dispensing services, noting the focus on the patient rather than the individual prescription. The consensus document also confirms the use of MTM as a label for a collection of services—a broad range of professional activities and responsibilities within the pharmacist's or other qualified health care professional's scope of practice. MTM describes efforts by pharmacists to improve medication use and advance patient care, from formulating a medication treatment plan to administering medications to providing education and training.

The pharmacy organizations recognized that the MTM program structure would have an important role in the success of these services. Thus, the consensus development process addressed criteria essential for MTM programs, including a preference for face-to-face interaction between the patient and pharmacist and the recognition that pharmacists and other health care professionals should be allowed to identify

Figure 3-1

Medication Therapy Management Services Definition and Program Criteria[a]

Medication therapy management is a distinct service or group of services that optimize therapeutic outcomes for individual patients. *Medication therapy management services* are independent of, but can occur in conjunction with, the provision of a medication product. *Medication therapy management* encompasses a broad range of professional activities and responsibilities within the licensed pharmacist's, or other qualified health care provider's, scope of practice. These services include but are not limited to the following, according to the individual needs of the patient:

a. Performing or obtaining necessary assessments of the patient's health status;

b. Formulating a medication treatment plan;

c. Selecting, initiating, modifying, or administering medication therapy;

d. Monitoring and evaluating the patient's response to therapy, including safety and effectiveness;

e. Performing a comprehensive medication review to identify, resolve, and prevent medication-related problems, including adverse drug events;

f. Documenting the care delivered and communicating essential information to the patient's other primary care providers;

g. Providing verbal education and training designed to enhance patient understanding and appropriate use of his/her medications;

h. Providing information, support services, and resources designed to enhance patients' adherence with their therapeutic regimens;

i. Coordinating and integrating medication therapy management services within the broader health care-management services being provided to the patient.

A program that provides coverage for *medication therapy management services* shall include:

a. Patient-specific and individualized services or sets of services provided directly by a pharmacist to the patient.[b] These services are distinct from formulary development and use, generalized patient education and information activities, and other population-focused quality assurance measures for medication use.

b. Face-to-face interaction between the patient[b] and the pharmacist as the preferred method of delivery. When patient-specific barriers to face-to-face communication exist, patients shall have equal access to appropriate alternative delivery methods. Medication therapy management programs shall include structures supporting the establishment and maintenance of the patient[b]–pharmacist relationship.

c. Opportunities for pharmacists and other qualified health care providers to identify patients who should receive medication therapy management services.

d. Payment for medication therapy management services consistent with contemporary provider payment rates that are based on the time, clinical intensity, and resources required to provide services (e.g., Medicare Part A and/or Part B for CPT[c] and RBRVS[d]).

e. Processes to improve continuity of care, outcomes, and outcome measures.

[a]*Approved July 27, 2004, by the Academy of Managed Care Pharmacy, the American Association of Colleges of Pharmacy, the American College of Apothecaries, the American College of Clinical Pharmacy, the American Society of Consultant Pharmacists, the American Pharmacists Association, the American Society of Health-System Pharmacists, the National Association of Boards of Pharmacy,* the National Association of Chain Drug Stores, the National Community Pharmacists Association, and the National Council of State Pharmacy Association Executives (now the National Alliance of State Pharmacy Associations). (*Organization policy does not allow the National Association of Boards of Pharmacy to take a position on payment issues.)*

[b]*In some situations, medication therapy management services may be provided to the caregiver or other persons involved in the care of the patient.*

[c]*Current Procedural Terminology.*

[d]*Resource-Based Relative Value Scale.*

candidates for MTM services. Finally, the groups approved an ongoing commitment to processes intended to improve continuity of care, outcomes, and outcome measures.

The final definition is applicable to all qualified health care professionals. The definition and program criteria should help CMS and Part D plans to further enhance the reality of MTM under the Medicare program.

References

1. 42 USC 1395c.
2. 42 USC 1395d.
3. 42 USC 1395j.
4. 42 USC 1395w-101.
5. Medicare Prescription Drug Improvement and Modernization Act of 2003. Pub Law 108-173.
6. *Federal Register.* 2005;70(Jan 28):4281.
7. Touchette DR, Burns AL, Bough MA, et al. Survey of medication therapy management programs under Medicare Part D. *J Am Pharm Assoc.* 2006;46:683–91.
8. Ketchum MB. Update on Medication Therapy Management (MTM) Programs in Part D: Centers for Medicare and Medicaid Services. Presented at: American Pharmacists Association and National Association of Chain Drug Stores Foundation Conference on Medication Therapy Management in Community Pharmacy: Building Process, Partnership and Outcomes, September 19–20, 2007.
9. The Lewin Group. Medication therapy management services: a critical review. *J Am Pharm Assoc.* 2005;45:580–7.
10. Bluml B. Definition of medication therapy management: development of profession-wide consensus. *J Am Pharm Assoc.* 2005;45:566–72.

Chapter 4

Incorporating Medication Therapy Management Services into Managed Care and Private Health Plans

Marialice S. Bennett and Brian R. Lehman

Rising health care costs are driving managed care and private health plans to explore new options for containing costs while still providing optimal care for those enrolled in their plans. To control their high costs for prescription drugs, plans have increasingly used generic product substitution, tiered co-payments, tighter formularies, and prior authorization for expensive medications. But new, unique approaches to containing costs are needed. Plans are beginning to shift their focus to services that keep their enrollees well and help them make the best use of their medications—an approach that may actually increase medication use and costs while decreasing total health care costs.

Wellness programs have been shown to decrease health plan costs by educating plan members to stay well and identifying those at high risk before complications become evident. Estimates of the return on investment for each dollar spent on such programs range from $1.40 to $13.[1–3] Lifestyle changes such as weight loss, increased exercise, and smoking cessation have been associated with decreased or at least delayed onset of many chronic diseases, including diabetes, heart disease, and lung disease.[4] Excess medical costs attributed to overweight and obesity have been estimated to be 21–36% higher than costs for persons who are not overweight.[5,6] Identifying the risks of the insured population is the first step in the design and implementation of programs and interventions to address these risks before complications arise.

Disease management and therapeutic drug monitoring programs help patients make better use of their medications. These programs typically result in better medication adherence and improved health care utilization—as well as additional fees for the provider offering the service.[7,8] Drug costs, provider fees, and procedure costs may rise while total health care costs decrease as a result of fewer emergency room (ER) and hospital visits and decreased costs related to complications of therapy. Additional benefits of such programs are decreased absenteeism and increased productivity while the employee is at work ("presenteeism").

Educating Payers

Community pharmacists are the health care providers best positioned to encounter a health plan's enrollees during their normal daily activities. Although pharmacists are well trained in pharmacology, pathophysiology, therapeutics, and drug therapy monitoring, payers' view of pharmacists practicing in community and home delivery settings is influenced mainly by personal experience and "education" from sources unfamiliar with the practice of pharmacy in the community setting. Pharmacists are recognized for dispensing and counseling members on medications and answering drug information questions, but the community pharmacist may be too busy with dispensing-related activities for in-depth consultation with plan members, and pharmacies are not open around the clock.

Pharmacy benefit managers (PBMs) want to increase the use of home delivery service. They use the following arguments in marketing home delivery to payers: the discount is greater with home delivery; dispensing errors are fewer; pharmacists are available to members by telephone around the clock; and PBMs have telephone or mail disease management programs. Because PBM representatives meeting with self-insured employers tend to emphasize medication discounts and the size and composition of their retail networks, employers often do not recognize the role pharmacists could play in medication therapy management.

Pharmacists, especially community practitioners, must educate payers about the impact pharmacists can have on plan members and on the bottom line. Community pharmacists can market the value of relationships with patients and face-to-face encounters in the environment where plan members live, work, and shop. This value can be documented by assessing the percentage of patients counseled, evaluating the results and impact of drug utilization review (DUR), and measuring the degree of plan member satisfaction with face-to-face encounters with the pharmacist. Economic impact can be evaluated in terms of generic medication substitution rates, generic dispensing rates, and cost savings and cost avoidance (see Chapter 1) associated with interventions secondary to patient interactions and DUR. Educating the payer could result in reimbursement for these activities. Conversely, pharmacies with poor performance in these areas could be excluded from the community pharmacy network.

Ultimately, plans could change their pharmacy benefit to enhance the delivery of pharmacists' services. They could reduce co-payment incentives for home delivery, remove mandatory home delivery of maintenance medications, and allow 90-day supplies of maintenance medications at community pharmacies. Or, maintenance medications could be filled centrally or by a home delivery service and distributed to the local pharmacy, where reimbursement would be based on services such as medication counseling, DUR, and medication management provided by the pharmacist.

With a better understanding of payers—how they perceive community pharmacy and how they came to that perception—pharmacists can develop a plan for marketing services that meet the needs of payers and their employ-

Figure 4-1

Current Managed Care Model for Medication Therapy Management Services (MTMS). In 2008, many health care purchasers were delivering a hybrid of MTMS using both the right and left sides of this model in some combination. PBM = pharmacy benefit manager.

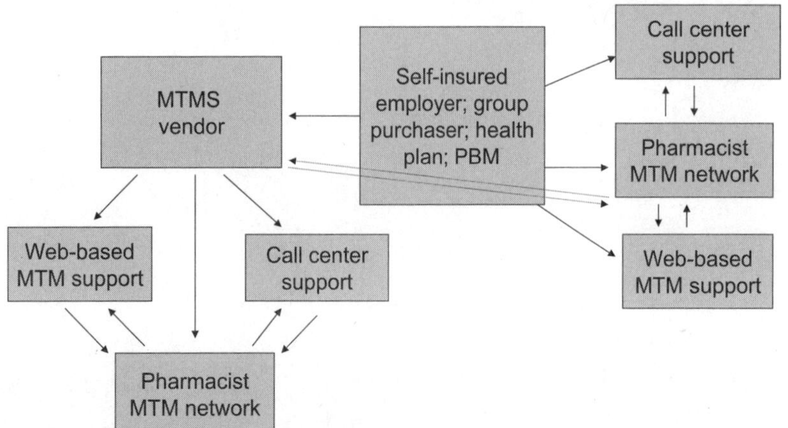

ees. Pharmacists and pharmacist networks can then formulate a business plan for delivery and reimbursement of medication therapy management services (MTMS). Medicare Part D positions pharmacists to become recognized providers and to develop networks of pharmacist providers to implement MTMS. National Provider Identifier (NPI) numbers and new pharmacy billing codes (Chapter 6) open the door for reimbursement for pharmacists' services. Figure 4-1 illustrates how managed care plans are beginning, in 2008, to cover MTMS and provide those services to individual members. As models for the provision of MTMS through managed care plans evolve, there are many opportunities for pharmacists.

Identifying the Plan's Need

The first step in incorporating MTMS into managed care and private health care plans is to identify the need of the plan. In what disease states, age groups, and employee populations are health plan costs most difficult to control, and which patients are at greatest risk for incurring high costs in the future?

Traditional health plans identify their needs by first examining aggregate data on the top reasons for and costs of ER and hospital visits. Costly diagnostic categories identified by many health plans include musculoskeletal, cardiovascular, and mental health conditions. Programs designed to emphasize prevention and adherence to a treatment plan will decrease the frequency and costs of ER and hospital visits.

Plans also focus on insured members with high expenditures; total health care cost, high-cost procedures, high-cost drugs, and high-risk drugs are frequently targeted. Tissue plasminogen activator, therapy for drug-induced anemias, and antibiotics are examples of drug therapies for which protocols and pharmacist-managed services can lead to more appropriate and cost-effective use. Examples of high-risk drugs include medications for HIV infection, oncology regimens, and anticoagulation therapies. Providers have documented improved care and cost savings when pharmacists' services focused on such therapies are implemented.[9] Conditions likely to affect absenteeism and presenteeism may also be targeted; for example, childhood asthma frequently requires a parent to miss work, and depression results in missed days or lack of attentiveness when the employee is at work.

Chronic diseases such as hypertension, diabetes, hyperlipidemia, and asthma frequently require lifelong treatment and are associated with serious complications if not managed properly. Programs designed to support patients with chronic diseases can have an impact on both present and future health care costs. For example, in the American Pharmacists Association program for diabetes patient self-management, total mean health care costs per patient for the initial year of enrollment were $918 lower than projections.[8]

Disease management programs offered at the work site require commitment from the employer, the patient, and the provider. The employer needs to market the program to employees, provide incentives for participation, and permit time away from work to participate. The employer also needs to reimburse the providers of service. The patient needs to actively engage in the program and be committed to change over a long period of time. The provider may need to commit to new delivery models such as an appointment-based practice at the work site or mobile care throughout the work site. For consistency of care, the provider needs to follow appropriate, accepted guidelines.

Wellness and prevention services allow health plans to proactively identify the risk of the insured population before expensive conditions or complications appear. Wellness and prevention services include health risk assessment (HRA) screenings, educational programming, intervention services, and follow-up management strategies. HRA identifies risks in individual plan members and in the aggregate insured population. Programs and services can then target the needs of the screened population (Figure 4-2). Incentives may be offered for lifestyle modifications and program involvement. Pharmacists can provide wellness and prevention services to help identify the health plan's needs and can design services to meet the identified needs (Table 4-1). HRA can also guide the design of the health plan itself (Figure 4-3).

With increasing demand to document outcomes, health care providers need to incorporate services that enhance the consistency and the quality of their practices. Quality-measurement organizations (e.g., the National Committee for Quality Assurance [NCQA]) and insurers themselves are setting quality indicators for practices, providers, and insurers. Pharmacist-provided MTMS can enhance outcomes. Pharmacists working in partnership with physician groups to provide disease management programs and drug therapy monitoring services can improve quality indicators for the physician group, increase access to the physician group, and decrease total costs to the health plan.[7,8]

Pharmacists need to partner with payers and employers to identify the needs of managed care plans, private health plans, and employees. Analysis of the health plan's aggregate data on ER visits, hospital admissions, high-impact disease states, high-use drugs, and high-cost drugs may be a starting point. Developing and implementing a wellness and prevention program or practicing within an existing program will help the pharmacist identify the needs of the insurer and design programs to meet those needs. Pharmacists can also incorporate MTMS into health plans by helping other health care providers meet the needs of their patients while controlling costs.

Designing Programs

Once the needs of payers and employees are identified, the pharmacist must design an intervention program to meet those needs. Pharmacist providers may

Figure 4-2

Wellness Model

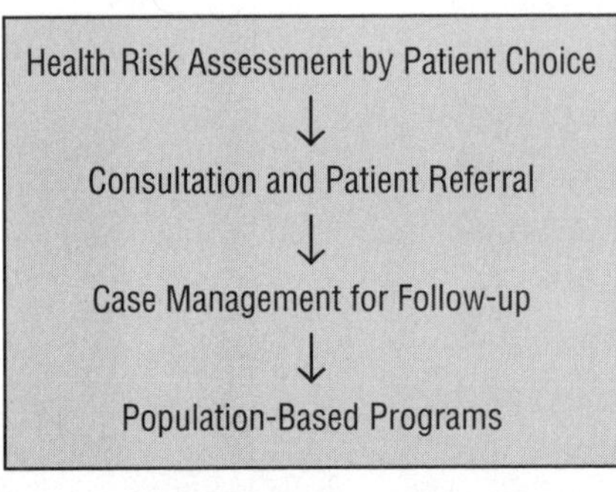

Figure 4-3

Health Plan Model

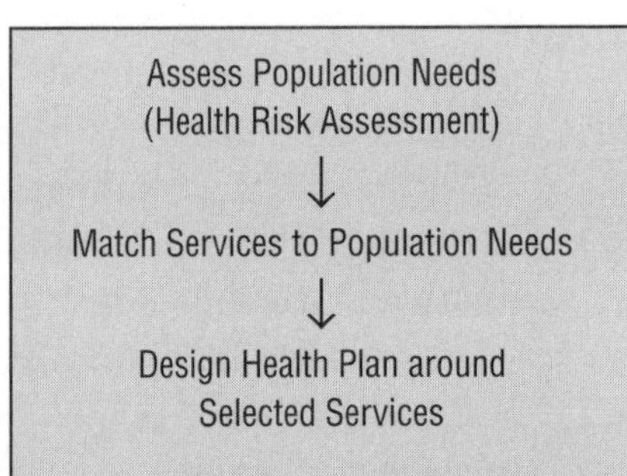

Table 4-1

Roles of Health Risk Assessment

Roles
Assess needs
Provide baseline data
Guide promotion activities and health education
Determine intervention strategies
Evaluate intervention strategies

develop disease management programs and therapeutic drug monitoring programs, or they may purchase them. The design of such programs involves identifying the level of intervention, developing a protocol, and determining the method of delivery. Characteristics of disease management programs are listed in Table 4-2.

Programs will need physician buy-in. Identifying a physician champion or opinion leader within the health plan will help drive the process. Physicians will value having input to the program; they will want to receive reports of the outcomes for their patients and the program. Physicians may receive incentives to participate.

Pharmacists may choose to work with other health care professionals to develop a clinically sound product using national guidelines and evidence-based medicine; current practice guidelines for virtually any therapeutic area can be found at www.guidelines.gov. An individual with a business background could give useful feedback on the value of the product to a payer. Alternatively, pharmacy providers may choose to purchase a medication therapy management program developed by a company, organization, or pharmacy network.

Whether created or purchased, such programs need to address different patient populations. Healthy employees need screening and awareness programs to identify risks before they are problems. Diagnosed employees need programs for disease management and therapeutic drug monitoring to reduce risks. The sickest employees need case management and intervention programs.

Table 4-2

Characteristics of Disease Management

Physician-directed care
Comprehensive care
Goal-oriented treatment guidelines
Patient-specific outcome goals
Patient education and empowerment
Population management
Evidence-based medicine

Four-Level Design

Programs can be designed at four levels (Figure 4-4). ***Level 1,*** assessment and awareness, can serve as an entry point.[10] At this level, persons in the health plan's insured population can complete an HRA that involves a detailed patient questionnaire addressing individual health risks, coupled with quantifiable screening tests. HRAs can be Web-based and permit aggregate compilation of the data.

An HRA questionnaire with breadth would include personal medical history, medication use, and recent hospitalizations or ER visits, along with targeted family history. Immunizations, preventive examinations, weight and nutrition history, exercise and fitness history, smoking and alcohol consumption, stress level and stress management techniques, automobile and home safety issues, and women's and men's health categories might also be included. Questions related to readiness to change in specific areas can help expedite and direct the counseling session to follow.

Blood pressure, height, and weight can be measured by the provider, and point-of-care testing devices can be used to measure cholesterol and glucose. (The provider performing point-of-care testing must follow current procedures specified by the Clinical Laboratory Improvement Amendments and the Occupational Safety and Health Administration.) The information can be added to the database and an individualized report can be produced for the participant.

Chapter 4

A wellness-focused health care provider identifies and discusses the potential risks with the patient and makes the appropriate interventions and referrals. The client enters the system to promote health rather than to prevent disease. The system is driven by a positive, holistic approach to health, rather than by fear of disease.

The physical entry point for Level 1 care may be a physician's office or clinic, a work-site health care clinic, or a community pharmacy wellness and patient care center. As a vital part of the wellness team, the pharmacist can provide health screenings, medication reviews, education, interventions and referrals to higher levels of care, and medication management for short-term care issues. Aggregate data for specific populations (i.e., an employer group) can identify risks and drive programming for the next levels of care.

Figure 4-4

Levels of Program Design

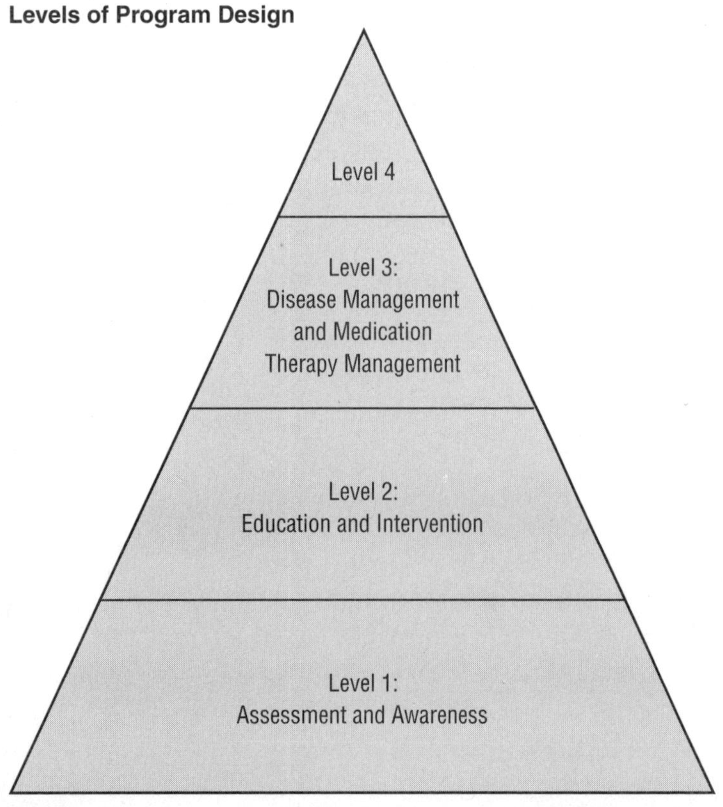

Level 2 care involves education and intervention. Participants with identifiable risks are referred to programs that provide education on their risks, lifestyle changes (e.g., nutrition, fitness, and smoking cessation), and stress management techniques, as well as support groups for dealing with issues such as divorce, death, and aging.

Educational programs on chronic diseases such as diabetes, hypertension, and dyslipidemia can be offered at the work site. Connections to resources that will help support behavioral change should be readily available and included as part of the health care benefit. Services such as weight loss, exercise, and smoking cessation programs can be made available at the physician's office, in the community where clients live, at local community pharmacy wellness and patient care centers, and at the work site. These services will usually be provided by physician extenders (including pharmacists) in collaboration with physicians on the team. Incentives can be provided for patients who can document sustained lifestyle changes.

In Level 2 care, the pharmacist can be part of the interdisciplinary team supporting behavioral changes. Along with providing program support, the pharmacist can assess patients' capability for self-care (i.e., whether they can treat their own symptoms or conditions) and assist patients in the selection of nonprescription medications. As more medications switch from prescription to nonprescription status, the pharmacist will have an important role in ensuring that nonprescription products are appropriately selected and monitored. Patients who are found to need more than self-care and assistance with nonprescription product selection may be referred by the pharmacist for Level 2, 3, or 4 care. The pharmacist may also provide medication management services for short-term issues and prevention. These activities need to be documented and shared with the payer.

Level 3 interventions involve disease and medication therapy management services. An interdisciplinary team provides collaborative care to best meet the needs of the patient. The providers serve as educators, coaches, and monitors of therapy in a consistent, more frequent manner than the current health care system generally permits. Policies, procedures, and protocols for all disciplines are driven by integrated, evidence-based medicine. Providers develop a deeper level of trust and a better understanding of the contributions of each discipline to the care of the patient. They begin to "share their borders," recognizing that they have a common professional interest in and knowledge base for obtaining the desired patient outcomes.[11]

Pharmacists can use their knowledge of medication therapy and monitoring to ensure that patients make the best use of their medications, focusing on chronic disease therapy, narrow therapeutic index drugs, polypharmacy, and adherence. Again, services can be provided from a physician's office or clinic, a work-site clinic, or a community pharmacy patient care center.

Level 4 care provides patients who do not respond to Level 2 or Level 3 care with more intensive evaluation and therapy. Patients who require urgent care, emergency care, or hospitalization may enter the system at this level. However, with proactive interventions at lower levels, Level 4 care will be required for fewer patients and at a later stage in life than in the current medical model, in which many patients wait to enter the system until prevention is less likely to be an option and expensive interventions are more likely. At this level, the pharmacist continues to act as the medication manager and has additional training to focus on areas of specialty care.

Several components of this care model are consistent throughout all four levels. Care is provided by interdisciplinary teams with shared borders. Pharmacists serve as personal medication managers for the patients under their care and are still connected to the medication product. Dispensing the medication at the site and time of care increases the opportunity for medication consultation, increases patient adherence, and decreases the patient's time away from work, school, or home. The pharmacist still oversees the medication distribution process, but most dispensing responsibilities are handled by support staff and technology.

The care at all levels of this model is driven by evidence-based medicine. Outcomes are measured and reported on a routine basis. A continuous quality improvement process is used. The overall goal is to increase wellness and prevention early in the lives of clients, decrease crisis management and health care utilization late in the lives of clients, and increase overall quality of life for the enrollees.

Work-Site Clinics

Employers may choose to offer these services at the work site. Pharmacists can partner with the payer and other health care providers to operate a work-site health clinic. The clinic may provide wellness and prevention services, walk-in urgent care, disease management services, and connections to the benefits of the health plan. Providers such as exercise physiologists, dietitians, behavioral health specialists, and alternative medicine providers may be part of the team. The care provided by an interprofessional team can enhance health outcomes, decrease absenteeism, and decrease overall health care costs. An example of such a work-site health center is Ohio State University's University Health Connection, which provides care for the university faculty and staff.

The pharmacist is a vital part of this delivery model. The work-site clinic may include both a dispensing pharmacy for easy access and a pharmacist who also provides MTMS.

In the case of large employers, mobile teams could provide services at various work-site locations as an extension of the clinic. A mobile team that meets the employee at his or her immediate work site enhances access and can help identify risks in employees who might not normally take advantage of the clinic services.

Exercise facilities, educational programming, immunization services, and health coaching may also be centered in the main work-site health clinic.

Implementing the Program

Once a disease management and therapeutic drug monitoring program is designed or purchased, a sound plan for putting it into action is needed. Strong leaders with business and health care skills are needed to ensure the success of pharmacist-provided MTMS. The organizational structure should not prevent the exchange of thoughts, ideas, and interactions between decision makers and providers. The organization should be driven from the bottom up, with pharmacist providers making suggestions to leaders.

Policies and Procedures

Each program will need policies and procedures to maintain consistency and reliability among providers of care. Table 4-3 lists important components to be included in a policy and procedure manual.

Outcomes for measuring success should be decided upon with the payer at the outset, with a timeline and system for periodic reporting to the payer. The outcome measures should indicate quality in existing programs and document value for the implementation of future programs. Outcomes can also be used to market services to other payers. Table 4-4 lists types of outcome measurements that might be considered.

Recruitment

The operations plan should include methods for recruitment or enrollment of eligible members. The employer may want to recruit through letters, informational meetings, advertisements, and physician referrals. Incentives for both the patient and the referring physician

Table 4-3

Policy and Procedures Components

Mission statement
Goals and objectives
Description of standards for the service
Description of service delivery
Evidence-based guidelines for the service

Table 4-4

Disease Management Program Outcomes

Clinical outcomes (e.g., A1c, blood pressure, lipid profile)
Adherence outcomes
Humanistic outcomes (e.g., patient and physician)
Economic outcomes (e.g., impact on total health care costs, emergency room visits, hospital visits)
Absenteeism and presenteeism
Access and enrollment data for the service

may support higher enrollment and better outcomes. Programs are more likely to be successful if the employer supports recruitment through on-site messaging or financial incentives than if the providers have to market directly to the insured population. The HRA and other screening events may help to identify patients who might not recognize the need for disease management or medication management programs. Education of the insured population is essential.

Pharmacy Network

The operations plan may also include the development of a network of pharmacies to provide MTMS. The primary channel of distribution for pharmacists' MTMS should be face-to-face encounters with members. Provision of MTMS exclusively by telephone or mail is possible but not optimal. Face-to-face encounters between the pharmacist and the plan member could take place in pharmacies, in physicians' offices, at the work site through video conferencing technology, or in private practices.

Participants in a network contract would need to agree on whether they are a vendor or a provider. Some entities must be a vendor and have a network of providers; alternatively, the vendor and the provider may be the same entity. A vendor would most likely be chosen through a competitive bidding process. A provider would be paid according to Current Procedural Terminology (CPT) codes or "dummy" National Drug Code (NDC) numbers, as described below.

Service Level

Human resources executives are concerned about the service level provided for employee plan members. A face-to-face encounter is perceived to be better than a telephone, mail, or Internet encounter because it strengthens the relationship with the member and produces better results. Payers will have a high customer service standard for pharmacists providing MTMS. For example, payers may want pharmacist accessibility by telephone or e-mail around the clock and access to a pharmacist in all areas where their employees live. Employers want to offer a better benefit than their competitors offer.

Reimbursement

The pharmacist may provide MTMS as a vendor (i.e., a pharmacy benefit) or as a provider (i.e., a medical benefit). If the pharmacist is considered a vendor, a contract is signed by the payer and vendor covering the services provided and payment amount to pharmacy providers. The payer reimburses the vendor, who distributes the money to pharmacist providers. Or, a dummy NDC can be processed though the PBM for reimbursement of the pharmacist provider.

If the pharmacist is considered a provider by the payer, reimbursement will be for the medical benefit. The pharmacist will need to be credentialed as a provider by the payer. The pharmacist will bill electronically or on a standard form such as Centers for Medicare and Medicaid Services form 1500 (see Resource E), using the new CPT codes for MTMS or the contracted or assigned reimbursement rate for the MTMS provided. The payer will reimburse the billing provider or the documented practice site.

Credentialing

The concept of credentialing and privileging by health care organizations has evolved in response to society's interest in protecting the public health, professional liability, and regulations that have emerged in response to these issues.

Credentialing is the process used by health care organizations to validate professional licensure, clinical experience, and preparation for specialty practice.

The standard credentialing for pharmacists in the current system typically has been limited to verification that the pharmacist has graduated from an accredited pharmacy college or university and is licensed to practice pharmacy in the state of employment. As pharmacists gain provider status, more specific competency assessment of individual practitioners may be required, as is done for other health care professionals. Additional credentials may include specified training for each MTMS or documentation of provision of a particular MTMS under supervision. In some health systems or organizations, additional credentials may include documentation of special education or training, such as board certification, competency-based continuing education, or fellowship or residency training.[12] Credentialing by health plans will follow the NCQA guidelines for credentialing nonphysician providers.[13] These guidelines include, minimally, verification of education and training, a current valid license, status of clinical privileges, board certification if applicable, work history, current and adequate malpractice insurance, and information on professional liability claims.

Privileging

Privileging is the process used by health care organizations to grant to a specific practitioner the authorization to provide specific patient care services. The facility granting the privilege has established the standard of care for the service. The privileging process ensures that the provider is competent to provide the specified service at the established standard for the facility. The concept of privileging in pharmacy is evolving. Both credentialing and privileging processes will become significant in the growth of MTMS.[12]

Contracts

Contracts must be drafted for any product or service sold to a payer. There are four main elements of a contract between a vendor and a payer.[14] First, the contract contains an agreement that includes intentions or deliverables of the vendor, definitions of terms, and acceptance of the offer. The second component is consideration; this section describes delivery of the services by the vendor and payment by the payer. The third section addresses contractual capacity, identifying that both parties have the capacity to enter into a contract; for example, that both parties are competent and are not minors. The last section states the legality of the contract. The contract must not violate any statutes or public policy. The contract basically delineates the terms of the relationship and prevents disagreement between the vendor and the payer.

Marketing

Pharmacist providers must market to payers directly or outsource selling their services to a marketing agency. It is critical that the marketer understand the needs of the payer (i.e., of the employee population). The marketing plan must be based on the identified need of the employee group. For example, does the employer have a young, healthy population; a middle-aged population with diagnosed chronic diseases; or an older population that is actively involved with physician visits, hospital visits, home health care visits, and high-cost health care?

In developing a marketing plan, pharmacist providers can do the following:

- List advantages of using MTMS provided by pharmacists in your system versus your competitors, focusing on the availability of face-to-face visits or the current standard of care.
- Discuss the credentials of your pharmacy providers, and share any documentation of outcomes from your existing programs or from pharmacists in published national programs.
- Develop a strong marketing strategy. Determine what will happen in a detailing visit to an employer or insurer. Plan the timeline for follow-up telephone marketing or an Internet message.
- Determine whether marketing in human resources magazines, on the radio, or on television would be profitable for your organization.
- Find champions to encourage the human resources decision makers to use MTMS provided by pharmacists. Champions could include the employees themselves or the medical director, manager of pharmacy benefits, or medical management director of the plan.
- Be prepared to share the expected and actual return on investment for your provided services.

When the payer decides to use the MTMS, help the payer market to employees. These services are an added health benefit for employees, in contrast to increased co-payments and deductibles that take away from employees.

The number and location of the pharmacist providers in the network will determine the market area for the network and the payers who would profit from the services.

Conclusion

The opportunity to provide MTMS opens the door for pharmacy to drive a new, more integrated health care delivery model.

References

1. Aldana SG. Financial impact of health promotion programs: a comprehensive review of the literature. *Am J Health Promot.* 2001;15(5):296–320.
2. Goetzel RZ, Juday TR, Ozminkowski RJ. What's the ROI?—A systematic review of return on investment (ROI) studies of corporate health and productivity management initiatives. *AWHP's Worksite Health.* 1999;6(summer):12–21.
3. Ozminkowski RJ, Dunn RL, Goetzel RZ, et al. A return on investment evaluation of the Citibank, N.A., health management program. *Am J Health Promot.* 1999;14(1):31-43.
4. Joint WHO/FAO Expert Consultation. *Diet, Nutrition, and the Prevention of Chronic Diseases.* Geneva: World Health Organization; 2003.
5. Sturm R. The effects of obesity, smoking, and drinking on medical problems and costs. *Health Aff.* 2002;21(2):245–53.
6. Erfurt JC, Foote A, Heirich MA. Worksite wellness programs: incremental comparisons of screening and referral alone, health education, follow-up counseling, and plant organization. *Am J Health Promot.* 1991:5(6)438–48.
7. Bluml BM, McKenney JM, Cziraky MJ. Pharmaceutical care services and results in Project ImPACT: Hyperlipidemia. *J Am Pharm Assoc.* 2000;40:157–65.
8. Garrett DG, Bluml BM. Patient self-management program for diabetes: first-year clinical, humanistic, and economic outcomes. *J Am Pharm Assoc.* 2005;45:130–7.
9. Schumock GT, Butler MG, Meek PD, et al. Evidence of economic benefit of clinical pharmacy services:1996–2000. *Pharmacotherapy.* 2003;23:113–32.
10. Bennett MS. Future challenges: changing health care delivery and advancing patient care. *J Am Pharm Assoc.* 2004;44:420–6.
11. Ray MD. Shared borders: achieving the goals of interdisciplinary patient care. *Am J Health Syst Pharm.* 1998;55:1369–74.

12. Galt KA. Credentialing and privileging for pharmacists. *Am J Health Syst Pharm.* 2004;61:661–70.

13. National Committee for Quality Assurance. *2006 MCO Standards and Guidelines.* 2006.

14. Cross FB, Miller RL. *West's Legal Environment of Business: Text and Cases—Ethical, Regulatory, International and E-Commerce Issues.* Mason, Ohio: Thomson South-Western; 2000.

Chapter 5

Educational Opportunities for Pharmacists Providing Medication Therapy Management Services to Seniors

John Feather

The establishment of medication therapy management services (MTMS) as part of the Medicare Part D prescription drug program opened up a tremendous opportunity for pharmacists to be paid for managing the medication needs of older adults. Working with older patients with complex needs has not been part of every pharmacist's training or experience, however. Some pharmacists may think they require additional education or objective evidence of their skills in order to take full advantage of the opportunity to provide medication therapy management (MTM). This chapter explores options for pharmacists who want to better prepare themselves to work with an aging population.

What Skills Will Pharmacists Need?

Most pharmacists, whether working in a community setting, managed care, a hospital, or long-term care, have a substantial proportion of older clients. Older people simply use more medications, on average, than younger people. The older the person, the more likely it is that he or she will use a large number of medications for a large number of medical problems. However, not all pharmacists have received training in the special needs of older patients, particularly those using multiple medications for multiple chronic conditions.

Pharmacists should consider the following questions:

1. Do I have the clinical skills needed to provide MTM for most older people?
2. Do I have the clinical skills to do so for patients with higher levels of need (i.e., the frail and medically complex)?
3. How can I best document to those who will pay for MTM (e.g., individual patients or families, insurance companies, prescription drug plans under Medicare Part D) that I have those skills?
4. How do I market my services to those who will pay for them?
5. Do I want to make MTM a major part of my practice? If so, how do I go about setting up such a practice?

These questions highlight several important points. First, the basic element of many MTM programs (including those under Medicare Part D) is providing clinical advice to seniors with greater than average needs. To receive MTMS under Medicare Part D coverage, clients must meet three criteria. They must be taking multiple prescription medications, have multiple chronic diseases, and be expected to have annual medication expenditures exceeding an amount set by the Department of Health and Human Services. Although open to interpretation by prescription drug plans, these criteria make many if not most Medicare Part

D beneficiaries ineligible for coverage of MTMS. Thus, the providers of MTMS under this program will be working with people whose needs are more challenging than usual, and those providers may require specialized training. Similarly, insurance companies and individual patients or families are most likely to seek MTMS when the older person has complex medication issues, rather than when the person simply needs advice on a single medication.

Many patients who do not qualify for payment under Medicare Part D may benefit from a pharmacist's MTMS, and, in fact, many insurance companies are looking at whether and how the Medicare MTMS models can be expanded to serve other clients. That leads to the second point: that these services cover a wide range, from programs for very frail and challenging patients to programs for those with less complex needs. The level of training needed by the provider may differ according to the level of service required by the clients. This may lead to differentiation of providers of MTMS and to the development of referral networks of practitioners in a community who can help patients access more specialized services.

Practitioners must be able to demonstrate to payers that they have the clinical skills to provide MTMS. Prescription drug programs under Medicare Part D will be regional or national in scope, so they will be looking for some objective way to know that the practitioners they hire are qualified to provide the service. Various approaches to demonstrating clinical skills are discussed below.

Questions 4 and 5 suggest that clinical skills are not the only area in which pharmacists may need or want training. If pharmacists want to make MTM a substantial part of their practices, they will need skills such as marketing, billing, negotiating, and documenting. Advanced training in business and management may be worthwhile for many pharmacists, especially those for whom MTM is a significant part of the practice.

Every MTM Program Is Different

The regulations implementing the Medicare Prescription Drug Improvement and Modernization Act of 2003 (MMA) gave Medicare Part D prescription drug plans (PDPs) and Medicare Advantage prescription drug plans (MA-PDs) broad authority to design their specific MTM programs, subject to Medicare's approval. The plans can define exactly which beneficiaries will receive MTMS, the range of services provided, and the educational requirements (if any) for those who are paid for providing the service.

The resulting differences among programs make it difficult for a pharmacist to determine the best educational strategy. Rather than asking "What is the best way for me to prepare educationally to meet the requirements to perform MTM?" the pharmacist should be asking how best to prepare for a particular PDP or MA-PD's program. A community pharmacist who has contracts with several PDPs or MA-PDs is likely to be receiving payment for different services provided to differently defined beneficiaries and may need to meet different educational requirements for each PDP or MA-PD.

The law makes it clear that not every beneficiary with Medicare drug coverage will meet the criteria to receive MTMS. Instead, the selection of clients will be determined by each PDP or MA-PD under guidance from the Centers for Medicare and Medicaid Services, and the way in which clients are defined will be critical in determining the level of expertise needed to provide the service. The plan's criteria for MTMS might include the total number of medications used, the cost of the drugs, the need for close monitoring to avoid adverse outcomes, and the potential for serious drug interactions.

Furthermore, some programs may have different tiers of clients, according to the complexity of their medication management issues. In this case, educational requirements might differ with different tiers of patients. PDPs may also divide MTM clients by particular disease states; for example, patients with diabetes would be in a different program than those with cancer, and the providers of MTM would need different training for each.

Credentials for MTM

The pharmacy profession offers many levels of educational programs to prepare practitioners who want to provide MTM, but the distinctions between those programs may not always be clear. The various types of educational programs and how they may be relevant to MTM are discussed in this section.

The Council on Credentialing in Pharmacy (CCP), a coalition of 12 national pharmacy organizations, published in December 2004 a comprehensive guide to all available voluntary credentialing programs in pharmacy. CCP makes the distinction between three types of credentials:

- Credentials needed to prepare for practice (academic degrees);
- Credentials needed to enter practice (licensure) and to update professional knowledge and skills (relicensure) under state law; and
- Credentials that pharmacists voluntarily earn to document their specialized or advanced knowledge and skills (postgraduate degrees, certificates, certification).

Since the first two types of credentials are basic requirements that have already been attained by any practicing pharmacist, the focus of education and training to provide MTMS will be on the last category, voluntary credentials.

Why should a licensed pharmacist want to have additional training? The CCP white paper "Credentialing in Pharmacy"—written before the advent of MTMS under Medicare prescription drug plans—gives this rationale:

> *Pharmacists who are providing cognitive services or specialized care should be compensated for the services they provide. Similarly, payers rightfully expect and deserve to receive validation that pharmacists are qualified to provide such services. Credentials, and in many cases, more specifically, certification, can help provide the documentation that Medicare and Medicaid, managed care organizations, and other third-party payers require of pharmacists today and in the future.*[1]

Without firm guidance on what will be required for specific MTM programs, the variety of education and training programs for pharmacists can be bewildering. It is important to understand how the following types of credentials differ:

- Continuing education credit
- Certificates of completion
- Certificate programs
- Traineeships
- Certification
- Residencies
- Postgraduate degree programs

Each of these is useful, depending on the level of specialization pharmacists wish to attain and how they plan to use their skills.

Continuing education credit (CE) is familiar to every pharmacist because a certain amount is required for relicensure by the state board of pharmacy. Most CE programs are short sessions (1 to 3 hours) consisting of a lecture by an expert on a particular topic, although CE is now provided for a range of activities, including Web-based programs. Most national and state pharmacy associations and academic institutions offer a wealth of CE programs on geriatric care or on disease states of particular importance to older persons. Even more programs will undoubtedly be offered as MTM becomes established and the demand for educational content grows.

CE programs that meet the requirements for licensure (and most likely for MTM programs developed by the PDPs and MA-PDs) are accredited by the Accreditation Council for Pharmacy Education (ACPE; www.acpe-accredit.org). It is important to look for the ACPE "seal of approval," which must be included in the promotional material for the program.

Certificates of completion may not be recognized by an outside accrediting body. Most CE programs provide a "certificate" attesting that the pharmacist attended the program, but they make no claim as to what the attendee learned. In addition, however, some training companies offer "certificates" to those who complete a series of courses, even though no testing takes place. Although the content may be excellent, it is not clear that a PDP or MA-PD will accept this type of certificate as evidence of competence and eligibility to be paid for MTMS.

Certificate programs, on the other hand, are accredited by ACPE. They are usually a minimum of 15 contact hours and require not only lectures but practice experiences and demonstration of the desired competencies. Delivering Medication Therapy Management Services in Your Community, described later in this chapter, is one example.

Traineeships are designed to provide intensive education for those who want to be able to provide a high level of patient care for a particular condition. They are usually of longer duration (a week or more) and combine lectures and hands-on patient care experiences. Many of the national pharmacy organizations offer traineeships; they can be contracted directly about current programs. The American Society of Consultant Pharmacists (ASCP) Foundation (www.ascpfoundation.org/traineeships/index.htm) offers a series of traineeships on geriatric-specific topics, including Alzheimer's disease and dementia, interdisciplinary geropsych/behavioral disorders, pain management, and Parkinson's disease. The American Society of Health-System Pharmacists (ASHP) Research and Education Foundation (www.ashpfoundation.org) administers clinical traineeships in areas including antithrombotic pharmacotherapy, cardiovascular risk/dyslipidemia, critical care, diabetes, oncology, and pain management.

Certification involves a rigorous test of a high level of competence in a particular specialty area; it usually requires a written examination and may include an experiential (hands-on) component. Periodic recertification, through retesting or some other method, is required to maintain the designation. It is possible that some PDPs may require or encourage certification, especially to receive payment for MTMS provided to more complex patients.

Two bodies currently certify pharmacists (Table 5-1). All of these certifications demonstrate high-level competence in a particular specialty, but they have slightly different aims. The Certified Geriatric

Pharmacist designation is awarded for competence across the broad area of geriatric practice, while Board of Pharmaceutical Specialties certification shows competence in specialty areas that cross the age span.

Residencies are postgraduate training programs in a defined area of pharmacy practice. Although only a few are specifically focused on geriatrics, many of them are relevant to the special needs of the elderly. Most of the programs are full-time for 12 continuous months, although some specialized residencies require 24 months for completion. ASHP (www.ashp.org) accredits these programs, which are offered in conjunction with other national pharmacy organizations, including the Academy of Managed Care Pharmacy (AMCP), the American College of Clinical Pharmacy (ACCP), the American Pharmacists Association (APhA), and ASCP. It is unclear whether PDPs or MA-PDs will require that some pharmacists (probably those who offer the most complex level of clinical service or who direct other pharmacists who work with the elderly) go through residency training.

Postgraduate degree programs, such as the PhD in pharmacotherapeutics or pharmacology, are unlikely to play a major role in MTM, although they will continue to be important in advancing the field of geriatric pharmacy.

Table 5-1

Certification Bodies in Pharmacy

- The Board of Pharmaceutical Specialties (BPS) (www.bpsweb.org) offers certification in five specialties: nuclear pharmacy, nutrition support pharmacy, oncology pharmacy, pharmacotherapy, and psychiatric pharmacy. Recertification is required every 7 years.
- The Commission for Certification in Geriatric Pharmacy (CCGP) (www.ccgp.org) offers the designation Certified Geriatric Pharmacist (CGP) for those who demonstrate a high level of competence in geriatric pharmacy practice, including geriatric pharmacotherapy and the provision of pharmaceutical care to the elderly. Recertification is required every 5 years.

Table 5-2

Pharmacy Associations Offering Training Relevant to MTM

- Academy of Managed Care Pharmacy (AMCP), www.amcp.org, 703-683-8416
- Accreditation Council for Pharmacy Education (ACPE), www.acpe-accredit.org, 312-664-3575
- American Association of Colleges of Pharmacy (AACP), www.aacp.org, 703-739-2330
- American College of Apothecaries (ACA), www.acainfo.org, 901-383-8119
- American College of Clinical Pharmacy (ACCP), www.accp.com, 816-531-2177
- American Pharmacists Association (APhA), www.aphanet.org, 202-628-4410
- American Society of Consultant Pharmacists (ASCP), www.ascp.com, 703-739-1300
- American Society of Health-System Pharmacists (ASHP), www.ashp.org, 301-664-8794
- National Association of Boards of Pharmacy (NABP), www.nabp.net, 847-391-4400
- National Association of Chain Drug Stores (NACDS), www.nacds.org, 703-549-3001
- National Community Pharmacists Association (NCPA), www.ncpanet.org, 703-683-8200

Educational Programs and Resources

Many in the pharmacy profession are working to create new programs for training pharmacists to meet the challenge of MTM for seniors. Any educational program that focuses on disease states prevalent in the elderly and the complex interactions found in geriatric patients is relevant to MTM. Specialized programs are likely to emerge as the specifics of Part D MTM programs become known. Educational programs focusing on the business side of providing MTM are also likely to be developed.

The first place to look for education relevant to MTM is the national and state pharmacy associations. All of these groups are likely to create new programs as the demand increases, so it is best to check their Web sites often for current offerings. Table 5-2 lists the national practitioner organizations. Information on state pharmacy associations can be obtained from the National Alliance of State Pharmacy Associations (www.ncspae.org, 804-285-4431). In addition, most schools of pharmacy offer a variety of programs that may be relevant to this population; contact your local school for more information.

The following paragraphs describe other resources; further information can be obtained from the sponsoring organizations. As MTM develops, more training programs for pharmacists will be created, not only by national associations but also by schools of pharmacy and commercial providers.

Delivering Medication Therapy Management Services in Your Community. This is an ACPE-accredited certificate program offered jointly by APhA and ASCP. It is intended to enhance pharmacists' clinical expertise in evaluating complicated medication regimens, identifying drug-related problems, and making recommendations to patients, caregivers, and health care professionals. Through self-study modules, case studies, and hands-on patient interview and assessment practice sessions, pharmacists can obtain the clinical knowledge, skills, and motivation needed to establish MTM services for Medicare Part D and other patients with complex drug regimens.

Framework for Community-Based MTM. In March 2005, APhA and the National Association of Chain Drug Stores (NACDS) Foundation released a model framework for implementing effective MTMS in the community pharmacy setting. That document, *Medication Therapy Management in Community Pharmacy Practice: Core Elements of an MTM Service Model,* outlined a process intended to "enhance patient understanding of appropriate drug use, increase patient compliance with medications, result in collaboration between pharmacists and prescribers, and improve detection of adverse drug events." Version 2 of that document, *Medication Therapy Management in Pharmacy Practice: Core Elements of an MTM Service Model,* was published in 2008. This model for practice (Resource A) has five core elements: (1) medication therapy review, (2) personal medication record, (3) medication action plan, (4) intervention and referral, and (5) documentation and follow-up. It is likely that pharmacy organizations will offer educational programs addressing each of the core elements.

Sound Medication Therapy Management Programs. This is a consensus document created by AMCP in conjunction with other pharmacy associations and with major aging and health groups. Now in its second edition, it addresses the features of a sound MTM program, including operational features. Although not an educational program per se, this document is a useful summary of the current state of thinking about what an MTM program should look like. It is available electronically at www.amcp.org/data/nav_content/websiteMTM-document.pdf.

Community Aging, Assisted Living, and Long Term Care (CAALTC) Certificate Program. The National Community Pharmacists Association (NCPA) has created the CAALTC Certificate Program, accredited by NCPA's National Institute for Pharmacist Care Outcomes (NIPCO). This program focuses on the business side of serving the elderly. It includes educational sessions on understanding this market and developing a business plan, efficient operations, contracting and pricing, automation and technology, and clinical protocols.

ASCP, whose focus is geriatric care, has a number of educational programs relevant to MTM. ASCP also has a variety of resources to help pharmacists evaluate their level of clinical knowledge and systematically work through a curriculum that eventually leads to taking the Certified Geriatric Pharmacist exam (www.GeriatricPharmacyReview.com). In addition, www.scoup.net offers a variety of free on-line educational resources on specific clinical conditions of the elderly.

Conclusion

As MTM programs evolve, so will pharmacists' needs for education and training and the available resources. Since the advent of Medicare Part D in 2006, MTM programs have varied widely. Over time, the requirements of Part D MTM programs should become more clear, and variation among the programs may decrease. With experience, pharmacists and PDPs and MA-PDs will learn which models work best for which patients.

Pharmacists interested in providing MTM through Medicare or another payment mechanism should begin now to prepare themselves. They will need a strong clinical background in geriatrics and diseases that affect the elderly. They will also need to understand how to practice most effectively in a variety of settings. With this preparation, pharmacists will be well on their way to successfully providing MTMS to the older persons who most need this assistance.

Reference

1. Council on Credentialing in Pharmacy. Credentialing in Pharmacy. July 2006. Available at: www.pharmacycredentialing.org.

Section II

Practical Guide to Billing for Medication Therapy Management Services

Editor: Michael D. Hogue

Chapter 6

Coding Principles for Medication Therapy Management Services: The ABCs of CPTs

Brian J. Isetts and Daniel E. Buffington

In order to submit compensation claims, health care practitioners need a system for describing and reporting the services they provide to patients. This chapter presents the history and background of the system used by physicians and many allied health care providers for coding and reporting health care services, and its application to medication therapy management services (MTMS) provided by pharmacists. The framework used to report and bill for professional services is described, with emphasis on use of pharmacists' reporting and billing codes.

The CPT Reporting System

The American Medical Association (AMA) publishes *Current Procedural Terminology (CPT)*,[1] sometimes referred to as the CPT manual or CPT codebook, a detailed coding system for describing and reporting health care services, procedures, and diagnostic testing. The CPT system for categorizing and describing health care services and medical procedures has evolved over many years and undergoes a rigorous annual review process.

The first edition of *CPT*, published in 1966, contained standard documentation terms and descriptors; it was intended to encourage the accurate communication of medical procedure and service information for insurance claims and for actuarial and statistical purposes.[2] In the first edition, a four-digit numerical system was used to classify a uniform nomenclature for describing and reporting medical, surgical, and diagnostic procedures. The "P" in CPT is noteworthy: it signifies that descriptions and codes for surgical and medical *procedures* dominated this early edition.

Since their inception, CPT descriptive terms and identifying codes have served a wide variety of functions. Administrative purposes such as claims processing are perhaps the most widely recognized use. CPT descriptive terms have also been used to develop guidelines for medical care review, national utilization comparisons, and medical education. Today, *CPT* has been expanded to describe numerous services provided by many different types of health care providers.

The second edition of *CPT*, published in 1970, expanded the system of terms and codes, introducing a five-digit classification system. The third edition was published in 1973 and the fourth in 1977. The fourth edition presented significant updates in medical terminology and a system for periodic updating. Since then, the CPT code set has been revised annually except in 1983.

The CPT system is maintained by a 17-member editorial panel. Two panel members come from the Health Care Professionals Advisory Committee, which represents health care professions other than medicine. Pharmacy was granted a seat on that committee in 2003. The work of the editorial panel is supported by a large body of advisors and staff. Specific procedures exist for addressing suggestions to revise *CPT*, add or delete a code, or modify existing nomenclature. The proposal to add MTMS to CPT progressed through the CPT code proposal submission process.

There are three categories of CPT codes. Category I CPT codes are assigned to procedures or services that are consistent with contemporary medical practice and are performed by many practitioners in multiple clinical practice locations. Most CPT codes are Category I.

Category II CPT codes are supplemental tracking codes. They can be used for performance measurement, to facilitate the collection of data about quality of care. They are not used for billing purposes.

Category III CPT codes are temporary codes that can be used to track and bill for new and emerging technologies and services. Category III codes are intended to be used to collect data (e.g., in the Food and Drug Administration approval process for devices) or to substantiate widespread usage. To be eligible for a Category III code, the procedure or service must be involved in ongoing or planned research; an example is new and revised immunization and vaccine product codes to facilitate reporting of immunizations. Category III CPT codes are functional for billing third-party payers, who incorporate them into their spectrum of service codes. Category III codes are effective for up to 5 years, permitting data to be gathered in support of a request for change to Category I status.

CPT and Medicare

Traditionally, a fee-for-service system of payment for physician services has been used. In 1956, the California Medical Association expressed interest in use of a relative value scale (RVS) as a basis for determining payments and fees. An RVS is a list of physicians' services ranked according to their value as defined by the scale.[3]

In 1969 a fee schedule system known as the California Relative Value Studies (CRVS), based on median charges reported by California Blue Shield, was implemented. Physician payment rates used by some state Medicaid programs and commercial insurers were based on the CRVS. In the late 1970s the Federal Trade Commission acted to suspend updating and distribution of the CRVS because of antitrust concerns.

When Medicare Part B was enacted in 1966, physician payment was based on a system of "customary, prevailing, and reasonable" (CPR) charges. The system was originally designed to reimburse physicians for services on the basis of their actual fees. It was based on the "usual, customary, and reasonable" charges used by many private health insurers. Problems with the CPR system, including varying payment levels across the spectrum of customary, prevailing, and reasonable charges, led Medicare to place a series of controls on CPR reimbursement levels. After weighing the evidence regarding payment reform, AMA concluded that an RVS based on relative resource costs, or a resource-based relative value scale (RBRVS), would more equitably cover physicians' costs of caring for Medicare patients.

In 1985, after extensive collaboration between AMA, the Health Care Financing Administration (HCFA; now known as the Centers for Medicare and Medicaid Services [CMS]), and the Harvard University School of Public Health, a national study was launched to develop an RBRVS system. In the Harvard RBRVS study, physicians ranked the overall work involved in their services without distinguishing between time and complexity. In 1988, Harvard researchers submitted the final report of the phase I RBRVS study to HCFA.[4]

The Harvard RBRVS study created a framework for establishing the value of physicians' services. In this framework, the cost of providing service includes three general components: physician work, practice expense, and professional liability insurance. Relative value units (RVUs) are calculated for each of the three service components through actions of the RVS update committee. This group (titled the AMA/Specialty Society—Relative Value Scale Update Committee) was formed by AMA to act as an expert panel in developing relative value recommendations to CMS. The committee's recommendations are forwarded to CMS each year, and CMS publishes final RVU recommendations, with associated monetary values, in the *Federal Register*.[5]

In the RBRVS system, payments for physician services are determined by the resource costs for providing them. The cost of providing each service is divided into its three components, each of which is resource-based. These factors are translated into RVUs, and payments are calculated by multiplying the combined RVUs for a service by a conversion factor (a monetary amount that is determined by CMS). Payments are also adjusted for geographical differences in resource costs.

Evolution of MTMS

Payment for pharmacists' services dates back to ancient times. Apothecaries in the early 20th century were paid by patients for providing essential health services. Historically, payment for pharmacists' services has most often been associated with the distribution of a medicinal product (e.g., botanicals, leeches, compounded medicines). Throughout the era of premanufactured dosage forms (i.e., from around 1950 to the present), payment for pharmacists' services has been embedded in the drug product dispensing fee. Only a handful of pharmacy pioneers imagined providing and billing for services separate and distinct from the business of dispensing.

The practice of pharmaceutical care emerged as a solution to the problem of mounting drug-related morbidity and mortality.[6] The missing link in a safe and effective medication-use system was the presence of a health care professional responsible for patients' drug therapy outcomes. However, compensation for pharmacists' services devoid of dispensing focused on pharmacists' specialty practices (e.g., warfarin monitoring, disease state management) or on consultation services in hospitals and long-term care facilities.

A description of MTMS provided within the practice of pharmaceutical care originated in federal health care legislation and congressional reports.[7] Medication therapy management (MTM) was characterized as an evolving patient care service, with drug therapy decisions being coordinated collaboratively by physicians, pharmacists, and other health professionals together with the patient. The literature and standards of practice pertaining to the provision of MTMS have been related to the development of pharmaceutical care practices.[8–10]

Genesis of MTMS CPT Code Proposal

The Health Insurance Portability and Accountability Act (HIPAA) has had a number of effects on health care beyond protecting patient privacy. One aspect of HIPAA that some pharmacists may not be aware of relates to rules mandating that all health claims submitted electronically follow precise electronic data interchange standards. This provision opened the door for pharmacists and other allied health professionals to submit claims for patient care services, ultimately leading to the creation of pharmacist billing codes and the assignment of pharmacist provider numbers.

The new professional opportunities presented by HIPAA caused the national pharmacy organizations to unite their efforts related to the provision of pharmaceutical care services through MTM programs. In October 2002, the major national pharmacy organizations joined together to begin work toward submitting a formal CPT code proposal to the CPT editorial panel. The history and progress of this effort are described on the Pharmacist Services Technical Advisory Coalition (PSTAC) Web site.[11]

After pharmacists were granted a seat on the CPT editorial panel's Health Care Professionals Advisory Committee, a CPT code proposal for MTMS was prepared and submitted to the editorial panel in 2004. Evidence of the effectiveness and safety of MTMS presented in the original CPT code proposal was derived from literature on the practice of pharmaceutical care. This evidence included the identification of MTMS as a distinct procedure provided within the practice of pharmaceutical care.[9]

Key components of the MTMS CPT code proposal were the specific rationale for requesting MTMS codes, a brief description of the service, clinical vignettes describing the service provided to a typical patient, and citations of medical literature supporting use of the service. The consensus definition of MTMS adopted by the major national pharmacy organizations[12] and standards of practice for the provision of pharmaceutical care[13] were used to support description of the service in the proposal. The code proposal recommended a five-level RBRVS[9] based on a patient's number of medical conditions, drug therapies, and drug therapy problems for the code descriptor nomenclature.

In 2005 the initial MTMS CPT code proposal was sent to a CPT editorial panel work group for discussion and modification with input from panel members and administrative members. These discussions resulted in the assignment of MTMS CPT codes to Category III,[14] the temporary status used for reporting new or emerging procedures and services.[2] Category III MTMS codes were approved in 2005 and published in *CPT 2006* and *CPT 2007*.

The description of MTMS in the CPT reference guide includes pharmacists' performing face-to-face comprehensive medication review and assessment to identify, resolve, and prevent drug therapy problems; formulating a medication treatment plan to achieve patients' goals of therapy; and monitoring and evaluating patient outcomes of therapy.[8,9,15] Two decisions made at the time Category III MTMS CPT codes were assigned have helped pharmacists report and bill for services. The first was the addition of "pharmacy" as a place-of-service code[16] in CPT, and the second was the ability of pharmacists to obtain a National Provider Identifier (NPI) number through the National Plan and Provider Enumeration System.[17]

The major reason cited by the CPT editorial panel for assigning Category III rather than Category I status was lack of evidence supporting widespread availability of MTMS. The temporary Category III MTMS CPT codes were time-based codes similar to CPT codes in use for a few other allied health care services (e.g., medical nutrition therapy).[1]

Soon after MTMS CPT codes were assigned Category III status, PSTAC launched a national effort to gather information on the availability of MTMS. Providers and payers of MTMS were identified, and a survey was designed to determine the nature and extent of MTMS throughout the nation. Survey data were collected from providers and payers in the summer and fall of 2006, and the results were used to support a code change proposal submitted to the CPT editorial panel in November 2006. Responses to the provider and payer surveys indicated that there were nearly 2.8 million MTMS encounters in the United States in 2004 and 2005, and that MTMS were available in all 50 states, Puerto Rico, and the District of Columbia.[9]

PSTAC members presented and defended the MTMS code change proposal at the February 2007 meeting of the CPT editorial panel. The panel voted to change ("migrate") MTMS CPT codes to Category I status. The panel also adjusted the MTMS coding nomenclature slightly to more accurately reflect contemporary CPT terminology pertaining to the definitions of new and established patients. The Category I MTMS CPT codes, general service description, and coding rationale are shown in Figure 6-1.

Figure 6-1

Category I MTMS CPT Codes (*CPT 2008*)

Medication therapy management service(s) (MTMS) describe face-to-face patient assessment and intervention as appropriate, by a pharmacist, upon request. MTMS is provided to optimize the response to medications or to manage treatment-related medication interactions or complications.

MTMS includes the following documented elements: review of the pertinent patient history, medication profile (prescription and nonprescription), and recommendations for improving health outcomes and treatment compliance. These codes are not to be used to describe the provision of product-specific information at the point of dispensing or any other routine dispensing-related activities.

99605 Medication therapy management service(s) provided by a pharmacist, individual, face-to-face with patient, with assessment and intervention if provided; initial 15 minutes, new patient

99606 initial 15 minutes, established patient

+99607 each additional 15 minutes (List separately in addition to code for primary service.)

(Use 99607 in conjunction with 99605, 99606.)

Rationale

A new subsection, guidelines, and three codes (99605–99607) have been established to report provision of medication therapy management services by a pharmacist. Code 99605 is intended to be reported for the initial encounter and review of the patient's medications. Code 99606 is reported for management sessions with the established patient. Codes 99605 and 99606 represent the initial 15 minutes for the service. Code 99607 is intended to report services requiring additional increments of 15 minutes beyond that reported with codes 99605 and 99606.

Guidelines have been added to define the circumstances under which these codes are or are not reported appropriately. The guidelines instruct that these services are performed at the request of the patient. Services provided are required to be documented and include review of the pertinent patient history, medication profile (prescription and nonprescription), and recommendations for improving health outcomes and treatment compliance. As indicated, these codes are not to be used to describe the provision of product-specific information at the point of dispensing or any other routine dispensing-related activities. Services provided subsequent to the initial patient service by the same business at a separate location should be reported with the established patient code 99606.

Use of the MTMS Codes

The MTMS codes were developed to be applicable for all pharmacy practice settings and payer types. Their use is not limited to Medicare MTMS. The codes were designed to describe face-to-face patient care services provided by a pharmacist to a patient for the purpose of optimizing medication therapy outcomes.

In 2005, the entities contracted by Medicare to provide the prescription drug benefit (Part D prescription drug plans and Medicare Advantage prescription drug plans) were faced with the immediate need to identify and use some type of CPT coding for receiving health care service claims and processing payment for beneficiaries in order to be HIPAA compliant. The lack of any defined CPT codes for pharmacists' services and the rapidly expanding use of those services in the commercial market and state Medicaid programs converged to stimulate the creation and subsequent approval of MTMS coding.

The CPT manual includes a distinct chapter of evaluation and management (E&M) codes, which are focused solely on cognitive health care services provided by physicians and other health care providers. Some pharmacists previously used E&M codes, at the lowest levels, to bill for cognitive services. Even though pharmacists typically provide cognitive rather than procedural services, the initial set of MTMS codes constructed and approved by the CPT editorial panel is time based, unlike E&M codes, and was modeled after other allied health care professional codes (i.e., medical nutrition therapy codes).

In the future, tiered-intensity (RBRVS) CPT codes may be re-evaluated as an additional set of codes to describe pharmacists' cognitive services, either replacing or augmenting the current MTMS CPT codes. For now, however, the focus should be on learning to apply the new MTMS codes. It is important to note that individual payers in the marketplace may elect to apply CPT codes at their own discretion. For instance, in the State of Minnesota—Medicaid Medication Therapy Management Care Program, pharmacists are compensated for services according to an RBRVS that is "cross-walked" to the time-based MTMS CPT codes.[18]

Pharmacists and their billing staff should be familiar with the mechanics and requirements of MTMS CPT coding. The time-based billing codes are designed to be applied in 15-minute increments. The two primary codes—99605, new patient (formerly, initial service) and 99606, established patient (formerly, reassessment service)—represent the first 15 minutes of service provided to a new and an established patient, respectively. If the service provided is longer than 15 minutes (i.e., 16–30 minutes total), then the incremental time extension code (99607) is applied for each additional 15-minute block of service. An initial service provided for a new patient that took 45 minutes would be billed using 99605 plus two units of 99607 codes, to represent the total of 45 minutes of service (Figure 6-1).

The rate billed for the service code or the collective set of individual service codes is determined by the practitioner and represents the practitioner's self-determined "fee structure" for the services provided. Fee structures are influenced by many variables: labor, overhead, liability, supplies, equipment, practice setting, and other practice-related expenses. However, payers often determine their own fee structures for the medical services provided for their beneficiaries, and these may vary from practitioners' self-determined fee structures. It is important for payers to use realistic fee structures that incorporate the many cost factors involved in delivering a particular type of health care service, such as MTMS. Concern over determining a realistic fee structure and code valuation is universal among physicians and allied health care practitioners.

Conclusion

The responsibility for providing MTMS according to the standards set forth in *CPT* rests squarely on the shoulders of pharmacists. Assistance in properly implementing the new MTMS codes is available from PSTAC and the national professional societies supporting PSTAC.

The migration of MTMS CPT codes to Category I status will help patients gain increased access to these services. It is anticipated that more pharmacists will provide MTMS, and more payers will compensate providers of these services described in *CPT*. The next steps will be to establish the relative value of the services. The pharmacy profession is expected to engage in a structured RVS survey in the near future to establish the value of MTMS.

References

1. *Current Procedural Terminology—CPT 2008.* 4th ed. Chicago: American Medical Association; 2008.

2. American Medical Association. CPT Process—How a Code Becomes a Code. Available at: www.ama-assn.org/ama/pub/category/3882.html. Accessed January 30, 2008.

3. *Medicare Physician Payment Reform: The Physicians' Guide.* Vol. 1. Chicago: American Medical Association; 1992.

4. Hsiao WC, Braun P, Yntema D, et al. Estimating physicians' work for a resource-based relative-values scale. *N Engl J Med.* 1988;319:835–41.

5. American Medical Association. AMA/Specialty Society RVS Update Process. Available at: www.ama-assn.org/ama1/pub/upload/mm/380/rvs_booklet_07.pdf. Accessed January 30, 2008.

6. Hepler CD, Strand LM. Opportunities and responsibilities in pharmaceutical care. *Am J Hosp Pharm.* 1990;47:533–43.

7. Medicare Payment Advisory Commission (MedPAC); Hackbarth GM, Chair. Report to the Congress: Medicare Coverage of Nonphysician Practitioners. June 2002:21–6.

8. Isetts BJ, Brown LM, Schondelmeyer SW, et al. Quality assessment of a collaborative approach for decreasing drug-related morbidity and achieving therapeutic goals. *Arch Intern Med.* 2003;163:1813–20.

9. Isetts BJ, Buffington DE. CPT Code Change Proposal: National data on pharmacists' medication therapy management services. *J Am Pharm Assoc.* 2007;47:491–5.

10. Isetts BJ, Schondelmeyer SW, Artz MB, et al. Clinical and economic outcomes of medication therapy management services; the Minnesota experience. *J Am Pharm Assoc.* 2008;48:203–11.

11. Pharmacist Services Technical Advisory Coalition. Medication Therapy Management Services CPT Billing Codes. Available at: http://pstac.org/aboutus/profsvc.html. Accessed January 30, 2008.

12. Bluml BJ. Definition of medication therapy management: development of profession-wide consensus. *J Am Pharm Assoc.* 2005;45:566–72.

13. Cipolle RJ, Strand LM, Morley PC. *Pharmaceutical Care Practice: The Clinician's Guide.* New York: McGraw-Hill; 2004.

14. *Current Procedural Terminology—CPT 2006.* 4th ed. Chicago: American Medical Association; 2006.

15. *CPT Changes 2006: An Insider's View.* Chicago: American Medical Association; 2005:309–12.

16. Pharmacist Services Technical Advisory Coalition. Place of Service (POS). Available at: http://pstac.org/services/pos-code.html. Accessed January 30, 2008.

17. National Plan and Provider Enumeration System. Available at: https://nppes.cms.hhs.gov/NPPES/Welcome.do. Accessed January 30, 2008.

18. Isetts BJ. *Evaluating Effectiveness of the Minnesota Medication Therapy Management Care Program.* December 14, 2007. Minnesota DHS Contract No. B00749. Available at: www.dhs.state.mn.us/main/groups/business_partners/documents/pub/dhs16_140283.pdf. Accessed January 30, 2008.

Chapter 7

Documenting Medication Therapy Management Services

Patty A. Kumbera and Brand A. Newland

Today's pharmacy practice model includes comprehensive systems for documenting and billing for product disbursement activities. A few minutes spent in nearly any community pharmacy provides evidence of the level to which product-specific documentation and billing—often controlled by advanced computer software—drive the practice of pharmacy. In the area of pharmacist services, however, documentation and billing are far less developed and integrated. The vast majority of pharmacy income today still derives from dispensing fees—predetermined payments pharmacies receive for each prescription dispensed. This model rewards pharmacies that can efficiently fill large numbers of prescriptions, but it does not provide a payment mechanism for the cognitive services delivered by the pharmacist.

Ample evidence suggests that pharmacist-delivered services could be quite valuable. From 1995 to 2000, increases in spending on prescription drugs were two to five times larger than increases in spending on hospital care and physician services. However, the growth in prescription volume has not been accompanied by more appropriate medication use. For example, 14–23% of elderly patients receive a medication that should not be prescribed for them.[1,2] As many as 40% of patients do not take their medications as prescribed.[3] This inappropriate use of medications does not come without consequences. In the Harvard Medical Practice study, 6% of all patients and 12% of patients age 65 and older experienced drug-related complications.[4] It has been estimated that drug-related morbidity and mortality add as much as $76 billion in costs to the health care system.[5,6]

The evidence is clear and overwhelming: medication use needs to be improved. Increasingly, pharmacists are taking advantage of opportunities to provide medication therapy management services (MTMS)—clinically oriented activities intended to improve medication prescribing, use, and outcomes. Examples of MTMS are wide ranging. A pharmacist–patient meeting during which the patient's medication regimen is reviewed and a personal medication record is created is one example. Another example is pharmacist collaboration with a physician to find an appropriate therapy option for a patient who has previously been prescribed a contraindicated medication. In both cases, because of unique positioning in the health care system and specialized training, the pharmacist is able to deliver high-quality, patient-oriented services. These services hold the potential not only to improve quality of care but also to reduce costs.

The value of MTMS has not gone unnoticed. The Medicare Prescription

The mention of any company or service does not constitute an endorsement by the authors or editors of any specific company. Information provided is current as of the time of writing. Readers are encouraged to evaluate all products and opportunities carefully.

Chapter 7

Drug Improvement and Modernization Act of 2003 (MMA) requires Medicare prescription drug plans to offer MTMS to select beneficiaries. Included as a means of improving the quality of care and reducing costs, MTMS may be new in name but certainly not in spirit. These services have existed for many years under banners such as "pharmaceutical care," "cognitive services," and "pharmacist care-based services." Yet, the MMA requirement for MTMS may provide the necessary impetus for more widespread adoption.

As pharmacists take advantage of this expanded opportunity for MTMS, the establishment of standard and appropriate measures for documentation and billing of their services is crucial. This chapter explains why documentation is so important to the success of MTMS. It describes several current models for documenting pharmacist-provided MTMS, illustrating a wide array of potential solutions.

Importance of Documentation

Consistency in documentation is perhaps the greatest adjustment a pharmacist must make in fully embracing MTMS. Pharmacists, by and large, have not incorporated documentation processes—essentially, the creation of patient charts—into their practices. This may be due to a perceived lack of necessity (pharmacy software adequately documents dispensing services provided to patients), a lack of training, or a combination of these factors and others.

However, with payment for MTMS now a reality, documentation of these services is of critical importance for four reasons. First, the creation of a documentation trail enhances patient care; records of the patient's care can be tracked, enhancing continuity of care. Patients for whom complete records of medication therapy management (MTM) have been maintained are likely to face less risk of medication-related problems, such as duplications of therapy and drug interactions.

Second, documentation allows the profession to continue to "tell the story" of pharmacist-provided MTM. Although MTM has been provided by pharmacists in various programs over the past 10–20 years, pharmacist-provided MTM has yet to be widely adopted in the health care system. Because pharmacist-provided MTM remains a novelty, the pharmacy profession must continue to prove itself by presenting detailed results of pharmacy services. It is true that other health care professionals may be faced with minimal documentation standards. Many of these professionals, however, have already been accepted as "mainstream" providers in the health care system. This is not yet true for pharmacists. In the coming years, pharmacists may need to document information such as lab values, cost avoidance figures, and patient quality of life indicators to support the value of the MTMS provided. (In fact, documentation requirements for other health care professionals may increase as pay-for-performance strategies are more widely adopted.)

Third, as pharmacists become more widely accepted as providers of MTMS, they will assume increased responsibility for positive patient outcomes. This has the potential to enhance the profession of pharmacy immeasurably (e.g., by earning greater respect from other health care providers, by improving pharmacist job satisfaction), but it also means that pharmacists may be held more accountable for their actions. Pharmacists will need to possess documentation to detail the therapeutic decisions made and recommendations presented that affected patient care.

Finally, documentation is critical for liability protection. In the absence of documentation of the actions involved in MTM, one person's word may be taken against another in a court of law, leaving the pharmacist on potentially shaky legal ground.

Maintenance of appropriate records of MTM is of great importance. At its simplest, documentation may take the form of progress notes. SOAP notes (subjective, objective, assessment, plan) allow a fair amount of flexibility. In this format, pharmacists may write comprehensive chart entries, or they may simply document the most critical information about the MTM intervention, such as date, patient name, pharmacist name, drug therapy problem description, pharmacist action, result (if known), and follow-up plan.

Documentation Systems

A handful of new companies that seek to help pharmacists gain compensation for MTMS have created unique documentation systems. A complete review of each system is outside the scope of this text, but the systems are briefly described here, and contact information for each organization is provided in the resources at the end of the book.

Outcomes Pharmaceutical Health Care introduced the first such system in 2000. The Outcomes MTM system, which is available at no cost to Outcomes network providers, assists pharmacists with documentation, billing, and administration of MTMS. In the Outcomes Web-based system, pharmacists document MTMS such as comprehensive medication reviews, prescriber consultations to resolve drug therapy problems, patient compliance consultations, and nonprescription medication consultations through use of a series of dynamic drop-down menus and split screens. For each service, pharmacists select Indication for Service (Reason), Professional Service (Action), and Outcome of Service (Result) codes. In addition to selecting Reason, Action, and Result codes, pharmacists must also select an appropriate Estimated Cost Avoidance (ECA) level for each intervention. Selection of an ECA level allows the pharmacist to quantify the dollar value of what the patient or payer (or both) avoided as a result of the pharmacist-provided MTMS. ECA levels range from Level 1, Improved Quality of Care, to Level 7, Life-Threatening. In addition to its documentation and billing system, Outcomes administers a nationwide network of MTM centers and markets its program—inclusive of the MTM system and network—to health plans, Medicare Part D plan sponsors, employer groups, and other payers.

Another documentation system is the Web-based system marketed by PharmMD Solutions, LLC. PharmMD's encrypted portal allows pharmacists to document their encounters from any location where Internet access is available. The company offers a documentation solution that allows the pharmacist access to existing medical and pharmacy claims if the company has a contract with the employer or health plan to receive such data. PharmMD also administers a network of pharmacist providers; it equips those pharmacists with clinical tools and intervention support to provide care to the employers and health plans with which the company has contracts.

Mirixa Corporation uses a large network of community pharmacy providers to provide service to contracted health plan and employer clients. Mirixa's unique documentation platform, MirixaPro, is a Web-based solution that allows pharmacists to receive MTM opportunities from the company as well as document their patient care interventions in a concise manner.

Finally, Medication Management Systems, Inc., markets a documentation system created by researchers at the University of Minnesota College of Pharmacy. Assurance Pharmaceutical Care is a computer-based system designed to support the practice of pharmaceutical care. It can be used to manage all of a patient's medications and to document drug therapy outcomes, cost savings, and clinical improvement in patient care. The program supports all reimbursement methods and supports the provision of MTMS to patients on a continuous basis, over repeated encounters, at multiple practice sites, and by multiple practitioners or a network of practitioners. Medicaid and Medicare Part D MTM billing forms are automatically generated for reimbursement.

APhA/NACDS Foundation Model

Documentation of MTMS may take numerous other forms. In 2005, the American Pharmacists Association (APhA) and the National Association of Chain Drug Stores (NACDS) Foundation convened a panel of community pharmacy stakeholders to create a model framework for pharmacist-provided MTM in the community.[7] This model described two documentation elements. The first of these elements, the personal medication record (PMR), is a patient-oriented medication therapy summary created at the completion of a medication therapy review between a pharmacist and a patient. The continuously updated PMR should include a comprehensive list of the patient's medications (prescription, nonprescription, herbals, nutritional supplements). This document may include the following information:

- Medication name and strength,
- Indication,
- Directions for use,
- Discretionary information,
- Pharmacist name,
- Prescriber name, and
- Date of PMR creation.

The second documentation element described by the APhA/NACDS Foundation model is the medication action plan (MAP). This document includes information for the patient to use in optimizing medication therapy. The MAP, which should also be continuously updated, may include the following:

- Patient identifier,
- Pharmacist identifier,
- Prescriber identifier,
- Medication therapy problems identified/resolved, and
- Date of MAP creation.

Copies of the PMR and MAP created for patients may be used to document MTMS provided. Version 2.0 of the APhA/NACDS MTM service model, which contains both the MAP and the PMR, was released in 2008.[8] It is included as Resource A at the end of this book.

Communication with Prescribers and Payers

Another area of MTM documentation is prescriber communication. Many pharmacies use a standard format for communicating with prescribers. This practice has become so widely accepted within health care that a group of national organizations has collaborated to create a pharmacy profession standard for fax communication between pharmacists and prescribers (Figure 7-1). The document allows a pharmacist or pharmacy staff member to document physi-

Figure 7-1

Standard Form for Fax Communication between Pharmacists and Prescribers

Request for Prescription Information or Change

Medicare Prescription Drug Coverage

Provider Communication Form

TO: (Prescribing Physician):____Date:______________

Fax:______________________________________ Phone:______________________________

Patient Name:____

Name of Drug Plan:____________________________ Phone (if available):___________________

Member Number:______________________________ Prescription Number :__________________

PRESCRIPTION ISSUES

The patient's drug plan has indicated that it will not pay for ___________________________________
___________________________________ for this patient because:

Prior authorization required

Step therapy required. Plan will pay for ______________________________________

Plan only authorizes___________________ dosage units (tablets/capsules) per prescription

Plan does not pay for drug in dosage/format prescribed

Drug is not on the formulary. NOTE:

Plan authorized one-time only payment for this drug

Plan did not authorize one-time payment

Other drugs on the formulary include (if available): __________________________
____

Other reason(s)____

The patient's drug plan covers this drug, but with a high tiered co-pay. Preferred drugs available at lower co-pay: ____

ACTION REQUESTED – Please Respond to Pharmacy:

Pharmacist Requesting Action:____

Urgent – patient is waiting

By next refill:_________________________ (Date)

Provide alternative medication: ____

Other recommended action:____

For Fax Back:
Physician Signature:_____________________________________ **Date:**______________

ACTION REQUESTED – Please Contact Drug Plan:

Request prior authorization

Request exception to formulary

INFORMATION ONLY – No Immediate Action Necessary

PLEASE NOTE: Medicare Part D does not pay for barbiturates, benzodiazepines, fertility drugs, drugs for weight loss or weight gain, drugs for hair growth, over-the-counter drugs, or prescription vitamins (except prenatal vitamins and fluoride preparations).

FROM: Pharmacy Name:____

Fax:____________________ Phone:____________________ e-mail:__________________________

Address:____ Phone: _____________

Information on this form is protected health information and subject to all privacy and security regulations under HIPAA.
Use of this form is endorsed by the Alzheimer's Association, American Medical Association, American Pharmacists Association, Center for Medicare Advocacy, Medical Group Management Association, National Community Pharmacists Association and the National Council on the Aging

cian information, patient information, prescription issues (such as prior authorization required or drug not covered on formulary), pharmacy-specific action requested, drug plan-specific action requested, and pharmacy information. A copy of this type of communication can be used to supplement the documentation of MTMS provided.

An additional mechanism for quick communication between pharmacist and prescriber is emerging. SureScripts is a Web-based platform initially created to help facilitate electronic prescribing. However, the platform also allows prescriber–pharmacist communication on patient-specific issues, and it can enable the pharmacist to view pertinent medical and laboratory data electronically. Pharmacies and physicians have been eager to sign on to this method of communication, although actual use is not yet at high levels.

Recently, Hogue and colleagues[9] proposed a model "superbill" (Resource F) that pharmacists can use to document for patients and third-party payers the types of MTMS provided. Superbills are commonly used in medical practices to provide the patient with a summary of services and to communicate with office staff the payment amounts for services rendered.

Paper or Electronic Documentation?

Regardless of the strategies used to document MTMS, pharmacies must decide how the information will be organized. Pharmacies, like other health care institutions, can choose paper charting or electronic charting.

In some pharmacies, paper charting allows easier access to patient information. Paper charts can be retrieved and taken virtually anywhere the patient may be. On the downside, paper charts take up space and become burdensome over time.

Electronic charting allows MTM documentation entered in a computer software program to be modified over time. If adequate computer equipment is already present in the pharmacy, the addition of an electronic charting system requires no additional pharmacy space. However, staff training is required for appropriate use of the software. And, unlike a paper chart, an electronic chart cannot go anywhere the patient may be.

Despite the potential drawbacks of electronic charting, pharmacies should favor electronic record keeping over paper-based documentation. The rest of the health care world is just beginning to face the challenge of converting years of paper-based records to an electronic format. Pharmacies should avoid this painful step and begin now to use electronic documentation of MTMS.

Conclusion

Effective documentation and billing, perhaps above all else, will be key to pharmacists' ability to capture roles as preferred providers of MTMS. Documentation may take many forms, but consistency is a must. The availability of pharmacist-specific Current Procedural Terminology (CPT) billing codes gives pharmacists a mechanism for capturing professional service fees; however, the billing codes have not yet been widely adopted. Much work remains to be done within the pharmacy profession, but the climate in the health care world has rarely before been so favorable for change.

References

1. Zhan C, Sangl J, Bierman AS, et al. Potentially inappropriate medication use in the community-dwelling elderly. *JAMA.* 2001;286:2823–9.

2. Aparasu RR, Mort JR. Inappropriate prescribing for the elderly: Beers criteria-based review. *Ann Pharmacother.* 2000;34:338–46.

3. Bond WS, Hussar DA. Detection methods and strategies for improving medication compliance. *Am J Hosp Pharm.* 1991;48:1978–88.

4. Rothschild JM, Bates DW, Leape LL. Preventable medical injuries in older patients. *Arch Intern Med.* 2000;160:2717–28.

5. Johnson JA, Bootman JL. Drug-related morbidity and mortality. A cost-of-illness model. *Arch Intern Med.* 1995;155:1949–56.

6. Ernst FR, Grizzle AJ. Drug-related morbidity and mortality: updating the cost-of-illness model. *J Am Pharm Assoc.* 2001;41:192–9.

7. American Pharmacists Association; National Association of Chain Drug Stores Foundation. Medication therapy management in community pharmacy practice: core elements of an MTM service model (version 1.0). *J Am Pharm Assoc.* 2005;45:573–9.

8. American Pharmacists Association; National Association of Chain Drug Stores Foundation. Medication therapy management in pharmacy practice: core elements of an MTM service model. (version 2.0). *J Am Pharm Assoc.* 2008;48:341–53.

9. Hogue MD, McDonough R, Bennett M, et al. A superbill for pharmacy practice. *J Am Pharm Assoc.* In press.

Chapter 8

Avoiding Fraud and Abuse

Alan R. Spies and Virgil Van Dusen

Health care fraud and abuse has become an area of critical concern to federal law enforcement agencies. Former Attorney General Janet Reno deemed it her "number two priority," second only to violent crime.[1] This statement may seem extreme, but the Centers for Medicare and Medicaid Services (CMS) estimates that by the year 2017, health care spending will reach \$4.3 trillion and will account for 19.5% of the gross domestic product.[2] In fiscal year 2003, federal Medicare and Medicaid expenditures topped \$435 billion, making CMS the world's largest single purchaser of health care.[3] The General Accounting Office (GAO; now the Government Accountability Office) estimated in 2001 that health care fraud and abuse account for up to 10% of total health care expenditures.[4] Given the fact that health care fraud costs taxpayers nearly \$100 billion a year,[5] federal and state agencies have made the prosecution of health care fraud a primary focus.[6]

This chapter first attempts to define what constitutes health care fraud, highlighting recent attempts by CMS to combat this problem. Next, it examines federal regulations addressing Medicare and Medicaid fraud. In addition, recent enforcement actions by the federal government against those engaged in health care fraud are discussed. Finally, several recent case examples are presented in an attempt to highlight the seriousness of this problem. The chapter concludes with practical tips that will help all pharmacists, regardless of practice setting, to identify and prevent fraudulent practices in the pharmacy.

CMS Definitions and Actions to Combat Medicare and Medicaid Fraud

Fraud is defined by CMS as "the intentional deception or misrepresentation that an individual knows to be false or does not believe to be true and makes, knowing that the deception could result in some unauthorized benefit to himself/herself or some other person."[7] According to Chris Ferrara, supervisor in the financial investigations department of Medical Mutual of Ohio, prescription drug fraud schemes may include generic limitations, kickbacks, diversion of drugs, and misrepresentation or falsification of trial data by pharmaceutical companies. Pharmacies may commit fraud by filling prescriptions with generic drugs but charging for brand name products or by taking prescriptions never picked up and returning the medication to stock (to be dispensed to other patients) while billing the health care plan for them. As discussed later in this chapter, one pharmacist has gone so far as to fraudulently dilute chemotherapy drugs.[8]

Auditors estimate that some \$12.1 billion in improper Medicare payments (ranging from services that were provided but inadequately documented to inadvertent mistakes to outright fraud and abuse) were made in fiscal year 2001.[9] What strategies is CMS using to combat this problem? In October 2005, CMS announced that it would use state-of-the art systems and expertise to prevent problems in the new Medicare prescription drug program:

> *Through a three-pronged approach, CMS will fight fraud and abuse and help people with Medicare protect themselves. The approach uses new and innovative techniques to monitor and analyze data to help identify fraud; work with law enforcement, prescription drug plans, consumer groups and other key partners to protect consumers and enforce Medicare's rules; and provide basic tips for consumers so they can protect themselves.*[10]

Preventing Fraud and Abuse

With recommendations from law enforcement experts and other fraud and abuse and program integrity experts and organizations, CMS is now working with eight Medicare Rx Integrity Contractors (MEDICs) that possess specialized skills enabling them to find fraud, waste, and abuse in the Medicare prescription drug program. These contractors assist CMS by

- Analyzing data to find problems that may indicate fraud or abuse could be occurring;
- Investigating potential fraudulent activities surrounding enrollment, eligibility determination, or distribution of the prescription drug benefit;
- Investigating unusual activities that could be considered fraudulent as reported by CMS, contractors, or beneficiaries;
- Conducting fraud complaint investigations; and
- Developing and referring cases to the appropriate law enforcement agency as needed.

The eight MEDICs (as of August 2008) are as follows:

- Delmarva Foundation for Medical Care, Inc. of Easton, Maryland
- Electronic Data Systems Corporation (EDS) of Plano, Texas
- IntegriGuard, LLC of Omaha, Nebraska
- Livanta, LLC of Annapolis Junction, Maryland
- Maximus Federal Services, Inc. of Reston, Virginia
- NDCHealth of Atlanta, Georgia
- Perot Systems Government Services, Inc. of Alexandria, Virginia
- Science Applications International Corporation (SAIC) of San Diego, California

CMS has also taken steps to resolve concerns about and premature marketing actions by prescription drug plans. It has issued warning letters to Part D contractors and worked with state regulators to enforce marketing agent licensure requirements.[10]

Working with Law Enforcement

CMS is continuing to take strong steps to combat waste, fraud, and abuse in Medicare and is incorporating those steps into the new drug benefit. Joining CMS in that effort are Medicare beneficiaries, health care providers, and state and federal law enforcement agencies such as the Department of Health and Human Services Office of Inspector General, the

Federal Bureau of Investigation, and the Department of Justice.

The expanded efforts are paying off. In one case, CMS referred to local law enforcement a reported scheme to sell drug benefit cards to people with Medicare; the beneficiaries were being asked for bank card information. In another case, which also was referred to law enforcement, individuals were asked for bank and other personal financial information during attempts to offer assistance with the new prescription drug coverage.[10] Additional cases involving prescription drug fraud are described later in this chapter. Before those cases are presented, however, let us examine some of the federal regulations that govern health care fraud.

Federal Regulations Governing Medicare and Medicaid Fraud

The federal government has achieved some success in recouping taxpayer dollars obtained by fraudulent means. In 2002, the government won or negotiated more than $1.8 billion in judgments and settlements in health care fraud cases and proceedings.[11]

The government's anti-fraud focus has varied from prescription drug sales and marketing activities in the early 1990s[12] to alleged improprieties by hospices and home health agencies in the mid 1990s[13] to nursing homes in the last part of that decade.[14,15] More recently, there has been renewed interest in the activities of prescription drug manufacturers, this time involving pricing practices in addition to sales and marketing activities.[16]

Health care fraud is addressed in several laws and regulations, both federal and state. In the following sections we discuss the most important regulations affecting pharmacy, including a provision for so-called *qui tam* actions, in which an individual bringing a suit under the False Claims Act may collect part of the settlement as a reward for "whistle-blowing."

The False Claims Act

The False Claims Act was enacted in 1863 in response to reports of "rampant fraud" perpetrated on the Union army during the Civil War.[17] This act reads in part:

(a) Liability for Certain Acts.
Any person who
(1) knowingly presents, or causes to be presented, to an officer or employee of the United States Government or a member of the Armed Forces of the United States a false or fraudulent claim for payment or approval;
(2) knowingly makes, uses, or causes to be made or used, a false record or statement to get a false or fraudulent claim paid or approved by the Government;
(3) conspires to defraud the Government by getting a false or fraudulent claim allowed or paid;...
(7) knowingly makes, uses, or causes to be made or used, a false record or statement to conceal, avoid, or decrease an obligation to pay or transmit money or property to the Government,
is liable to the United States Government for a civil penalty of not less than $5,000 and not more than $10,000, plus 3 times the amount of damages which the Government sustains because of the act of that person...
(b) Knowing and Knowingly Defined.
For purposes of this section, the terms "knowing" and "knowingly" mean that a person, with respect to information
(1) has actual knowledge of the information;

(2) *acts in deliberate ignorance of the truth or falsity of the information; or*

(3) *acts in reckless disregard of the truth or falsity of the information,* and no proof of specific intent to defraud is required. [emphasis added][18]

This last provision is especially noteworthy. The fact that no proof of specific intent to defraud is required makes it much easier for the government to win a case against a potential defendant. Thus, it is quite conceivable that a defendant pharmacist could be found guilty of violating the act if he or she were deliberately ignorant of the law in defrauding the government.

Violators are subject to a civil penalty of $5,000 to $10,000 per claim, plus three times the amount of damages incurred by the government. Because of the way health care services are billed, penalties can accrue quickly. Most health care providers generate a bill for each occasion of services rendered to each patient, resulting in the submission of thousands of claims per year.[19] Fraud usually involves seemingly insignificant amounts, such as a few cents or a few dollars per claim, but the amounts can potentially total millions of dollars. For example, a psychiatrist was accused of submitting 8,002 claims, each inflated by approximately $30, for total damages of $245,000. At trial, the government requested penalties of $10,000 per claim, for a total of $81 million.[20]

Qui Tam Provision

The False Claims Act goes further by stating in 31 U.S.C. §3730(d) that:

(1) If the Government proceeds with an action brought by a person under subsection (b), such person shall, subject to the second sentence of this paragraph, receive at least 15 percent but not more than 25 percent of the proceeds of the action or settlement of the claim, depending upon the extent to which the person substantially contributed to the prosecution of the action…

(2) If the Government does not proceed with an action under this section, the person bringing the action or settling the claim shall receive an amount which the court decides is reasonable for collecting the civil penalty and damages. The amount shall be not less than 25 percent and not more than 30 percent of the proceeds of the action or settlement and shall be paid out of such proceeds…[21]

Since amendments in 1986[22] modernized the act and made it more lucrative to pursue *qui tam* actions, the number of health care-related False Claims Act suits has grown exponentially. In 1993, there were 132 *qui tam* actions. By 2002, this number had jumped to approximately 320.[23] This powerful civil law can be invoked not only by federal prosecutors but also by competitors, employees, and even patients and their families.[24]

Medicare and Medicaid Anti-Kickback Statute

The Medicare and Medicaid Patient Protection Act of 1987, as amended (the "Anti-Kickback Statute"), provides, in part, that:

(1) whoever knowingly and willfully solicits or receives any remuneration (including any kickback, bribe or rebate) directly or indirectly, overtly or covertly, in cash or in kind

(A) in return for referring an individual to a person for the furnishing or arranging for the

> *furnishing of any item or service for which payment may be made in whole or in part under [Medicare] or a State health care program, or*
>
> *(B) in return for purchasing, leasing, ordering, or arranging for or recommending purchasing, leasing, or ordering any good, facility, service, or item for which payment may be made in whole or in part under [Medicare] or a State health care program, shall be guilty of a felony and upon conviction thereof, shall be fined not more than $25,000 or imprisoned for not more than five years, or both.*[25]

Unlike the False Claims Act, the Anti-Kickback Statute is a criminal law specifically targeting improper activities involving health care items and services. This federal statute attempts to cover a vast range of financial relationships that include health care providers and their patients and manufacturers or suppliers from whom the health care providers obtain their products. Furthermore, this law strives to limit the influence of financial incentives over health care decisions, demanding that such decisions be made solely on the basis of which products and services best serve the patient's interests.[26,27]

Before specific enforcement actions by state and federal governments are discussed, it is important to emphasize some points regarding the Anti-Kickback Statute. First, the law prohibits both the offer and the payment of remuneration and, as such, subjects both parties to prosecution (provided they have the requisite intent). It should be noted that remuneration is defined rather broadly to mean not only the exchange of money, but anything of value or any type of benefit offered to the referring party, including relieving that party of an existing financial burden.

There are exceptions under the act for a few categories of activities, known as "safe harbors," that are deemed to "pose little or no threat of abuse or to be otherwise desirable or legitimate arrangements."[28] However, the safe harbor requirements are very narrow and do not provide protection for many real-life business arrangements.[29] Each safe harbor has specific criteria, but common requirements include (1) a signed written agreement, (2) a minimum 1-year term, (3) payment consistent with "fair market value," and (4) compensation set in advance and not dependent on the volume or value of referrals or other business between the parties.

In determining whether to prosecute under the statute, the Office of Inspector General has stated that it will look to a variety of factors, including (1) the potential for increased charges or costs to payers, especially the government, (2) the potential encouragement of overutilization (e.g., the ordering or performance of health care services beyond those that are medically necessary), (3) the potential for adverse effects on competition, and (4) the intent of the parties.[30]

Applying the above regulations to the pharmacy profession, the Office of Inspector General noted the following in a 1994 Special Fraud Alert on prescription drug marketing schemes:

> *Traditionally, physicians and pharmacists have been trusted to provide treatments and recommend products in the best interest of the patient. In an era of aggressive drug marketing, however, patients may now be using prescription drug items, unaware that their physician or pharmacist is compensated for promoting the*

selection of a specific product.[31]

It is imperative that pharmacists use their professional judgment in making appropriate drug therapy decisions for their patients. Failure to do so may result in action by the federal or state government.

Federal and State Enforcement Actions

When Congress enacted the Medicaid and Medicare programs in 1965, it failed to concurrently implement safeguards against potential fraudulent practices. During the first decade of these widely popular programs, in the absence of a specific state or federal law enforcement agency responsible for providing oversight, there was widespread fraud by some in the health care community. New York was the first state to establish an independent counsel's office to combat this type of health care fraud. That office's efforts and results were remarkable; within a few years, millions of dollars in restitution and fines was recovered.[32]

Because of the positive outcome in New York, Congress passed legislation in 1977 that provided the impetus for efforts in other states. By providing up to 90% of the funding for the first 3 years of operation of state anti-fraud units, followed by 75% thereafter, this legislation spurred the individual states to investigate and prosecute health care fraud. That funding continues today. As required by the legislation, the state fraud task forces consist of teams of attorneys, investigators, and auditors who are highly trained to both investigate and prosecute health care fraud. Over the years these teams have proved to be extremely successful in completing their mission.

Currently, the country has 48 Medicaid fraud units, organized under the umbrella of the National Association of Medicaid Fraud Control Units, which is headquartered in Washington, D.C.[32] These units routinely recover millions of dollars through both civil prosecution and criminal restitution. Criminal conviction for fraudulent practices results in more than mere fines. Convicted health care practitioners are required to be excluded from participation in federal health care programs such as Medicaid and Medicare. Such a requirement can be financially devastating to an organization that relies heavily on Medicaid and Medicare patients.

Coordination of Resources

It is not uncommon for a state's Medicaid fraud unit to join forces with the regional U.S. Attorney's office for the purpose of collaborating on matters of mutual interest. One such example is the 2004 case of *United States v Raphael Farra, MD.* In this case, the U.S. Attorney's office alleged that the defendant submitted false claims under the Medicare program. Prior to trial, the U.S. Attorney was able to reach a settlement with the defendant for $285,000. Because of the defendant's fraudulent conduct, the Medicaid program of the state of New Hampshire was also negatively affected, and the state was permitted to recover Medicaid damages in a parallel settlement. This coordination of federal and state authorities will probably continue to have synergistic outcomes in the prosecution of health care fraud cases.

Surveillance and Utilization Review Subcommittee

One of the current requirements under federal Medicaid law is that states establish a unit to stamp out fraudulent and improper billing practices. These units are identified as a surveillance and utilization review subsystem (SURS). One method by which these units operate is to distribute explanation of benefits notices to consumers. These notices specifically ask the beneficiary to review the services claimed by the provider. If a discrepancy is noted, the beneficiary is to report it to the SURS unit.[32]

Pharmacies providing services to Medicaid recipients should understand that the state agency will rely heavily on consumer reports in determining if such services were, indeed, provided. Because Medicaid is a state-run program that is federally funded but often has significant funding from the individual states as well, both the federal government and state governments are interested in fraud cases. Considering all the different types of cases that a U.S. Attorney's office can pursue, will pharmacies be prosecuted for fraudulent activities? With recent audits indicating that improper Medicare payments amount to $12 billion a year, the government simply cannot afford to ignore fraud. Much of the cost of the new Medicare prescription drug program could potentially be funded by an influx of penalties recovered for fraudulent behavior. Great care must be taken to ensure that the benefit has in fact been provided for all claims submitted for payment. If a pharmacist is convicted of Medicaid fraud, the fines are costly. Of even greater cost is the exclusion from Medicaid participation, which is both mandatory and permanent. The CMS Web site (www.cms.gov) offers useful tips for both providers and beneficiaries on preventing fraud and reporting suspected fraudulent activities. The sidebar on page 66 lists salient points for beneficiaries, including information on an incentive program for reporting suspected fraud (Figure 8-1).

Figure 8-1

Medicare's Incentive Reward Program for Fraud and Abuse. (Developed by the Health Care Financing Administration [now the Centers for Medicare and Medicaid Services], Program Integrity Group, Baltimore, Maryland, December 1998.)

YOU CAN HELP FIGHT MEDICARE FRAUD AND ABUSE!

MEDICARE'S INCENTIVE REWARD PROGRAM FOR FRAUD AND ABUSE

TO HELP FIGHT MEDICARE FRAUD AND ABUSE FOLLOW THESE 3 EASY STEPS:

STEP 1: Compare your Medicare statement with the services you received from your doctor or other health care provider. If you have questions about the statement or the services provided, talk first to your doctor or health care provider.

STEP 2: If you still have questions after talking to your doctor or provider, contact your Medicare contractor. The telephone number is listed on your Medicare statement. The contractor will follow up on your questions and will determine if an investigation is necessary. If the investigation leads to the recovery of at least $100 from a health care provider, you may be eligible for a reward.

STEP 3: If you feel further action is needed in dealing with Medicare fraud or abuse, call the Medicare fraud hotline at 1-800-447-8477. Your call will be taken seriously. If a review of your complaint leads to the recovery of at least $100 from a provider, you may be eligible for a reward.

TO BE ELIGIBLE FOR A REWARD:

- The initial complaint must be received on or after July 8, 1998;
- The information you give must lead to a recovery of at least $100;
- The information must not be related to a fraud investigation already under way; and
- You must not be related to an employee of certain federal government agencies.

If the information you provide makes you eligible for a reward, you will be mailed a letter after all Medicare funds have been recovered. Please be aware that investigations take a long time to complete; some take several months or years. The amount of the reward you may receive will not be more than 10% of the Medicare funds recovered in the case, or $1000, whichever is less.

**REMEMBER, MOST HEALTH CARE PROVIDERS ARE HONEST.
MANY QUESTIONS OR CONCERNS END UP BEING HONEST CLERICAL ERRORS.**

Fraud Case Review

Health care fraud enforcement is flourishing. It appears that this trend will continue in spite of the human resources currently allocated to the war on terrorism. Furthermore, leaders of the enforcement movement, such as those at the Office of Inspector General, the Department of Justice, and the U.S. Attorneys' offices, usually are not political appointees and will not be swayed by views of the executive branch of government. These government groups have developed proactive initiatives targeting particular sectors of the health care industry for intensive scrutiny. The first such action of this type was known as Operation Restore Trust.[24] Its purpose was to provide a coordinated effort between state and federal groups that focused on fraud by home health agencies, nursing homes, hospices, and durable medical equipment providers. Subsequent initiatives continue and, in the future, specific sectors of the health care industry will be targeted, including pharmacy practice and the pharmaceutical industry.

Tips for Beneficiaries

- Any Medicare beneficiary who suspects fraud should call 1-800-MEDICARE (1-800-633-4227), the local State Health Insurance Assistance Program, or a local law enforcement agency. Figure 8-1 outlines a Medicare incentive program to help fight fraud and abuse; a reward is given for information leading to the recovery of Medicare funds from health care providers who engage in fraud and abuse against the Medicare program.
- Medicare beneficiaries need to be aware of how to protect themselves against identity theft. "Quick Facts about Medicare Prescription Drug Coverage and How to Protect Your Personal Information" (www.medicare.gov/publications/pubs/pdf/11147.pdf) will help beneficiaries learn key ways of protecting themselves.
- Anyone with Medicare who finds that someone is inappropriately using his or her personal information should call 1-800-MEDICARE and the Federal Trade Commission's identity theft hotline at 1-877-438-4338 to make a report (TTY users should call 1-866-653-4261). Beneficiaries who feel themselves to be in danger for any reason should call their local police department immediately.[10]

While the government is a key component in the enforcement of laws and the prosecution of violators, a new force has emerged. Private individuals known as *relators* provide information to the government that can result in prosecution, conviction, and fines. In most cases, if the lawsuit filed by the relator or information conveyed to the government results in a settlement or judgment, the relator is entitled to a share of the recovery. Some relators have reaped multimillion dollar recoveries by using the False Claims Act. Although one might like to think that such individuals are altruistic, the U.S. Supreme Court has concluded that "*qui tam* relators are... motivated primarily by prospects of monetary reward rather than the public good."

TAP Pharmaceuticals

The case of *TAP Pharmaceuticals v U.S. Department of Health and Human Services* is a straightforward example of health care fraud.[33,34] Federal government health care programs have traditionally reimbursed physicians on the basis of actual charges or 95% of the average wholesale price (AWP) for drugs sold or administered in the office setting. The AWP was typically based on information contained in pharmaceutical pricing publications and databases, which in turn received information directly from the manufacturers. If the actual acquisition price was less than the AWP listed price, then reimbursement by the government based on an AWP billing resulted in a nice profit—or kickback. This was evident in the present case. In effect, the government paid millions of dollars more than it should have to physicians to acquire the product at prices below AWP.

There is a significant difference between this case and typical pharmacy reimbursement involving AWP less a percentage. The government is aware of discounts given by manufacturers and wholesalers to pharmacies. This knowledge is based on a requirement under the Omnibus Budget Reconciliation Act of 1990 that obligates manufacturers offering discount pricing to anyone to make that information available, while giving that same pricing to government programs. In the TAP case, the true pricing structure of its product was concealed from Medicare and, furthermore, the company wrongly advised its customers to report AWP rather than the actual drug price.

In October 2001, TAP Pharmaceutical Products agreed to pay a record $875 million to settle both civil and criminal fraud allegations. This was a *qui tam* suit filed by TAP's former vice president of sales, who claimed to have quit because of concerns about the company's sales and marketing practices. Another *qui tam* suit was filed by a physician, who reported that he had been offered an "education grant" if he would reverse a decision that provided HMO coverage for a less expensive drug from a competitor. The whistleblowers shared approximately $95 million from the proceeds of the recovery.

Hospital Corporation of America, Inc. (HCA)

The amount of the settlement in the TAP case may seem almost beyond belief, but another case actually resulted in a $1.7 billion payout.[35] HCA, Inc. (formerly known as Columbia/HCA and HCA—The Healthcare Company) agreed to pay civil penalties and damages arising from false claims the government alleged HCA submitted to Medicare and other federal health programs in addition to possible kickbacks to physicians. This settlement was also the result of a *qui tam* action. The whistleblowers received a combined share of $151,591,500, the highest combined *qui tam* award ever paid out by the government.

Caremark, Inc.

United States v Caremark, Inc. was a case more directly related to the practice of pharmacy. Caremark, Inc., a major health care corporation, pleaded guilty to fraud in its home infusion, oncology, hemophilia, and human growth hormone businesses. The organization was guilty of paying kickbacks to physicians and others in order to entice referrals and for using certain products, such as Protropin (Genentech, Inc.), a human growth hormone. Caremark agreed to pay $161 million to the federal and affected state governments in fines, restitution, and damages.[36] As part of the settlement, Caremark sold its home infusion business and canceled contracts with physicians and other referral sources. It also agreed that its remaining businesses would comply with a "corporate integrity plan" that spells out measures to ensure future compliance with health care laws and regulations.

As noted in the Caremark case, one of the most significant developments in settling health care fraud allegations is the requirement that health care providers enter into corporate integrity agreements. Common elements of the agreement include the appointment of a compliance officer, compliance training procedures, methods for employees to report violations, and reports to the government documenting the provider's compliance efforts. In return, the government agrees not to seek the provider's exclusion from federal health care programs. Oversight and reporting requirements typically last 5 years. Compliance program guidelines are available from the government for health care providers that are required to establish such programs.

Wal-Mart and Rite Aid

Both Rite Aid and Wal-Mart have also found themselves faced with charges of fraudulent billing.[37,38] Their fines, while not as significant as in the three previously cited cases, certainly must force every pharmacist to stop and rethink the issue of fraudulent billing.

Unlawful fraudulent practices, innocent as they might appear, resulted in Rite Aid paying out $7 million to the federal and state governments. Wal-Mart paid $2.8 million. Why? Each of these retail giants billed government programs for drugs that were never delivered to beneficiaries. In most of the fraud issues addressed, the government was billed for full quantities of patient prescriptions when only partial amounts of the prescriptions were dispensed. This practice stemmed from medicine shortages when patients came to pick up prescriptions. Only a portion of the prescription was filled, but the patient never returned later to pick up the rest of the medication. Although there may have been no intent to defraud, the government determined that such actions were indeed fraudulent in nature and deserving of penalties. Whistleblowers, once again, brought this activity to the attention of the government and received a portion of the settlement in each of these cases; one individual received more than a million dollars.

How do pharmacies prevent such claims? Policies and procedures need to be in place to address billing for partial prescription dispensing. In the future, pharmacies should bill only for the exact amount of medication that is actually picked up by the patient. Compliance with such policies should be reviewed on a periodic basis. Employee training should emphasize past penalties and the possibility of future consequences for failure to recognize that such activities are fraudulent.

Implications for Pharmacists

Although the cases cited above were directed toward corporate entities, the individual pharmacist must realize that many fraud claims can result from what might appear to be innocuous acts. For example, the switching of tablets to capsules (of the same drug and same strength) may not appear to be significant, until you consider the following case.

Omnicare Pharmacy of Maine is a company that filled orders for long-term care facilities statewide. During the time in question, state officials noticed the percentage of patients taking capsules of ranitidine climbed from less than 5% in March 2000 to 95% 3 months later. The switches came in response to a federal rule change that capped the Medicaid reimbursement for tablets but not for capsules.[39] The pricing difference was significant. Reimbursement for the capsules was fixed at $82.77 per month, whereas the tablets would be reimbursed at only $15.10 per month. It was later determined that Omnicare filed for reimbursement for 2,129 prescriptions for the capsules that were illegal prescriptions because the prescribers either did not authorize them or authorized them on the basis of misrepresentations by Omnicare. The company agreed to settle the case (while denying any wrongdoing) by making payments of $60,000 to patients or their insurance companies that were not covered by Medicaid but received the capsules and $614,740 to the state Medicaid program, plus other fines and penalties. The simple act of changing a prescription medication from a tablet to a capsule can result in charges of fraud.

In another case involving Omnicare, a whistleblower reported that a supplier of drugs to Medicaid-eligible patients in long-term care facilities located in New Jersey failed to provide full credit for returned medications, which were subsequently dispensed again.[40,41] Omnicare's practice was to send Medicaid a check for 50% of the cost of the returned medication and keep the other 50% to cover the expense of restocking and redispensing the medication. Was this action fraudulent? The court ruled that it was not. The court's rationale was based on a New Jersey regulation that required reversal when "services were not provided." The regulation did not state that "services are not provided" when medications are dispensed and subsequently returned, meaning that no mandate exists to reverse a claim once a medication has been returned. Certainly the organization was benefiting financially by giving only partial credit, but the court seemed to hold that no reimbursement was actually required. Although it may appear that the government was cheated, the wording of the regulations was used to show that there is no fraud if no intentional misrepresentation, concealment, or nondisclosure is made at the time of dispensing.[42]

Pharmacist Robert Courtney

No discussion of pharmacy fraud is complete without a review of the *Robert Courtney v United States* case. Courtney was an independent pharmacy owner in Kansas City, Missouri. Local, state, and federal investigations revealed that Courtney intentionally diluted chemotherapy drug products for many patients over the span of several years.[43] His scheme began to unravel when a sales representative for Eli Lilly and Co., which makes Gemzar (gemcitabine), found a discrepancy between the amount of Gemzar the pharmacy ordered and the amount it billed a Kansas City-area physician. In July 2001, the Federal Bureau of Investigation's Kansas City division discovered, through a sting operation, that prescriptions prepared by Courtney contained anywhere from 39% to less than 1% of the active ingredient, instead of the 100% they should have contained. Authorities estimated that Courtney diluted 98,000 prescriptions, potentially affecting about 4,200 patients.

Courtney pleaded guilty to 20 federal counts of tampering and adulterating or misbranding the chemotherapeutic agents Taxol (paclitaxel), Gemzar (gemcitabine), Platinol (cisplatin), and Paraplatin (carboplatin). Courtney's pharmacy license was revoked, and he was forced to sell his two pharmacies. Federal authorities seized Courtney's assets, totaling about $12 million, and set up a victims' fund. Courtney faced some 300 lawsuits accusing him of fraud and wrongful death. One of those suits was brought by a 42-year-old woman suffering from cancer who had bought Gemzar and Taxol from Courtney. She alleged both a shortened life span and posttraumatic stress disorder. The jury awarded the woman damages in excess of $2.225 billion.[44]

As in most fraud cases, greed was a primary motivator. Court records indicated that Courtney "diluted the strength of the chemotherapy drugs out of greed and in order to make more money."[43] How much did Courtney profit from his actions? Federal authorities claim that the dilutions would have saved Courtney hundreds of dollars per dose. For instance, Courtney would have saved about $780 for a single order of Gemzar. Multiplying this amount by the estimated thousands of suspected dilutions gives an indication of the potential profit margin with these fraudulent actions.

Patients have traditionally placed their trust in their pharmacist. Actions by individuals such as Robert Courtney erode that trust. It is incumbent on each pharmacist to adhere to the highest standards—ethically, morally, and legally. The public expects nothing less of us, and our oath requires it.

Practical Tips for Pharmacists

The best insurance against fraud and abuse liability is to implement an effective fraud and abuse compliance program. Margit Nahra,[45] an attorney who specializes in health care fraud and abuse counseling, offers some practical tips that all pharmacists, regardless of practice setting, can use to avoid liability:

1. Stay informed about applicable payment rules and developments in the fraud and abuse laws, and liberally use the resources offered by professional associations. Being overwhelmed by the onslaught of changes is not a defense against liability.
2. Exercise appropriate oversight of staff, and scrutinize contractual relationships.
3. Encourage open staff communication. Employees who feel comfortable discussing possible violations with management are less likely to file *qui tam* suits.
4. Enlist outside assistance as necessary and appropriate. Realistic assessment of what can and cannot be accomplished in-house is critical; potential issues should not be ignored just because you are busy or assistance is costly. The cost of legal defense in a government investigation or prosecution is likely to be far greater than the cost of obtaining help to take the steps necessary to avoid such scrutiny.

References

1. 1994 Annual Report of the Attorney General of the United States. Available at: www.usdoj.gov/ag/annualreports/ar94/finalag.txt.
2. Centers for Medicare and Medicaid Services. National health expenditure projections 2007–2017. Available at: www.cms.hhs.gov/NationalHealthExpendData/Downloads/proj2007.pdf.
3. *A Closer Look: Inspectors General Address Waste, Fraud, Abuse in Federal Mandatory Programs: Hearing Before the House Committee on Budget.* Testimony of Dara Corrigan, Acting Principal Deputy Inspector General, Department of Health and Human Services, before 108th Congress; 2003:82.
4. Matthew DB. Tainted prosecution of tainted claims: the law, economics, and ethics of fighting medical fraud under the civil false claims act. *Indiana Law J.* 2001;73:525–89.
5. Krakoff DS, Holloran MC. The accidental kickback. *Legal Times.* September 15, 1997.
6. Department of Health and Human Services. A comprehensive strategy to fight health care waste, fraud, and abuse. March 9, 2000. Available at: www.hhs.gov/news/press/2000pres/20000309a.html.
7. Centers for Medicare and Medicaid Services. Medicare manual system; pub 100-08, Program Integrity. July 25, 2003. Available at: www.cms.hhs.gov/Transmittals/Downloads/R47PI.pdf.
8. Mass A. Pharmaceutical fraud: Rx for trouble. *Employee Benefit News.* October 1, 2004.
9. Department of Health and Human Services Office of Inspector General. Improper fiscal year 2001 Medicare fee-for-service payments. No. A-17-01-02002. February 2002. Available at: http://oig.hhs.gov/oas/reports/cms/a0102002.pdf.
10. Centers for Medicare and Medicaid Services Office of External Affairs. *The New Medicare Prescription Drug Benefit: Attacking Fraud and Abuse* (Medicare Fact Sheet). October 7, 2005.
11. U.S. Department of Health and Human Services and Department of Justice. Health care fraud and abuse control program annual report for FY 2002. Available at: www.oig.hhs.gov/reading/hcfac/HCFAC%20Annual%20Report%20FY%202002.htm.

12. Department of Health and Human Services Office of Inspector General. Promotion of Prescription Drugs through Payments and Gifts. OEI-01-90-00480. 1991. Available at: http://oig.hhs.gov/oei/reports/oei-01-90-00480.pdf.

13. Department of Health and Human Services Office of Inspector General. Special fraud alert: physician liability for certifications in the provision of medical equipment and supplies and home health services. January 1999. Available at: http://oig.hhs.gov/fraud/docs/alertsandbulletins/dme.htm.

14. Department of Health and Human Services Office of Inspector General. Publication of OIG special fraud alert: fraud and abuse in nursing home arrangements with hospices. *Federal Register.* 1998;63(Apr 24):20415.

15. Department of Health and Human Services Office of Inspector General. Publication of the OIG compliance program guidance for nursing facilities. *Federal Register.* 2000;65 (Mar 16):14295 n.49. Available at: http://bulk.resource.org/gpo.gov/register/2000/2000_14295.pdf.

16. Department of Health and Human Services Office of Inspector General. OIG compliance program guidance for pharmaceutical manufacturers. *Federal Register.* 2003;68 (May 5):23731.

17. The False Claims Act. History of the law. Available at: www.allaboutquitam.org/fca_history.shtml.

18. 31 USC §3729(a)(1-3, 7)(b)(1-3).

19. Bucy PH. The PATH from regulator to hunter: the exercise of prosecutorial discretion in the investigation of physicians at teaching hospitals. *St. Louis Univ Law J.* 2000;44:3–50.

20. *United States v Krizek.*111 F3d 934, 936 (DC Cir 1997).

21. 31 USC §3730(d)(1-2).

22. False Claims Amendments Act of 1986, Pub L No. 99-562, 100 Stat 3153.

23. Taxpayers Against Fraud. *Qui Tam* Statistics. Available at: www.taf.org/statistics.html.

24. Krause JH. A conceptual model of health care fraud enforcement. *Brooklyn J Law Policy.* 2003;12:55.

25. 42 USC 1320a-7(b).

26. Bulleit TN Jr, Krause JH. Kickbacks, courtesies, or cost-effectiveness? Application of the Medicare Antikickback Law to the marketing and promotional practices of drug and medical device manufacturers. *Food Drug Law J.* 1999;54(3):279–323.

27. Department of Health and Human Services Office of Inspector General. Medicare and Medicare Programs: Fraud and Abuse; OIG Anti-Kickback Provisions. July 29, 1991. Available at: www.oig.hhs.gov/fraud/docs/safeharborregulations/072991.htm.

28. Boese JT, McClain BC. Why Thompson is wrong: misuse of the False Claims Act to enforce the Anti-Kickback Act. *Ala Law Rev.* 1999;51(fall):1–55.

29. 42 C.F.R. 1001.952(d).

30. Medicare and State Health Care Programs. *Federal Register.* 1991;56:35954–6.

31. Office of Inspector General. Special fraud alert: prescription drug marketing schemes (August 1994), reprinted in Publication of OIG Special Fraud Alerts. *Federal Register.* 1994;59(Dec 19):65372–6. Available at: www.oig.hhs.gov/fraud/docs/alertsandbulletins/121994.html.

32. Cahill JS. Combating health care fraud and patient abuse: the role of the Medicaid fraud unit. *New Hampshire Bar J.* 2004;45(spring):71 at 72.

33. *Re: Lupron® Marketing & Sales Practices Litig,* 245 F Supp 2d 280 (D Mass 2003).

34. *TAP Pharmaceuticals v United States Department of Health and Human Services.* 163 F3d 199; 1998 US App LEXIS 30447; 59 Soc Sec Rep Service 532 (4th Cir 1998).

35. United States Department of Justice. Largest Health Care Fraud Case in U.S. History Settled. HCA Investigation Nets Record Total of $1.7 Billion. Available at: www.justice.gov/opa/pr/2003/June/03_civ_386.htm.

36. United States Department of Justice. 1995 Annual Report. Chapter I Making America Safe. Available at: www.usdoj.gov/ag/annualreports/ar95/chapter1.htm.

37. Wal-Mart to pay $2.8 million for allegedly dispensing partial prescriptions & billing U.S. health programs for full amounts [news release]. U.S. Department of Justice; June 25, 2004. Available at: www.usdoj.gov/opa/pr/2004/June/04_civ_446.htm.

38. Rite Aid to pay $7 million for allegedly submitting false prescription claims to government [news release]. U.S. Department of Justice; June 25, 2004. Available at: www.usdoj.gov/opa/pr/2004/June/04_civ_445.htm.

39. Drug switch resolved for $1M. Omnicare unit settles claims. August 26, 2004. Available at: www.enquirer.com/editions/2004/08/26/biz_biz2omni.html.

40. *Re: Quinn (Omnicare)*, 382 F2d 423, 3rd Cir, 2004 US App Lexis 18474 (applying New Jersey law, September 1, 2004).

41. *Re: Genesis Health Ventures*, Slip Op No. 03-2313 (October 12, 2004), 2004 Lexis 21170 (also applying New Jersey law).

42. Vivian JC. Medicaid fraud or not? *US Pharmacist.* 2004;29(12):55–6,58. Available at: www.uspharmacist.com/index.asp?show=article&page=8_1398.htm.

43. *United States v Courtney,* 362 F3d 497; 2004 US App. LEXIS 6409 (8th Cir 2004).

44. Jury Awards Woman $2.2 Billion in Diluted Drug Case. Available at: www.usatoday.com/news/nation/2002-10-10-diluted-drugs-case_x.htm.

45. Nahra M. New developments in federal fraud and abuse law: what every consultant pharmacist needs to know. *Consult Pharm.* 1997;12:1087–99.

Section 

Practical Implementation Strategies for Medication Therapy Management Services

Editor: Michael D. Hogue

Chapter 9

Providing Medication Therapy Management Services in Community Pharmacy Practice

Jean-Venable "Kelly" Goode and Bradley P. Tice

Community pharmacists will be the primary pharmacy provider of medication therapy management services (MTMS), because both pharmacists and patients are in the community setting. In 2006, pharmacists held 243,000 jobs, and 62% of those were in a community pharmacy (independent, chain, supermarket, or mass merchandiser).[1] Approximately 65% of physician visits end with a prescription being written—and usually filled at a community pharmacy. Of 3.4 billion prescriptions written in 2006, for example, 81% were filled at community pharmacies.[2]

The focus of this chapter is helping the community pharmacy practitioner implement MTMS. Several key elements must be in place for MTMS to be successful in a community setting: development of the product or service, preparation of the site, training, reporting, monitoring and tracking, and marketing. This chapter systematically describes the tasks involved in planning and implementing MTMS.

The chapter integrates two basic project management tools to help readers effectively visualize how to implement MTMS in a timely and efficient manner. The first is the work breakdown structure (Figure 9-1), a tool used to define all aspects of a project. Each component of the project is identified. Then, subtasks specific to each practice site can be identified. Implementation thus can be broken down to the lowest level, with tasks that can be achieved within a 2-week period and assigned to a single person. For instance, 1.0 Develop Products might be broken into 1.1 Services, 1.2 Documentation, 1.3 Policies and Procedures, and so on. Similarly, 3.0 Training might comprise 3.1 Define Objectives, 3.2 Identify Trainers, 3.3 Develop Training Program, and so on. Each component of Figure 9-1 is discussed in a section of the chapter.

The second project management tool we will use is the critical path diagram (Figure 9-2), which, using the work breakdown structure components, illustrates the sequence of events in MTMS development and implementation. As you determine how long each task will take, you will be able to determine how long it will take to prepare to offer your services.

Develop Products or Services (1.0)

The first block on the critical path diagram is Develop Products or Services (1.0). The pharmacy profession has created a comprehensive working definition of MTMS,[3] and most pharmacists have been involved to some degree in informal MTMS in their practice. To prepare for a service that will be compensated, however, changes in current practice may be necessary. The following tips will be helpful in preparing for change:[4]

Warren Narducci, PharmD, Nishna Valley Pharmacy, and Anne Burns, BPharm, American Pharmacists Association, are acknowledged for their thoughts and contributions to this chapter.

1. Examine your corporate/business culture to discover any impediments to change. Some traditions and practices may need to be re-engineered to meet the new service needs.
2. Talk regularly about change so that employees think in terms of change and help to make the change happen.
3. Make expectations clear. Key employees should know that embracing change is part of their responsibility.
4. Monitor company/business procedures and systems to be sure they support change.

Pharmacists may offer all of the components of medication therapy management (MTM) in their practice, or only a few. An important step will be deciding the type of product or service to offer patients.

Before addressing the type of product or service they will develop, pharmacists need to assess the patients they serve and their practice environment. Typically, this involves a needs assessment and SWOT (strengths, weaknesses, opportunities and threats) analysis (Table 9-1).[5] A needs assessment helps to identify gaps between what products and services are available and what should be available for patients. Surveys, questionnaires, and focus groups may be used in the assessment. If patients do not recognize that they need a service or product, it will be very hard to market and sell.

Figure 9-1

Work Breakdown Structure

Numbering is for reference purposes only and does not indicate a sequential order of completion.

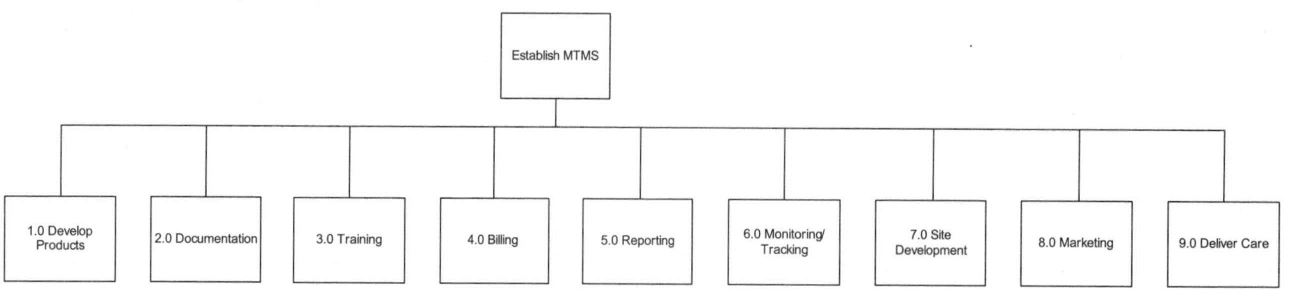

Figure 9-2

Critical Path Diagram

Numbers refer to location in the work breakdown structure. The numbers are not sequential; they are for reference and grouping, not for indicating chronological order for completion.

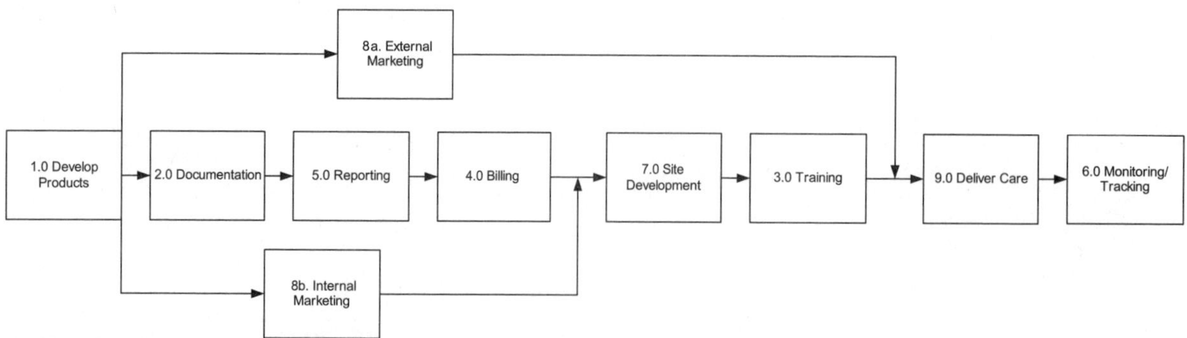

Table 9-1

Example of a SWOT Analysis for an Independent Pharmacy

Strengths	Weaknesses	Opportunities	Threats
Private consultation area	Not using consultation area for anything but storage	Large number of Medicare patients	Takes up possible sales floor space
Pharmacy in convenient location	Staffing is low	No other pharmacies in the vicinity	Local health plan pushes mail order

Pharmacists must also evaluate other factors that may affect the type of product or service that is offered, such as the following:[6]

1. Are there staffing constraints?
2. How much time will it take to offer the service?
3. Will the service take place at the point of dispensing or during appointments?
4. Will all pharmacists be required to provide MTMS?
5. Will funds be needed to redesign space or purchase equipment?
6. How will the service be marketed?
7. Will the product generate revenue?
8. Will additional training be needed?

The Centers for Medicare and Medicaid Services (CMS) MTMS final regulations[7] give pharmacists a target population (individuals with multiple chronic diseases who are taking multiple Part D covered drugs and are likely to incur annual costs that exceed a certain amount). However, pharmacists should not limit product or service development to these patients only. Other patients who might benefit from MTMS may include those who

- Receive medications from more than one prescriber,
- Receive a medication that requires laboratory monitoring for efficacy or adverse effects,
- Do not adhere to medications or lifestyle changes,
- Have recently been discharged from a hospital, or
- Are disabled.

After defining the target patient population, pharmacists must develop a process for identifying these patients in their practice. Most often, this is done by having patients complete an intake sheet (Figure 9-3) when they present to the pharmacy. Information on the intake sheet can be used to identify potential patients for MTMS.

The American Pharmacists Association and the National Association of Chain Drug Stores Foundation have adopted a joint model for basic MTMS in pharmacy practice (Resource A). *Medication Therapy Management in Pharmacy Practice: Core Elements of an MTM Service Model (Version 2.0)* involves patients in decision-making to optimize medication use.[8] The model is intended to be used for all patients who can benefit from pharmacist-provided MTMS, regardless of whether they are in public or private health plans or self-paying. The five core elements in the model are as follows:

- Medication therapy review,
- Personal medication record,
- Medication action plan,
- Intervention or referral, and
- Documentation and follow-up.

Medication therapy review is the foundation of the model. The review can be either comprehensive or targeted. In

Figure 9-3

Sample Patient Information Sheet

Name: ______________________________ M/F: ___ Date of Birth: __________

Address: ____

Home Phone: __________________ Office Phone:_________________________

Employer: ______________________ Job Title: _________________________

Height: ______ Weight: ________Race: _________ Pregnant? ☐ Yes ☐ No

Medical History
Please check all that apply:

☐ Alzheimer's	☐ Depression	☐ Kidney disease
☐ Angina	☐ Diabetes	☐ Liver disease
☐ Anemia	☐ Emphysema	☐ Lung disease
☐ Arthritis	☐ Headache/migraine	☐ Nervous disorders
☐ Asthma	☐ Heart condition	☐ Parkinson's disease
☐ Blood disorder	☐ High blood pressure	☐ Ulcers
☐ Cancer	☐ High cholesterol	☐ Other:

Medication History
Please list any medication you are currently taking that we do not have on record:

____

What problems are you having with your medications?

____

What nonprescription medications, supplements, or herbals are you currently taking?

____

Are you allergic to any medications?__________ If yes, please list medication and type of reaction experienced:

____

Are there any medications that you cannot tolerate? __________ If yes, please list medication and the type of reaction experienced:

____

Lifestyle History
Do you use tobacco?(check all that apply): ☐ None ☐ Smoke ☐ Chew ☐ Other:_____How often?_____
Do you consume alcohol? ☐ Yes ☐ No If yes, what type of beverage? ______ How often?_____
Do you exercise? ☐ Yes ☐ No If yes, what type of exercise? ___________ How often?_____

Since health information may change periodically, I will attempt to notify the pharmacist of any changes in my medical conditions, medications, or allergies.

____
Signature   Date

a comprehensive review, the pharmacist assesses the patient's overall health and reviews all of the patient's medications (prescription, nonprescription, herbal and other dietary supplements) for appropriateness and to identify any medication-related problems. The model recommends that patients receive an annual comprehensive review and additional comprehensive reviews after events such as discharge from a hospital on new medications, an emergency department visit, or admission to or discharge from a long-term care or assisted living facility. Throughout the year, the patient receives targeted medication therapy reviews to address new medication problems or for follow-up monitoring. Targeted reviews are performed for patients who have received a comprehensive review in the past year.

According to the model, after a comprehensive medication therapy review the patient should receive a personal medication record—a complete list of all medications, including all prescription and nonprescription medications, herbal products, and dietary supplements. This record is intended to be used by the patient and shared with other health care providers to promote continuity of care. The personal medication record should be updated as necessary.

After all medication therapy reviews, the patient should also receive a medication action plan—a plan written in patient-focused language and intended to assist the patient in medication self-management.

If problems with medication therapy or other health problems are identified, the pharmacist will intervene or refer the patient to the appropriate health care provider. Collaboration with physicians and other health care providers is an important component of MTMS.

The pharmacist documents the MTM visit in a specific format for ongoing monitoring and billing and schedules a follow-up visit for the patient if necessary.

The most basic MTMS should involve a medication therapy review, repeated at least annually and more frequently if the pharmacist believes this is necessary. In the patient interview, the pharmacist should assess overall health status, including current and previous disease states or conditions. If necessary, the pharmacist should obtain permission from the patient to seek additional information from the patient's other health care providers (Figure 9-4). The pharmacist should then assess whether the patient has any medication therapy problems, such as[9]

Figure 9-4

Sample Consent for Release of Medical Information

CONSENT FOR RELEASE OF MEDICAL INFORMATION

I hereby authorize the release of medical information, including but not limited to laboratory results, to XXX Pharmacy.

Date: ______________ Signature: ______________________________

Printed name: ___________________________

1. Taking a drug without an indication,
2. Not receiving needed drug therapy,
3. Receiving the wrong drug therapy or product,
4. Receiving too low a dose,
5. Receiving too high a dose,
6. Not adhering to the drug therapy regimen,
7. Experiencing adverse effects, or
8. Experiencing a drug–drug, drug–laboratory test, or drug–food interaction.

Figure 9-5 shows a template pharmacists can use when conducting the medication therapy review. This form should be used in combination with the patient information sheet (Figure 9-3).

After the assessment, the pharmacist formulates a plan that includes resolution of any medication therapy problems, education and training on appropriate medication use and the importance of medication adherence, counseling on preventive services for any chronic diseases, and education and training on appropriate lifestyle modifications and the importance of adherence to lifestyle changes. The plan must include any patient-specific goals and take into account the patient's ability to carry out the goals (ultimately, the patient is in control of his or her own health care). The pharmacist should communicate appropriate information to the patient's other health care providers, including any recommendations for resolving medication therapy problems. The initial interview should include a schedule for

Figure 9-5

Sample Medication Regimen Review Template

Patient name: ____________________ Date: ________ Chief complaint: ________________

Problem	Drugs	Drug-Related Problem	Intervention	Desired outcome/ Follow-up
1.				
2.				
3.				
4.				
5.				
6.				

Subjective: ____

____

Objective: ____

Assessment: ____

____

____

Plan: ____

____

____

Follow-up appointment: ____________________ Phone follow-up: ________________

Pharmacist: ________________________ Signature: ________________________

monitoring and follow-up. Pharmacists should document all MTMS provided for patients (see Chapter 7). Figure 9-6 is an algorithm for pharmacists' patient care process.

Other services may be incorporated during the regular workflow of the pharmacy. These include antibiotic callback (pharmacists check with patients 3 to 5 days into therapy to verify that the infection is resolving and there are no adverse effects), adherence or compliance aids, special medication packaging, and resolving problems with new prescriptions.

Pharmacists wishing to offer higher-level services may need to obtain more training or specialty certification (see Chapter 5). Higher-level services may include disease management, therapy monitoring (blood pressure, blood glucose, cholesterol, liver function), and wellness and prevention programs (screenings and immunizations). Pharmacists should develop a business plan for any new product or service to help ensure its success.

Documentation (2.0)

The maxim "If it was not documented, it was not done" applies to any MTMS delivered by pharmacists. Services can be documented with pen and paper or with electronic programs or databases. It is important to remember that all documentation, including documentation with portable electronic devices that may be transported away from the practice site, must be compliant with the Health Insurance Portability and Accountability Act.

Most pharmacy computer programs are not equipped to handle detailed patient care documentation, and most electronic patient care programs do not integrate with the pharmacy dispensing system.

Figure 9-6

Patient Care Process

Adapted from: American Pharmacists Association. Positioning Your Practice for Pharmaceutical Care: An Individualized Blueprint for Change. 1996.

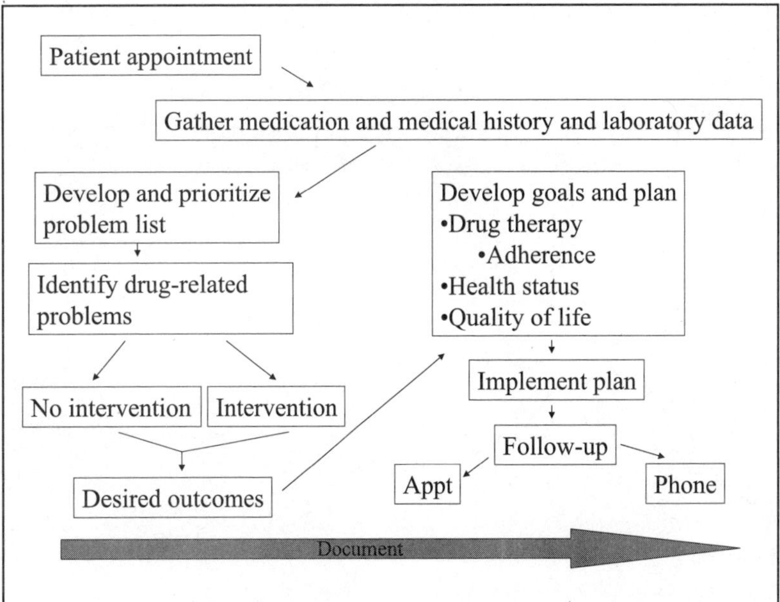

Any patient care documentation should include the following components:

- Patient data,
- Name of the pharmacist,
- Patient problems (dates),
- Desired patient outcomes,
- Pharmacotherapeutic assessment,
- Pharmacotherapeutic plan,
- Dates of problem resolution,
- Patient outcomes, and
- Patient follow-up.

Many pharmacists choose to create a chart to keep the patient information and any documentation organized in one place. The patient chart should contain the following:

- Name
- Address
- Telephone number
- Sex
- Age (birth date)
- Marital status

- Occupation
- Weight
- Height
- Allergies
- Chronic illnesses
- Special notes on previous interventions
- Special warnings or precautions
- Referred-from history
- Medication history
- Physicians/other care providers
- Third party/insurance profile
- Pregnancy/breastfeeding status
- Kidney, liver, cardiac function
- Nutrition status
- Patient's expectations for care
- Other (e.g., race, religion, birthplace, immune status)

The medication regimen review form (Figure 9-5) can be used to document basic MTMS; a similar form (Figure 9-7) might be used for follow-up consultations. Pharmacists might use another form (Figure 9-8) to document brief encounters such as phone calls. Separate forms might be used for specific disease management programs; these are particularly useful if pharmacists are new at providing patient care, because they provide prompts to gather specific information. Forms and documentation procedures should be consistent for everyone involved in the MTMS.

When establishing a documentation system, it is important to take billing requirements into consideration. Although

Figure 9-7

Sample Medication Review Follow-up Template

Patient name: ____________________ Date: ________ Chief complaint: ____________________

New/Unresolved Problem	New Drugs	New/Unresolved Drug-Related Problem	Intervention	Desired outcome/ Follow-up
1.				
2.				
3.				
4.				
5.				
6.				

Subjective: ____

____

Objective: ____

Assessment: ____

____

____

Plan: ____

____

____

Follow-up appointment: ____________________ Phone follow-up: ____________________

Pharmacist: ____________________ Signature: ____________________

Figure 9-8

Sample Telephone Call Documentation Form

Patient name: ______________________________ **Page** ___ **of** ___

Date: ____________________ Initials: ________

Complaint/reason for follow-up: ______________________________

____

Plan/resolution: ______________________________

____

____

____

- -

Date: ____________________ Initials: ________

Complaint/reason for follow-up: ______________________________

____

Plan/resolution: ______________________________

____

____

____

- -

Date: ____________________ Initials: ________

Complaint/reason for follow-up: ______________________________

____

Plan/resolution: ______________________________

____

____

____

the specific requirements may be determined by payers, pharmacists now have Current Procedural Terminology (CPT) codes to use in billing for MTMS (see Chapter 6). The MTMS CPT codes are used for the following documented elements: review of the pertinent patient history, medication profile (prescription and nonprescription), and recommendations for improving health outcomes and treatment compliance. Pharmacist providers using these codes need to make certain that documentation of the services matches the level of services provided. Billing with these codes is in 15-minute increments. When a service takes longer, the documentation must accurately reflect the need for the length of the service.

Another important part of documentation is ensuring that patients receiving services have signed all necessary consents. The claim form that pharmacist providers will most often use to bill for MTMS (CMS form 1500; see Resource E at back of this book) contains two statements that must be signed by the patient to ensure compliance with Medicare billing rules. This form and its electronic equivalent are used in billing both private and public claims, so the patient's signature is required on any claim for MTMS provided. It is not necessary for the patient to physically sign this form, but the pharmacist or pharmacy must have a signature on file for these statements (blocks 12 and 13 of the form).

Marketing (8.0)

Marketing is essential to the success of any business, yet pharmacists often do not understand the need for or the "how to's" of marketing. A marketing plan will equip pharmacists with a systematic approach that enables them to stay within the budget, track results to determine what is working and not working, and make changes in the marketing strategy as necessary. This section provides a few basics of marketing, differentiates service marketing from product marketing, and describes practical plans for marketing MTMS and patient care services.

Marketing is the process of creating customers for your product—communicating what you are offering (your product) and the value or benefit the customer (patient) will receive from purchasing it. Product marketing usually involves comparisons between similar items; for example, companies may compare razor blades on the basis of how close they shave or how long they last. There are two types of products: commodities and services. Pharmacists are used to selling commodities: prescription medications, nonprescription medications, and related products. Although MTMS and patient care are products, they differ from commodities in that they are also services.

Five P's of Marketing

The marketing of products, whether commodities or services, generally involves the "five 5 P's": product, price, promotion, place, and positioning.

Product. Development of products or services (discussed earlier in this chapter) includes defining each of your products, whether you will have one or more than one, and any ancillary services related to the products.

Price.[10] What is your pricing strategy? Although this will be defined in part by payers, it is good to have a general background in pricing strategy. The two basic types of pricing are cost-plus pricing and value-based pricing.

Cost-plus pricing is the most common method used, but it is actually the most detrimental to delivering profits. Cost-plus pricing is product focused; it involves determining how much the product will cost and adding what the seller determines is a fair or desired markup. There are many problems with this method. First, it implies that it is possible to accurately determine how much a product costs (or a service costs to deliver), even though the cost is usually variable depending on volume. In addition, this method predetermines who your customers will be and sets the quantities that will be sold.

Customers do not base their purchasing decisions on how much the item costs to produce. Rather, purchase decisions are based on the value the customer perceives that he or she will receive from the purchase. Costs must play a role in your pricing strategy; you must make sure that you cover your costs. But which costs must you consider?

To remain profitable, you must consider *avoidable* or *future* costs. In other words, it is not the cost at which the item was purchased (or the cost to deliver the service) that matters; it is the cost of replacing that item or service. For example, if you purchase drug A for $10 and price it at $20 but it costs you $25 to replace drug A to sell the next time, have you made a profit? Will you be able to stay in business?

Value-based pricing is used by profitable businesses. It is customer focused; it involves looking at a customer who has satisfactorily received the product and determining how much that customer would be willing to pay. This is difficult, but here are some starting points.

First, what is the "reference value"—the value of a competing product that the customer views as the best substitute or alternative? Second, what is the "differentiation value"—the value of the benefits your services deliver to the patient? For example, compare your MTMS and a visit to the patient's physician. If the patient pays $15 for a physician office visit, that may be the reference value. If he or she earns $20 per hour and has to take off from work for 3 hours for the office visit, the differentiation value would be $60. This is one reason it is important to identify your target customer.

Promotion. This is the most traditional or visible aspect of marketing. It involves radio, newspaper, and television advertising; coupons; direct mail; store signage; and other means of promoting a business or product. Without a plan, promotion can be costly and ineffective. The approach you take with your business or service will likely depend on your experience, ability to measure results, access to resources, and tolerance for ambiguity. Key points to remember include the following:

- Repetition is important. A person may need to see or touch an advertisement 7 to13 times before buying into it.
- If you are uncomfortable with marketing, start slowly. You may be better able to measure the results of your marketing if you change only one aspect of it at a time. You may want to find a good, all-encompassing strategy; leave it in place for a designated time period; and measure changes in service or product business from the time it was implemented. Then, make a single change at a time to measure the effects.
- Word of mouth can be the most effective and least expensive promotional tool, although generating positive word of mouth can be difficult. In one example of effective use of this tool, a restaurant owner invited a select group of people to special events to sample the food and service before opening his new restaurant. He chose to invite hairdressers, because they talk to many different people during their day's work. Giving these key people a taste of the restaurant helped the word to spread quickly.

Place. Place is where you provide the service. Will you have a private or semiprivate sit-down counseling area? Will it be in the view of other customers? This may seem unimportant, but placing your service in view of other customers helps create customers' expectation for the service and understanding that it is a significant part of your business.

Positioning. Positioning describes how you want your service or business to be viewed by others. Do you want to be viewed as a specialty pharmacy, caring, high-cost, low-cost, accessible, or customer friendly? Think about what these descriptions imply for different aspects of your business: pricing; hours of operation; the look of your business, inside and out; and the amount of time spent with customers.

Unique Aspects of Service Marketing

Marketing services differs in four ways from marketing commodities.[11] Services are intangible, inseparable, variable, and perishable.

Intangible. A patient cannot touch or feel the service. A big part of the challenge of marketing services is to enable the customer to "see" what it is the service looks and feels like, to create a vision in the patient's mind of what he or she will get by purchasing the service.

Inseparable. Services are typically produced and consumed at the same time. Because of this, both the client and the server affect the service outcome, and buyers are highly interested in who the provider is.

Variable. Services vary according to who offers them and when they are offered. Unlike a commodity, which can be produced in exactly the same fashion time after time, services vary each time they are offered, depending on who is providing the service and who is receiving it. Services can even vary when provided by the same individual at different times. For instance, a pharmacist who is fresh and excited about providing a service to a patient is likely to deliver service somewhat different from what he or she provides when stressed or not feeling well.

Perishable. Unlike products, services cannot be stored or inventoried. When demand for services fluctuates, it can be difficult to staff efficiently. This is one of the most difficult challenges in initiating new services. Demand may be low at first, and paying someone to staff an empty appointment book can be costly. Think of examples of how others in service industries (e.g., dentists, veterinarians) encourage people to make and keep appointments.

Features, Advantages, and Benefits

One common mistake pharmacists have made in trying to sell their services is focusing on the features, or aspects, of the service. Going back to the razor blade example, the features would include the number of blades a razor uses, how much it costs, and how much time it takes to shave using that razor. For services, the features would include the time it takes to deliver the service, how the service is delivered, when the service is delivered, and the price of the service. The problem with using features is that it gives people the opportunity to raise objections, such as "It takes too long" or "It costs too much."

Marketers often lump together the advantages and benefits of their product or service, but an approach called "solution selling"[12] distinguishes between the two. For example, an advantage of a pharmacist's service might be that it takes less time than a physician visit. However, this is a benefit only if the shorter time expenditure is something the patient wants; some might prefer the longer visit.

Selling Statements

Although salespeople as a group are often thought to be quick tongued or witty, it is more likely that they simply are well prepared with "selling statements." They have identified what the potential customer's objections and interests may be and developed responses in advance.

A selling statement can generate awareness of and interest in your services. It should get your main message across in 30 seconds or less—about the length of a person's attention span.[13] The key is to identify your objective and stay focused on it. If possible, develop a "hook" to get the customer's attention; for example, "Just the other day, we were able to save a patient $160 per month on her medications." This hook would be immediately followed by "When is the last time you had your medications reviewed for serious interactions and possible cost savings?" The pharmacist could then provide answers to the customer's "what, who, where, when, why, and how" questions and finally could ask, "When can we schedule an appointment?"

The pharmacist should have one or two probing questions ready to use if the customer does not accept the offer—but should realize that marketing involves repetition. The pharmacist has planted a seed that will grow. It may take several attempts, but the more often the offer is repeated, the more likely it is to be accepted.

Budget for Marketing

It may seem that more is better when it comes to marketing, but no business can afford to spend foolishly. A break-even analysis will help determine what is reasonable to spend on marketing. The first step is to determine your costs for providing the MTMS you have decided to offer. Next, develop assumptions about what your service volume will be. This may not be easy, but it will allow you to set goals for your business as well. On the basis of these projections, determine your return on investment by subtracting your costs from your projected revenues for providing MTMS. Then, determine what percentage of the extra revenues you can use or will need to generate that level of business. The important part will be tracking your results to see the effects of your spending, determining what works and what does not, and fine-tuning your marketing accordingly.

Internal and External Marketing

In the critical path diagram (Figure 9-2), marketing is divided into two categories, internal (8b) and external (8a), shown below and above the main line. Marketing is no less important than the items on the main line; the difference is that those items are dependent upon each other and sequential in their development. It is possible to develop and deliver MTMS without marketing; however, any pharmacist who tries that will be relying on the "build it and they will come" philosophy, which has not proven highly successful for pharmaceutical care over the past 15 years. Patients must see and understand the value of MTMS, and marketing is essential to establishing that value.

Internal Marketing (marketing within your organization). The first step is to identify all of the people or positions in the organization that will be touched by the new service. In an independent pharmacy, it may be only a pharmacy technician and a store clerk. In a chain pharmacy, a greater number of people will be involved at the corporate level, making this step more time consuming. However, in many companies internal marketing is performed from the corporate level. At the store level, you will still want to consider all staff in the pharmacy and any staff for the general merchandise or front-end parts of the store. Store-level staff members need to see the new service as an enhancement to their jobs, not just another task to be done.

Once you have identified the target audience for your internal marketing, you can determine how you will market to those individuals. This will depend on your budget. You may simply explain the new services at a staff meeting. One key to success is being prepared to answer the question, "What's in it for me?" To encourage staff to promote the service products, you may want to develop a contest or incentive. Research findings suggest that for a bonus to drive performance, it needs to be anywhere from 3–5%[14] to 20–40%[15] of base pay. At a pharmacist's salary, this may be excessive, but for technicians it may be achievable and effective. Smaller incentives may also work; the key is to make them meaningful to the person receiving them.[16] You will also need to decide whether to use the incentive just to get started or continue it over the long term—and you will need to clearly communicate this decision. As will be discussed later, however, results will be the driver of your success, not incentives.

External Marketing. Before developing your external marketing plan, you need to determine who your stakeholders and target customers are. Your stakeholders are the people who can influence others (groups of people) either positively or negatively toward your business or service. For example, a local school principal or superintendent may have an influence on whether the school's employee health plan uses your business. Key physicians may also be stakeholders; if you are targeting a specific disease state, a physician who specializes in that area is a stakeholder. You will need to develop marketing materials directed toward stakeholders, such as printed material (brochures, folders, or binders) or small items left with stakeholders to remind them of your business or service. You may choose to set up a meeting or group session to describe and promote your business or service.

Marketing to customers involves all aspects of how you deliver and promote your services. It is useful to ask yourself, "What do my customers expect when they walk through the doors of my pharmacy?" If they simply expect to receive a bag with a bottle of pills in it from across the pharmacy counter, you will need to change their expectations. To promote services, which are intangible, you must find ways to make them tangible to customers. These will likely include signage inside and outside the store and in-pharmacy marketing such as bag stuffers, buttons on staff lab jackets, or pens. Take some time to brainstorm ideas for marketing.

To control your budget and make your marketing more effective, identify the target customers for your service and focus on them. Consider characteristics such as income level, disease category, age, and medications used. The target customers for MTMS may be patients over 65 years of age who take multiple medications. Some pharmacists, when starting a new service, prefer to focus on a specific group of patients, such as those with a certain disease, because they feel most confident in their ability to provide MTMS to that group. This can be a beneficial way to get started, because the pharmacist's confidence is important in making the new service successful. The better you understand your target customer, the more efficient and successful your marketing efforts will be.

Finally, on the basis of your marketing budget, your stakeholders, and your target customers, you will need to determine what marketing methods you will use for the next 12 months. List the methods you will use (e.g., in-store sign, brochure, radio, bag stuffer) and the cost for each month a given method will be used, as shown in Figure 9-9.

Figure 9-9

Sample Worksheet for Projecting Costs for Various Marketing Methods

Projected Costs

Method	Month											
	1	2	3	4	5	6	7	8	9	10	11	12
Bag stuffers	$200	$200		$200		$200						
Radio	$400	$400	$400	$400	$400							
Total	$600	$600	$400	$600	$400	$200						

Reporting (5.0) and Billing (4.0)

Both internal and external reporting are essential to the success of MTMS. External reporting will consist primarily of reporting outcomes of the services. Outcomes reporting will be particularly important in the initial stages of MTMS as companies are looking to justify the costs for providing the services. Reported outcomes will include costs prevented or controlled; for example, prevented additional physician visit or emergency room visit, decreased days missed from school or work (Table 9-2). Outcomes may also include improvements in therapeutic targets, such as laboratory test values tied to disease outcomes or preventive services. Lab values may be available for tests run in the pharmacy, or results can be obtained from the lab or physician's office. Monitoring/Tracking is the last box on the critical path diagram (Figure 9-2), but as part of reporting you need to decide what to monitor and how you will track it.

Internal reporting will be used for performance evaluation and business analysis. These reports may include number of patients seen, number of follow-ups performed, customer satisfaction, and quality indicators similar to those used in other areas of the health care industry (e.g., how frequently various tests are performed; drugs started since an event, such as beta-blockers after myocardial infarction).

Internal reporting can be electronic or manual. Electronic reporting saves time and offers other efficiencies. The use of a simple database (e.g., Microsoft Access, FoxPro) and possibly a separate reporting tool (e.g., Crystal Reports) can significantly enhance reporting capabilities. Training in the use of these programs may be needed.

Table 9-2

Reportable Outcomes

Clinical	Humanistic	Economic	
		Direct Costs	Indirect Costs
Cure disease	Increase quality of life	Increase prescribed drug costs	Decrease days missed from work
Reduce or eliminate symptoms	Decrease quality of life	Decrease prescribed drug costs	Increase days missed from work
Increase or worsen symptoms	Increase patient satisfaction	Increase nonprescription drug costs	
Arrest or slow a disease process	Decrease patient satisfaction	Decrease nonprescription drug costs	
Patient deceased		Prevent physician visit	
Prevent or slow a disease process		Cause additional physician visit	
Worsen or speed up disease process		Increase lab costs	
Improve compliance		Decrease lab costs	
Improve safety		Prevent emergency room visit	
Improve efficacy		Cause emergency room visit	
		Decrease hospital length of stay	
		Increase hospital length of stay	

Regardless of how it is done, reporting is a key aspect of MTMS delivery. Reports are essential for measuring business performance, understanding how pharmacist recommendations are affecting patient care, and making improvements in both of these areas.

Chapters 6 and 7 address coding and other types of documentation involved in billing for MTMS.

Site Development (7.0)

The pharmacy location offering MTMS will need to consider some re-engineering to prepare; the extent of preparation will depend on the type of product or service that will be offered. For any new product of service, it will be necessary to

1. Enhance or adjust workflow (see workflow algorithm in Figure 9-10)
2. Establish a new labor model to fit the new product or service
3. Establish a fee structure
4. Establish a documentation system (discussed above)
5. Develop policies and procedures (process planning)
    a. Practice plan
        i. Product or service to be offered
        ii. Service delivery method
        iii. Dates/times for service delivery
        iv. Practice standards
        v. Patient education materials
        vi. Communication and/or referral
        vii. Follow-up
        viii. Patient chart method
        ix. Continuous quality improvement
    b. Laboratory manual (if applicable)
        i. Standard operating procedures for equipment
        ii. Quality control
    c. Pharmacy job descriptions
    d. Billing procedures
    e. Performance evaluations
6. Establish a marketing plan (discussed above)

Changes made in preparation for MTMS should be consistent across the organization and should not burden an already stretched staff. Job descriptions may need to be retooled and tasks redesigned. The workflow process needs to be changed so that pharmacists perform only those tasks that state law says must

Figure 9-10

Pharmacy Workflow Algorithm

Adapted from: American Pharmacists Association. Positioning Your Practice for Pharmaceutical Care: An Individualized Blueprint for Change. 1996.

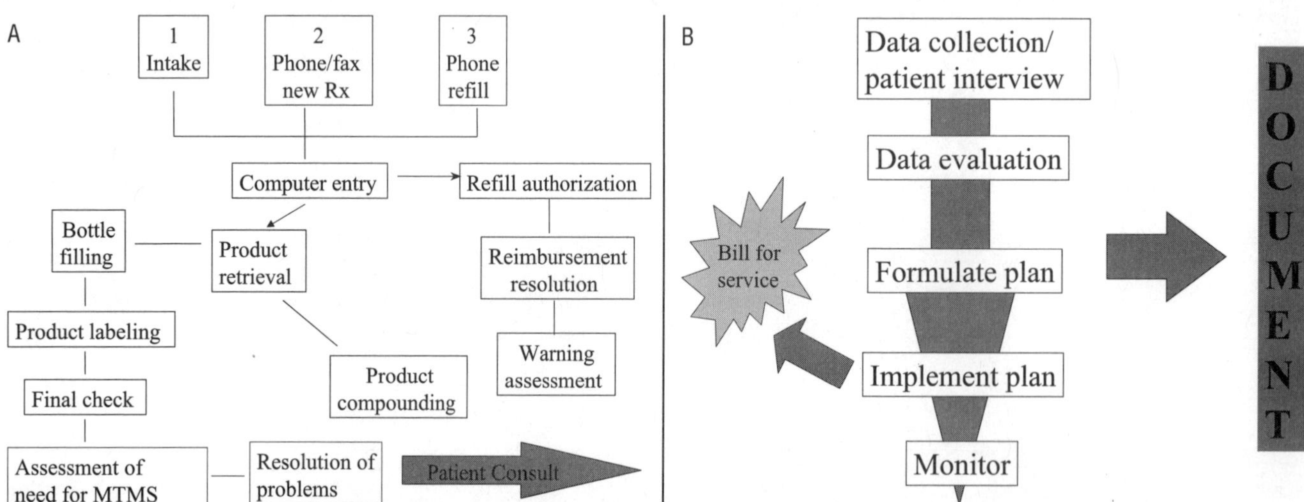

be performed by a pharmacist; this will free up time to conduct MTMS. Patient care associates (technicians) should perform all of the nonprofessional tasks, including prescription intake, order entry, filling of product, restocking shelves, and answering the telephone. Pharmacists should be assessing the intake form, reviewing the medication profile, providing counseling, identifying patients for MTMS, and providing MTMS.

Many community pharmacists will need to slightly modify their work space to create a private or semiprivate area for providing basic MTMS. Adding dividers is the least expensive way to create a semiprivate space. Unless patient records will be kept electronically, a file cabinet will also be needed.

If high-level MTMS will be offered, a private space is preferred. The space should have at least two chairs, a table or desk, a file cabinet, a sink if laboratory testing is performed, a computer (for access to pharmacy records and electronic patient records), and monitoring equipment such as a blood pressure cuff and blood glucose meter). In some states, pharmacies may have devices for anticoagulation monitoring and for testing cholesterol, liver function, and A1c.

Training (3.0)

The pharmacy profession defined basic MTMS so that any pharmacist should have the knowledge and skill to provide these services for patients.[3] However, some pharmacists may need a refresher in therapeutics, geriatric pharmacotherapy (see Chapter 5), or communication skills. Training may also be needed in the process for delivering care and in how to implement that process. Nonpharmacist staff and management personnel will also need training as pharmacies prepare to deliver MTMS.

Training should take place before implementation of MTMS, but ongoing training and education must be incorporated to ensure continued competence. Regardless of practice setting, several issues need to be considered in implementing training for pharmacist and nonpharmacist personnel. Pharmacists must consider the content of the training and the delivery methods. Large chains may have the resources and expertise to develop their own training programs, while independent practices and smaller chains may have to rely on available programs. The training method should be appropriate for the desired outcome. For example, if skill development is needed, live instruction is usually appropriate. Instruction in skills such as critical thinking and problem solving may be available via the Internet. Internet, CD-ROM, or print materials can be used to increase knowledge. Traineeships may also be considered; these allow pharmacists to spend time seeing patients under the direction of skilled or certified pharmacists. Traineeships usually last 1 to 4 weeks and require an investment of pharmacist and company time. Table 9-3 lists advantages and disadvantages of different types of training delivery methods.

Pharmacist Training

Training programs for pharmacists may be available through professional associations, universities, industry groups, and foundations. As mentioned, training may be needed in the process for delivering care, incorporating MTMS into workflow, identifying patients for MTMS, planning, documenting, and billing. Given the definition of MTMS adopted by the profession, pharmacists may need training in patient interviewing and assessment; patient education and adherence strategies; pharmacotherapy of conditions such as diabetes, hypertension, hyperlipidemia, arthritis, chronic obstructive pulmonary disease, osteoporosis, vascular disease, congestive heart failure, Alzheimer's disease, Parkinson's disease, men's health, and women's health; and criteria for appropriate drug use in the elderly.[17]

Several types of credentials are available for pharmacists wishing to specialize in a specific area (Table 9-4). However, specialization is not necessary for pharmacists wishing to provide MTMS in community practice.

Nonpharmacist Training

Pharmacy support personnel, storefront personnel, store management, district or regional management, and upper management should receive training. Pharmacy support personnel should have training in communication, marketing, and how to identify patients for MTMS.

Storefront personnel and store management should have communication and marketing training to enable them to answer basic questions for interested patients. All company management should receive training in order to understand the concept of MTMS and how it affects the direction and future of the company.

All personnel should receive training about the MTM program and the company policies and procedures for MTMS, as well as the importance of the change in direction for the company or business.

Table 9-3

Training Delivery Methods

Method	Advantages	Disadvantages
Live programming	Skill development Interaction with expert Timely information	Time consuming Scheduling of personnel
Internet	Can be completed at any time Fewer scheduling conflicts Newer technologies may allow patient simulation and skill development Information usually timely	Must have basic computer skills May not have easy access Technology does not always work well
CD-ROM	Generally self-paced Can be completed at any time Fewer scheduling conflicts Generally for knowledge enhancement, but can allow for skill development	Depending upon complexity of material and program used, some operating systems may be impossible to run Lack of opportunity for personal interaction to resolve questions
Print materials	Can be completed at any time Fewer scheduling conflicts Knowledge enhancement only	May be costly Information may be out of date
Traineeships	Knowledge and skill development Practice with real patients	Costly Time consuming

Deliver Care (9.0)

After completing the tasks on the critical path to this point, the pharmacy and staff will be ready to deliver MTMS. It is best to perform several dry runs before initiating the service. Taking the time to practice will ensure that the providers have a full grasp of the process before actually working with a patient. Furthermore, everyone involved needs to understand how to schedule patients and the process to be followed when a patient arrives for an appointment.

As previously noted, patients' judgment of the service will be based on several intangible aspects. It is important to help the patient feel comfortable. Make certain that the provider introduces himself or herself. Also, make certain that the provider is professionally dressed and the area in which the service is being provided is clean and neatly organized. It may be a good practice to give the patient an overview of what will be done and what to expect from the service. The service will likely be new to patients; providing this explanation will help them feel at ease in the new situation.

The provider will have to manage the time allotted for the service. Patients often have many questions and enjoy the opportunity to discuss their health care with a willing professional. It may be difficult to strike a balance between answering all questions and providing the service in a manageable time frame. It may be helpful to explain to the patient that the service is expected to last for a preset period of time; for example:

Mrs. Smith, I want to provide you with the best help that I can. Our appointment is scheduled to last 30 minutes. If you have any questions that are really important to you, please do your best to ask them while we have time to discuss them.

You may choose to say this in a different way, but the point is that you need to set boundaries that are fair to both parties and let the patient work within those boundaries.

At the conclusion of your session, make certain that any necessary follow-up is understood and agreed upon, set a follow-up date if appropriate, and pleasantly thank the patient. The way the service ends will significantly influence the patient's overall impression of it.

Monitoring/Tracking (6.0)

Monitoring progress of your MTMS and tracking results will be an integral component of the success of your program over the long term. Monitoring should include both the operational aspects and the patient-specific outcomes of the service.

Operational monitoring will focus on delivery of an efficient service product within the constraints of the business. As pharmacies become more involved in service delivery, business metrics specific to services need to be integrated into the everyday tracking of the business's performance. Community pharmacies typically use measures such as prescription volume, inventory turns, and generic usage that are focused on a retail product and a distributive business model. Service delivery metrics may include number of appointments, length of appointment, number of patients seen per day, number of no-shows, and number of repeat visits/patient retention.

As providers and payers look to establish the value of MTMS, it will be important to follow up with patients to monitor outcomes of the services and to document those outcomes. Table 9-2 lists measures that might be used in outcomes assessment. Outcomes may be difficult to quantify, but pharmacists should use their best professional judgment.

Table 9-4

Selected Specialty Certifications

Specialty	Designation	Organization
Pharmacotherapy	BCPS	Board of Pharmaceutical Specialties (www.bpsweb.org)
Geriatrics	CGP	Commission for Certification in Geriatric Pharmacy (www.ccgp.org)
Disease management	CDM	National Institute for Standards in Pharmacist Credentialing (www.nispcnet.org)
Diabetes education	CDE	National Certification Board for Diabetes Educators (www.ncbde.org)
Advanced diabetes management	BC-ADM	American Association of Diabetes Educators and American Nurses Credentialing Center (www.diabeteseducator.org/ProfessionalResources/Certification/)
Anticoagulation	CACP	National Certification Board for Anticoagulation Providers (www.ncbap.org)
Asthma		National Asthma Educator Certification Board (www.naecb.org)

Chapter 9

Case Study

Bird Pharmacy is a regional chain with 150 stores in two states, serving a large and diverse population. The chain employs 450 pharmacists and 1500 pharmacy support personnel. Approximately 90% of the chain's prescription business is third party. Before the Medicare Prescription Drug Improvement and Modernization Act of 2006, the chain performed basic community pharmacy services: profile review and drug interaction assessment, prescription counseling, and nonprescription counseling. Bird Pharmacy management decides to change the current practice environment to provide MTMS for its Medicare population. The pharmacist management team begins with basic MTMS.

The pharmacy receives a notification that one of its patients, Isabelle Johnson, a 78-year-old African American, is eligible for MTMS. Today, Ms. Johnson visits her local Bird Pharmacy with a new prescription from Dr. Scott for cephalexin 500 mg (#21), 1 cap tid.

Her profile shows the following medications:

Nystatin/triamcinolone cream 30 g
Apply as directed
Dr. Jones

Premarin vaginal cream 42.5 g
Use as directed
Dr. Smith

Propoxyphene napsylate/APAP (40)
1 tab q6h as needed
Dr. Leonard

Lotrel 5/10 capsule (30)
1 tab qd
Dr. Leonard

Lexapro 10 mg (30)
2 tabs qd
Dr. Smith

Actonel 35 mg (4)
1 tab every week
Dr. Leonard

Astelin nasal spray (1)
2 sprays bid
Dr. Gold

Loratadine 10 mg (30)
1 tab qd
Dr. Gold

The pharmacist initiates the MTMS marketing strategy by presenting Ms. Johnson with a "selling statement," which ideally will be reinforced by signage and other pieces of the marketing plan that are in place throughout the pharmacy. Ms. Johnson agrees to participate in a medication review and makes an appointment with the pharmacist. Meanwhile, Ms. Johnson's cephalexin prescription is entered in the antibiotic call-back program. The pharmacist will call Ms. Johnson after 3 days to assess the effectiveness of the antibiotic, adherence, and whether adverse effects have occurred.

References

1. US Department of Labor. Bureau of Labor Statistics. Pharmacists. Available at: www.bls.gov/oco/ocos079.htm.

2. National Association of Chain Drug Stores. Facts and Resources. Available at: www.nacds.org/user-assets/pdfs/Pharmacy/2006CommunityPharmacyResults.pdf.

3. Bluml BM. Definition of medication therapy management: development of profession-wide consensus. *J Am Pharm Assoc.* 2005;45:566–72.

4. SCORE, Counselors to America's Small Business. Five tips on preparing for change. Available at: www.score.org/5_tips_bp_8.html.

5. Knowlton CH, Thomas OV, Zarus SA, et al. Planning for new pharmacy services. *J Am Pharm Assoc.* 1998;38:626–7.

6. Marcrom RE, Horton RM, Shepherd MD. Create value added services to meet patient needs. In: *The Dynamics of Pharmaceutical Care.* Washington, DC: American Pharmaceutical Association; 1992.

7. Centers for Medicare and Medicaid Services. 42 CFR Parts 400, 403, 411, 417, and 423 Medicare Program; Medicare Prescription Drug Benefit. Available at: http://edocket.access.gpo.gov/2005/pdf/05-1321.pdf.

8. American Pharmacists Association and National Association of Chain Drug Stores Foundation. Medication therapy management in pharmacy practice: core elements of an MTM service model (version 2.0). *J Am Pharm Assoc.* 2008;48:341–53.

9. Strand LM, Cipolle RJ, Morley PC. Drug-related problems. Their structure and function. *Drug Intell Clin Pharm* 1990;24:1093–7.

10. Nagle TT, Holden RK, *The Strategies and Tactics of Pricing.* Upper Saddle River, NJ: Prentice Hall; 2002.

11. Kotler P. *Marketing Management.* Upper Saddle River, NJ: Prentice Hall; 1998.

12.Bosworth MT. *Solution Selling: Creating Buyers in Difficult Selling Markets.* New York: McGraw-Hill; 1995.

13. Frank MO. *How to Get Your Point Across in 30 Seconds or Less.* New York: Pocket Books; 1986.

14. Garver R. Employee incentive programs reap big rewards. *American Banker.* April 18, 2006.

15. Shea G. *Leading Organizational Change.* SmithKline Beecham/APhA/Wharton Executive Management Program for Pharmacy Leaders. September 13, 2000.

16. Motivation/Incentives. *S&MM Pulse.* 2006;158(3).

17. Beers MH. Explicit criteria for determining potentially inappropriate medication use by the elderly. An update. *Arch Intern Med.* 1997;157:1531–6.

Chapter 10

Providing Medication Therapy Management Services in Ambulatory Care Clinics

Timothy E. Welty and Melody H. Ryan

For effective, legal, and safe provision of medication therapy management services (MTMS), an infrastructure is needed that provides the pharmacist with the necessary financial, data, record-keeping, and quality control support to meet government regulations and—most important—improve patient care. Without this infrastructure a pharmacist may have difficulty providing effective service and may not receive proper reimbursement. In part because it has such an infrastructure, the ambulatory care clinic setting affords pharmacists the most natural environment for providing MTMS.

Most often, ambulatory care pharmacy is practiced in the context of a multiphysician or multidisciplinary clinic. The pharmacist has direct access to the patient and to physicians, nurses, and other health care professionals (e.g., therapist, physician assistant, social worker, dietitian). This gives the pharmacist an opportunity to be a part of the initial therapeutic decision-making process and facilitates continuous involvement in the pharmacotherapeutic management of a patient from the initiation of therapy. The pharmacist is able to communicate directly with other health professionals and discuss concerns and proposed solutions to problems that are identified. Pharmacy practice in an ambulatory care clinic also provides the pharmacist with easy and direct access to the patient's original medical record, greater ability to order laboratory or other tests needed for monitoring pharmacotherapy, easy access to test results, and the ability to document interventions in the patient's medical record.

An ambulatory care environment provides a supporting structure important to the overall administration of an effective MTMS program. Mechanisms to ensure high-quality services are usually in place. Quality assurance controls are required by accrediting bodies and government agencies (e.g., the establishment of standards of care and treatment protocols, peer review of care provided by practitioners in the clinic group, and outcome assessment). A successful ambulatory care practice will make provisions to ensure that the best possible quality is maintained in all clinic operations.

Another area of support that is essential to the successful provision of MTMS is billing and financial services. To properly obtain reimbursement and ensure maximal payment for services rendered, support is needed for proper coding of services provided, timely filing of claims, tracking of reimbursements, and responding to claim denials. The financial viability of an MTMS program will depend upon the ability to manage the process for reimbursement (see Chapter 6). Many ambulatory care clinics have departments that handle all billing concerns or have contracts with companies to provide these services. This allows the pharmacist to focus on providing MTMS and not spend an inordinate amount of time on billing issues.

The ambulatory care setting is an optimal environment for the provision of MTMS for many reasons. In most cases the pharmacist should be able to work within existing organizational structures to establish an effective MTMS program.

Description of Ambulatory Care Practice

Ambulatory care practice settings range from solo medical practices to large multispecialty clinics. They can be publicly funded clinics such as those operated by a public health service, privately owned and operated clinics, or a mix often associated with a state university-affiliated clinic. The implementation of MTMS in ambulatory care will take different forms to meet the unique needs of the varied practice environments and their patients.

General versus Specialty Clinics

An ambulatory care site may be a general medical clinic or a specialty clinic. A general medical clinic typically is staffed by primary care physicians and health care professionals who diagnose and manage patients with a wide range of medical problems. Most such clinics limit their practice to either adult or pediatric patients, but they do not limit their practice according to diagnosis. A pharmacist who provides MTMS in this setting needs to be familiar with the pharmacotherapy of a wide range of diseases and equipped to manage a broad spectrum of patients. Although this type of clinic gives the pharmacist exposure to many patients with multiple chronic diseases who receive multiple medications, the breadth of patient needs may limit the depth of care that can be provided. For example, the pharmacist in this type of clinic may be ill equipped to provide MTMS to a patient who has difficult-to-control diabetes, coronary artery disease complicated by chronic heart failure, and renal dysfunction. Such a patient may require more intensive MTMS by a specialty pharmacist or pharmacists. Another problem that may be encountered in the general clinic environment is identification of patients eligible for Medicare Part D coverage of MTMS. Because patients with simple acute illnesses are likely to be treated in these clinics, the pharmacist and clinic personnel will need to carefully screen patients for eligibility in accordance with Centers for Medicare and Medicaid Services regulations.

Specialty clinics are most often organized around the well-defined medical specialties (e.g., cardiology, pulmonary medicine, neurology, dermatology, oncology, and endocrinology). Within the groups of physicians and health care providers in these clinics, individuals may subspecialize to manage patients with specific diseases. Patients seen in specialty clinics are typically referred because of the complexity of their disease or because they have been diagnosed with a rare or unusual disorder. Care or pharmacotherapy that is provided in specialty clinics is focused only on the disease related to the specialty area. For example, a patient with chronic heart failure and Parkinson's disease might see a neurologist or a neurologist subspecializing in movement disorders for management of the Parkinson's disease, but the neurologist would not intervene in the management of the chronic heart failure unless it directly affects the Parkinson's disease. In this case, the neurologist would consult with either the primary care physician or cardiologist regarding the way treatment of chronic heart failure affects treatment of Parkinson's disease. Potential difficulties in providing MTMS in a specialty clinic setting involve ensuring that patients meet their insurer's chronic disease and medication criteria for eligibility to receive MTMS and that MTMS is focused on the disease being managed in the specialty clinic. Some patients, however, may be willing to pay for specialty pharmacy services even if they do not meet their insurer's eligibility criteria. Specialty-focused MTMS does not preclude the possibility of addressing pharmacotherapy issues that are outside the realm of the particular specialty area, but interventions should be left to the physician or pharmacist responsible for managing the diseases to which these issues relate.

As the pharmacy profession develops approaches to providing MTMS, it is conceivable that an ambulatory care model similar to that of medicine will be followed. In that model, general MTMS programs would be provided by pharmacists with a broad knowledge of pharmacotherapy and the skills necessary to manage a variety of diseases. Those pharmacists would manage patients whose disease processes are relatively uncomplicated. Patients who have a complicated, unusual, or rare disease would be referred to specialized pharmacists who possess the depth of knowledge and skills needed to properly manage the specific complicated disease. For management of the other chronic diseases and medications, a specialty pharmacist would defer to a pharmacist in a general or primary care program or a pharmacist in another specialty area. As in medicine, a difficulty with this model of care is coordination and continuity of treatments and interventions. For example, if a cardiologist is managing the patient's coronary artery

Figure 10-1

Potential Model for Generalist and Specialist Pharmacist Care

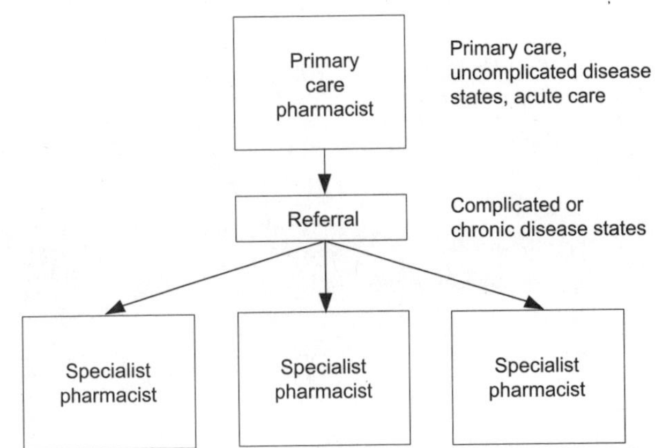

disease, that physician or a cardiology-specialized pharmacist may decide on an intervention that conflicts with or is problematic for the management of the patient's epilepsy. Thus, there is a need for someone, usually the primary care or general medicine health care provider, to coordinate and oversee the patient's care. It would seem reasonable for pharmacists committed to providing general MTMS to fill this role (Figure 10-1).

Pharmacists' Activities

The activities of pharmacists providing MTMS in the ambulatory care environment will vary greatly depending on the type of clinic, the existing programs in the clinic, and the availability of other health care professionals in the practice site. A variety of services could be provided by a pharmacist in an ambulatory care MTMS program, but four basic skills (Table 10-1) are essential to master. These are skills that any pharmacist should possess, but the ambulatory care setting presents special challenges because of sometimes limited availability of data, gaps in information due to the intermittent nature of clinic visits, and short, intense interactions with patients during a clinic visit. A strong MTMS program in the ambulatory care setting

Table 10-1

Basic Clinical Skills for Ambulatory Care

Collection of patient-specific data essential to understanding the patient
Assessment of the available data, leading to the development of a patient problem list and care plan
Reporting to the physician regarding patient data, problems identified, and recommended interventions
Education of the patient or caregivers on treatment plans, medications, and health-related items

Table 10-2

Pharmacists in Ambulatory Care Practice[1]

Clinic Type	% of Institutions
Anticoagulation	36
Oncology	28
Primary care/family practice	23
Diabetes	23
HIV/AIDS	17
Medication management	16
Smoking cessation	15
Dyslipidemia	14
Pain management	12
Asthma/pulmonary	12
Congestive heart failure	12
Psychiatry	9
Hypertension	7
Neurology	4

should include mechanisms for providing more consistent, frequent contact with patients and gathering as much patient information as is necessary for good decision-making.

Implementation of Ambulatory Care Pharmacy Practice

In 2004, the American Society of Health-System Pharmacists conducted a survey of institutions regarding pharmacist involvement in ambulatory care practices. At approximately half of the teaching institutions and integrated health networks or HMOs that responded, pharmacists were involved in ambulatory care practice.[1] Direct comparison with a similar survey conducted in 2001[2] is difficult because of differences in reporting, but it appears that the number of institutions supporting ambulatory care pharmacist involvement is increasing. In 2004, the greatest pharmacist involvement appeared to be in clinics focusing on specific diseases or specialties, although 23% of institutions had pharmacists involved in primary care or family practice clinics (Table 10-2).[1] The activities reported by responding institutions indicated that many ambulatory care pharmacists were already offering services that directly correspond to MTMS elements, such as providing oral counseling with each new prescription, monitoring compliance, and monitoring patient outcomes (reported by 52%, 47%, and 44% of responding institutions, respectively).[1] With the advent of MTMS, many institutions are likely to expand their clinical pharmacy programs to include more pharmacist-directed clinics. Both administrators and clinicians may need direction in establishing these clinics.

Methods of establishing pharmacist-directed clinics have been described in several articles and books.[3–5] All suggest determining the need for the service, establishing relationships, developing a business proposal, establishing clinic procedures, planning for outcomes assessment, and marketing the clinic. Needs assessments generally begin informally with discussions of patient needs or provider interests. Eventually, a formal needs assessment should be conducted to determine the number and types of patients that might be seen by the clinic, provide information for the business plan, and establish baseline data for tracking outcomes (Table 10-3).

Building support for the clinic is extremely important. Physician support is often emphasized and may already exist, but it is also important to assess the support available from administrators, nurses, laboratory personnel, and individuals in business and billing offices. The impact of the pharmacist-directed clinic on each of these groups should also be assessed. Administrators and business and billing personnel may be

Table 10-3

Sources Describing Needs Assessment Methods

Reference	Description
Hawtin et al.[4]	Describes methods for planning, conducting, and presenting the needs of a community for new services
Abramson[5]	A comprehensive description of research in community settings, including the methods for conducting needs assessments
Gupta[6]	Describes the basics of needs assessment and includes sample tools for modification

able to provide expertise for developing a sound business plan for the clinic that is consistent with the organization's business model. Business plans often include the clinic's purpose, background, and structure; implications; assessment methods; billing issues; a financial summary; resources needed; and supporting documents.[7]

Procedures for the clinic should cover all aspects of the patient–clinic interface. The following procedures might be included: methods for patient referral, patient registration, documentation of the clinic visit, patient education materials, methods for referral to other services, methods of patient follow-up, and billing. Assessment of all outcomes for the clinic should be considered during clinic development. Important outcomes may include clinical outcomes, adherence to medication regimen, compliance with national guidelines, quality of life, financial solvency of the clinic, and impact of the clinic on other institutional services. The assessment parameters should be incorporated into the daily operation of the clinic, if possible; this important step will aid the clinic in performing regular outcome assessments and reporting them efficiently. Finally, a comprehensive marketing plan for the clinic should be devised. Whether aimed at other health care providers or potential patients, the marketing message should be clear, direct, and frequently repeated.

The literature has described methods used to establish pharmacist-directed clinics, including general clinics, disease-specific clinics, and even clinics for specific medications. Kuo et al.[3] described the process for establishing a pharmacist-directed clinic within a family medicine practice.

Disease-specific clinics for anticoagulation, headache, seizure disorders, and HIV have been described.[8–11] The development of an anticoagulation clinic in a private community hospital was described in detail by Norton et al.[9] Planning for the clinic included gathering baseline data, obtaining physician input, visiting an established anticoagulation clinic, formulating a business plan, forming collaborative relationships with hospital departments, and developing clinical protocols. Physicians and patients were satisfied with the clinic, the number of warfarin-related bleeding admissions to acute care decreased, and the clinic was financially solvent.

At a specialty headache clinic, patients were scheduled for 60-minute appointments with the pharmacist after referral from primary care physicians.[11] The pharmacist discussed the headache diagnosis and medication plan with the referring physician. The plan was presented to the patient, who was asked to keep a headache diary. Follow-up appointments were scheduled in 2 to 4 weeks and as needed thereafter. Under the clinic's protocol, 70% of patients reported that headache frequency and severity decreased.

When pharmacist-directed clinics are focused on monitoring specific medications, the most commonly chosen medication has been warfarin. Many warfarin or anticoagulation clinics have been described in the literature. Ernst and Brandt[12] described one such clinic conducted in a private physician's office. Patients were referred by their primary care provider, and point-of-care anticoagulation monitoring was performed and interpreted by the clinical pharmacist. Billing for the interaction was treated as incident to a physician's services, under Medicare guidelines. The establishment of a pharmacist-directed clinic for teriparatide in a private endocrinology practice has also been described.[13] Patients to be started on teriparatide were referred to the clinic, their charts were reviewed for contraindications, lifestyle changes were suggested, drug information was provided, and patients were taught good injection technique. Follow-up was provided in a telephone call.

Issues to Consider in Providing MTMS in the Ambulatory Care Environment

As can be appreciated from the literature examples, development of a pharmacist-directed clinic requires consideration of several issues. The desire to provide care for patients is an important requirement, but without consideration of surrounding issues, the clinic's success cannot be assumed. Both an understanding of the issues described in the following section and clear communication of needs between all parties are necessary.

Space and Scheduling

A space for the clinic is essential. Finding even a single examination room within a large clinic may be difficult in some settings. When space is at a premium, clinic directors may be reluctant to relinquish any space that is not directly related to billing at the highest possible level. If dedicated space within a physician's office is required, the pharmacist should engage in negotiation to determine the most appropriate days and times for the clinic (e.g., when a certain physician also has clinic or when the clinic space is most available). The pharmacist should also consider any other space needs, such as an area for conducting point-of-care testing or for medication storage or administration. In settings that accept pharmacy students on rotation, it is also important to consider what students' role in seeing patients will be and whether more space will be required for student participation (for example, a space in which a student can conduct medication histories while the pharmacist is seeing another patient).

It is difficult to know exactly how much time will be required for each patient interaction in the clinic. New patients usually require more time than patients returning for follow-up appointments. It is advisable to consult practitioners in similar pharmacist-directed clinics to determine appointment length. Initially, it is best to schedule patient appointments slightly further apart than might be necessary, to allow the pharmacist to establish a work pace that fits the particular clinic and patient needs. The spacing of appointments may occur naturally; patients may be referred sporadically at first and then more frequently as the clinic becomes established. Financial projections made in developing the clinic business plan will also help the pharmacist determine how much time can be allotted to each patient if the clinic must be fiscally stable within a set period of time.

Documentation of Service Provided

The importance of appropriate documentation cannot be overemphasized. In billing federal agencies for services rendered, documentation is important not only for clinical and legal purposes but also to support the level of billing and avoid charges of fraud. Standardized methods of documentation should be developed for the clinic. The advantages of standardizing the documentation form or notes are to make it simpler for the practitioner, decrease the likelihood of forgetting an important element of the visit, allow another pharmacist to seamlessly provide care, and make any necessary chart reviews for quality assurance, outcomes measurement, or research easier. If a documentation system has not already been specified by the organization, the pharmacist is advised to develop note templates or checklist-type documentation systems.

Pharmacists may not be familiar with the idea that documentation is needed to support the level of billing, but federal and many private payers require that billing be based on the time spent with a patient and the complexity of the service provided. Therefore, it is helpful for the documentation format to incorporate the time and key elements supporting the complexity of the visit (see Chapter 6).

Fiscal Issues

Patients Qualified for Service

If the primary goal of the clinic is to provide MTMS, the targeted beneficiaries under this plan must be considered in the needs assessment. The Medicare final rule for MTMS states that the targeted beneficiaries will be those with multiple chronic diseases who are taking multiple medications and who are likely to incur annual costs for medications that exceed a specified level. The beneficiary's chosen prescription drug plan determines how many chronic diseases and medications the patient must have to qualify for payment. For 2006, the cost of medications had to exceed $4,000 for the beneficiary to be eligible, and that threshold is expected to remain through 2009. Pharmacists may offer and provide MTMS to nontargeted beneficiaries, but the beneficiary must be informed that the services are not covered by Medicare and that he or she will be responsible for 100% of the cost.

Given the Medicare rules, it is important to screen patients who are referred to the pharmacist-directed clinic to determine whether they are eligible for MTMS payment. One reported example of such screening was an HIV/AIDS clinic in which the pharmacist selected patients to see immediately after their physician appointments.[10] The patients selected had multiple medications, adherence problems, new medication therapies, potential adverse effects, potential drug–drug interactions, or drug toxicities or had been recently discharged from a hospital or emergency department. In contrast, a patient with well-controlled disease and five or more prescription medications might not be selected for MTMS. The composition of patient populations in the ambulatory care setting should be considered in determining personnel needs for MTMS. It may be most expedient to have technical, clerical, or billing personnel screen patients for eligibility and inform those who do not meet eligibility requirements of the payment conditions of the clinic visit.

Methods for Billing

Fee structures must be developed for billing clinical services. Two basic methods of billing are likely to be of most use in the pharmacist-directed clinic. The first is to bill according to the length of the visit. Often the time is billed in increments of 15 minutes. The second billing method is to bill according to the type of service provided.[14] In this method, the patient would be billed for a "hypertension visit" or a "multiple medication consult," for example. The method by which the pharmacist bills for MTMS will likely be determined to some degree by the insurer. The Current Procedural Terminology (CPT) codes for MTMS (Chapter 6) allow pharmacists to bill in 15-minute increments, up to a total of 45 minutes. Pharmacists must carefully select billing methods and, when necessary, establish rates that are appropriate for billing all patients the pharmacist sees. To bill different amounts for different insurance carriers may constitute fraud.

The usual case for pharmacists working with a medical group or an institution is that a billing system is already in place. The billing office generally will review the billing codes submitted by the provider for completeness and correctness. In addition, it will likely submit the bill to the appropriate payer, track reimbursement status, and deal with any disputed charges. It is important for the pharmacist to ensure that the billing personnel understand the services to be provided by the pharmacist-directed clinic and the method of billing for these services. Educating these individuals about other successful clinics and their billing structures is very important to the success of the clinic; the pharmacist may wish to provide articles about or business plans from other clinics.

Application of Billing Codes

Most billing codes in use at present are the CPT codes. These five-digit codes are used on billing documents to indicate the service or procedure that the provider performed.[14] Different codes are used depending on whether the patient is new to the practice or already established. Other defining factors are complexity of the problem, level of detail in the history or examination, and time spent with the patient. Basic standards of documentation for each CPT code and level of service (see Figure 6-1, page 47) are also established. To ensure proper reimbursement, it is imperative that each billable encounter with a patient be carefully documented in the medical record, with the required elements clearly noted. Most large clinics have a billing compliance officer who can provide guidance and instruction on items essential to proper documentation and billing.

Revenue Flow

Although it is frequently a contentious subject, there is very little literature describing exactly how revenue generated by pharmacist-directed clinics is distributed. In the setting where the pharmacist is the employee of a physician group, money generated will likely go to the group practice. In many practice settings, the individual practitioner is paid a negotiated salary that is based upon the projected income that individual should produce. Funds generated by individual practitioners do not go directly to support the salary of the individuals. Certainly there is a relationship between what an individual practitioner is paid by the group and what funds that practitioner generates, but monies generated by the practitioner generally do not directly go into the practitioner's paycheck. The pharmacist should participate in any bonus plans the practice has, if the income generated is in excess of the amount spent on supplies and the pharmacist's salary and benefits.

If the pharmacist is employed by an institution's department of pharmacy or a college of pharmacy, the distribution of revenue is more complex. If the employer rents clinic space for the pharmacist, the employer will likely receive most of the money collected from MTMS. On the other hand, if the pharmacist sees patients within the clinic area of another practice (e.g., in the family practice clinic) or uses the services of another department (e.g., billing or collection services, nursing services), that clinic or department may ask for some reimbursement for the resources expended on the pharmacist-directed clinic. It is extremely important to address these issues in the business plan developed for the pharmacist-directed clinic.

Clinic Administration

Credentialing and Provider Numbers

Credentialing is the process by which a specific health care professional is recognized to provide care. Providers are frequently credentialed for an institution or for an insurer. Determining the manner in which other nonphysician health care professionals are credentialed in the organization may provide some guidance to the pharmacist. The pharmacist may be asked to provide documentation of graduation, state licensure, residency or fellowship completion, board specialty certifications (e.g., by the Board of Pharmaceutical Specialties or other organizations listed in Table 9-4, page 93), and any advanced training certificates (e.g., completion of the Antithrombotic Pharmacotherapy Traineeship offered by the American Society of Health-System Pharmacists Research and Education Foundation).

National Provider Identifier numbers are available for pharmacies and individual pharmacists. Alternatively, some insuring organizations will provide the health care practitioner, once credentialed, with a provider number. Either way, the provider number is used on billing documents to link the provider to the patient encounter. The organization's billing office will also use this number to track billing to the provider and to assess the level of payment the provider receives. Often a figure utilizing the provider numbers and connected coding (e.g., amount collected divided by amount billed) is generated by the billing office to compare providers and detect problems with the billing system.

Protocols for Providing Service

Many pharmacist-managed clinics have established protocols for providing services. Some of these are more general, but most are disease specific. Reichert and Hammond[15] have described a general method for developing clinic protocols; they make recommendations for developing protocols, presenting the protocols to the approving persons, and updating the protocols annually. The following protocol sections are suggested: introduction, general approach to the patient, protocols for managing chronic diseases, and protocols for managing acute diseases. Reilly and Cavanagh[16] described in detail a clinic focused on preventing second cardiovascular events. In that clinic, the pharmacist proactively searched for patients with coronary artery disease and scheduled them for a 15–20-minute intake visit with a specialist nurse and a follow-up visit with the nurse and pharmacist. Recommendations were forwarded to the primary care physician for approval, and follow-up visits were scheduled. Bozovich et al.[17] described another example of a protocol for a lipid clinic in a private cardiology group office.

Scope of Practice in Different States

While the MTMS regulations pave the way for more compensation in recognition of pharmacists' clinical skills, they do not authorize pharmacists to participate in activities not allowed by state pharmacy practice acts. More than 75% of states have made changes that allow more pharmacist participation in the management of patient therapy.[18] Pharmacists providing MTMS will need to consult with their state board of pharmacy to determine what activities are covered under the scope of practice for the state. Recognition of the provision of MTMS under the Medicare regulations may encourage more states to revise their pharmacy practice acts.

Quality Assurance Measures

Quality assurance is an important evaluation step for all clinic practices. Through quality assurance, the clinic can hone its processes and measure progress toward standardized goals. Quality assurance can be accomplished in a variety of ways, but these should be specified during the planning process for the clinic. The quality assurance measures may also form some of the outcomes for the clinic.

As a method of quality assurance, many organizations choose to determine the degree to which patient care conforms to one or more national guidelines. One example is comparison of pharmacist-directed patient medical records with American Diabetes Association practice guidelines.[19] One clinic used this strategy to demonstrate the effectiveness of pharmacist versus physician management of patients. In another example, a clinic set a threshold for the percentage of patients achieving National Cholesterol Education Program low-density lipoprotein goals.[17] Clearly, this form of measurement can be used only where guidelines exist. In the absence of established guidelines, comparisons of laboratory or clinical measures with literature values may be acceptable. Anticoagulation clinics may choose to compute the amount of time patients spend in the established therapeutic range for international normalized ratio, the number of thrombotic events, and the number of bleeding events for comparison with other clinics.[20]

The Health Plan Employer Data and Information Set (HEDIS) guidelines are another nationally accepted quality measurement system that will be easily recognized by various administrative groups within an organization.[21] Specific measures for comparison exist for the following medication-related situations: annual monitoring for patients on persistent medications, antidepressant medication management, appropriate treatment for children with an upper-respiratory infection, avoidance of antibiotic treatment in adults with acute bronchitis, beta-blocker treatment and persistence of beta-blocker treatment after a heart attack, cholesterol management for patients with cardiovascular conditions, comprehensive diabetes care, controlling high blood pressure, disease-modifying antirheumatic therapy in rheumatoid arthritis, flu shots for adults, follow-up after hospitalization for mental illness, follow-up care for children prescribed medication for attention deficit hyperactivity disorder, initiation and engagement of alcohol and other drug dependence treatment, medical assistance with smoking cessation, medication management in the elderly, osteoporosis management in women who have had a fracture, and use of appropriate medications for people with asthma.

Accreditation

Although not all ambulatory care organizations elect to seek accreditation, the Joint Commission has accreditation standards for these organizations, published in the *Comprehensive Accreditation Manual for Ambulatory Care.*[22] Some of these standards are applicable to the pharmacist-directed clinic and will be briefly discussed.

The standards for providing care, treatment, and services stress the development of an individualized plan for care for each patient in an interdisciplinary, collaborative manner. The pharmacist providing MTMS can play an important part in care plan development and execution. The standards also emphasize the importance of providing education and training specific to the patient's needs. Again, the pharmacist can provide important information to the patient regarding his or her health and treatment.

The Joint Commission has many standards specific to medication management. Most relate to the procurement, storage, and dispensing of medications and may not pertain to the pharmacist-directed clinic. However, there are standards for safely and accurately administering medications, monitoring medication effects, and responding to adverse drug events and medication errors. As in the inpatient setting, the pharmacist providing MTMS in an ambulatory care environment should be intimately involved in meeting these standards.

Some pharmacist-directed clinics may be involved in testing under waiver of the Clinical Laboratory Improvement Amendments (CLIA-waived testing). In that case, there are specific Joint Commission standards to which the clinic must adhere. If the clinic is instead directing patients to a clinic-based laboratory, the laboratory will be responsible for attaining and maintaining the necessary certifications and accreditations.

Potential Problems with MTMS in Ambulatory Care

Who Provides the Service?

Although the Medicare Prescription Drug Improvement and Modernization Act of 2003 does not limit who can provide MTMS, the legislation recognizes that this service can be best provided by pharmacists. This lack of clarity in the legislation may cause difficulties for pharmacists who are confronted with other health care professionals who desire to provide MTMS. When working with clinic administrators, a pharmacist will need strong data supporting the provision of MTMS by a pharmacist and a clear business plan. The pharmacist's positioning to provide these services may be bolstered by creation of the new CPT codes (Chapter 6). Only pharmacists can use the MTMS CPT codes. Claims submitted with these codes by any health care provider other than a pharmacist will be rejected and not paid; pharmacists must educate clinic administrators on this restriction.

In addition, it is important to ensure that the same services are not being provided to the same patient by different pharmacists within the clinic. It is conceivable that the same patient could receive MTMS from different pharmacists on the same day. This might occur when pharmacists with different areas of specialization or different levels of expertise encounter the patient. For example, a pharmacist specializing in pulmonary disease might see a patient for chronic lung disease, and a pharmacist specializing in cardiovascular disease might see the same patient for hypertension. The different disease states necessitate the involvement of pharmacists with different specialty areas. It is also conceivable that a specialty pharmacist could provide MTMS for a specific disease while a general pharmacist addresses the patient's other MTMS needs. Problems, including accusations of fraud, could arise if two specialty pharmacists provided MTMS to the same patient for the same diagnosis on the same day. Similar issues are possible if a specialty pharmacist provides MTMS for a specific disease and a general pharmacist also provides MTMS for that disease on the same day.

Additional Documentation

To avoid problems in determining who provides service, it is important that documentation beyond notes in the patient's medical record be provided. This documentation may take the form of a letter or other written communication to other health care providers, especially other physicians and other pharmacists, involved in the patient's care. This type of communication will typically summarize the patient-specific database, problems that have been identified, and the intervention or treatment plans. It will also delineate the providers who are responsible for managing aspects of the treatment plan. Written communication may be viewed by some as simply a courtesy, but it helps avoid duplication of efforts, conflicting treatment plans, confusion on the part of the patient, and duplication of billing. The pharmacist should also remember that this type of documentation will often be incorporated in the patient's medical records, so the communication should be complete and appropriate for this type of documentation.

Determining a Usual and Customary Fee

In order to receive proper reimbursement and to avoid accusations of fraud, it is imperative that a proper fee be charged for MTMS rendered. Usually this fee is associated with a specific CPT code and is set on a national basis. However, a pharmacist may perform certain procedures that fall outside the typical codes used for billing purposes. In this case, careful documentation of the costs incurred in performing the procedure and a survey of what other pharmacists are charging for the service should be performed. These will assist in the determination of a normal and customary fee in negotiations with third-party payers. In 2005, the American Pharmacists Association (APhA) commissioned a study by the Lewin Group to examine the value of MTMS provided by pharmacists. A summary of the study report is included as Resource B.

Staffing Issues

The initiation of a new service involves not only a carefully developed business plan but also thorough consideration of human resources required for the service. If insufficient staffing is available to provide the service, then patients will be dissatisfied and individuals involved in providing the service will be frustrated. If too many individuals are involved in providing the service, then the program may fail financially. Human resource needs should be determined as part of the plan for starting MTMS in an ambulatory care setting. This should include a survey of the number of potentially eligible patients in the clinic, a projection of the time involved in providing MTMS to each patient, a projection of how frequently each patient will visit the pharmacist, and consideration of coverage for vacations and time off from the clinic. In addition, there should be an assessment of the need for support personnel (e.g., appointment scheduling, triage of phone calls, billing, clinic nurses or medical assistants). Well-developed clinics should have this infrastructure available and have a good understanding of support personnel needs.

Conclusion

The ambulatory care clinic setting may provide the optimal environment for the provision of MTMS. Access to the patient, medical records, and physicians and other health care professionals and the administrative infrastructure that exists in most clinics should make the development and provision of MTMS relatively easy. To practice effectively in the ambulatory care environment, a pharmacist must possess basic clinical skills, the ability to work closely with other health care professionals, and good clinical decision-making skills. In addition, the pharmacist will need to develop a sound business plan and anticipate solutions to potential barriers or problems in providing services. As MTMS develops and changes, the business plan may need to be altered to meet the requirements of various agencies and the expectations of patients. Therefore, a pharmacist practicing in the ambulatory care setting should balance providing well-developed MTMS and dealing with the business and administrative demands of practice management.

References

1. Knapp KK, Okamoto MP, Black BL. ASHP survey of ambulatory care pharmacy practice in health systems—2004. *Am J Health Syst Pharm.* 2005;62:274–84.

2. Knapp KK, Blalock SJ, Black BL. ASHP survey of ambulatory care responsibilities of pharmacists in managed care and integrated health systems—2001. *Am J Health Syst Pharm.* 2001;58:2151–66.

3. Kuo GM, Buckley TE, Fitzsimmons SD, et al. Collaborative drug therapy management services and reimbursement in a family medicine clinic. *Am J Health Syst Pharm.* 2004;61:343–54.

4. Hawtin M, Hughes G, Percy-Smith J. *Community Profiling: Auditing Social Needs.* Buckingham, England: Open University Press; 1994.

5. Abramson JH. *Survey Methods in Community Medicine.* 4th ed. London: Churchill Livingstone; 1990.

6. Gupta K. *A Practical Guide to Needs Assessment.* San Francisco: Jossey-Bass Pfeiffer; 1999.

7. Snella KA, Sachdev GP. A primer for developing pharmacist-managed clinics in the outpatient setting. *Pharmacotherapy.* 2003;23:1153–66.

8. McCants ER, Emanuel AM, White WM. Provision of Pharmaceutical Care in a Seizure Clinic: From Inception to Implementation. Paper presented at: 36th Annual ASHP Midyear Clinical Meeting; 2001; New Orleans, La: MCS-11.

9. Norton JL, Gibson DL. Establishing an outpatient anticoagulation clinic in a community hospital. *Am J Health Syst Pharm.* 1996;53:1151–7.

10. Colombo J. Establishing pharmaceutical care services in an HIV clinic. *J Am Pharm Assoc.* 1997;NS37:581–92.

11. Weitzel KW, Presley DN, Showalter ML, et al. Pharmacist-managed headache clinic. *Am J Health Syst Pharm.* 2004;61:2548–50.

12. Ernst ME, Brandt KB. Evaluation of 4 years of clinical pharmacist anticoagulation case management in a rural, private physician office. *J Am Pharm Assoc.* 2003;43:630–6.

13. Stroup J, Kane MP, Busch RS. Pharmacist-run teriparatide clinic. *Am J Health Syst Pharm.* 2003;60:2247–9.

14. Snella KA, Trewyn RR, Hansen LB, et al. Pharmacist compensation for cognitive services: focus on the physician office and community pharmacy. *Pharmacotherapy.* 2004;24:372–88.

15. Reichert SL, Hammond RW. Developing a protocol for collaborative drug therapy management. *Am J Health Syst Pharm.* 1999;56:1715–7.

16. Reilly V, Cavanagh M. The clinical and economic impact of a secondary heart disease prevention clinic jointly implemented by a practice nurse and pharmacist. *Pharm World Sci.* 2003;25:294–8.

17. Bozovich M, Rubino CM, Edmunds J. Effect of a clinical pharmacist-managed lipid clinic on achieving National Cholesterol Education Program low-density lipoprotein goals. *Pharmacotherapy.* 2000;20:1375–83.

18. Hammond RW, Schwartz AH, Campbell MUJ, et al. Collaborative drug therapy management by pharmacists—2003. *Pharmacotherapy.* 2003;23:1210–25.

19. Nowak SN, Singh R, Clarke A, et al. Metabolic control and adherence to American Diabetes Association practice guidelines in a pharmacist-managed diabetes clinic. *Diabetes Care.* 2002;25:1479.

20. Willey ML, Chagan L, Sisca TS, et al. A pharmacist-managed anticoagulation clinic: six-year assessment of patient outcomes. *Am J Health Syst Pharm.* 2003;60:1033–7.

21. National Committee for Quality Assurance. The State of Health Care Quality 2007. Available at: www.ncqa.org/tabid/543/Default.aspx.

22. Comprehensive Accreditation Manual for Ambulatory Care. Oakbrook Terrace, Ill: Joint Commission; 2008.

Resources

Medication Therapy Management in Pharmacy Practice

Core Elements of an MTM Service Model

Version 2.0 March 2008

Medication Therapy Management in Pharmacy Practice: Core Elements of an MTM Service Model

Version 2.0
A joint initiative of
the American Pharmacists Association and
the National Association of Chain Drug Stores Foundation

Acknowledgment

The American Pharmacists Association and the National Association of Chain Drug Stores Foundation respectfully acknowledge the contributions of all individuals and organizations that participated in the development of *Medication Therapy Management in Pharmacy Practice: Core Elements of an MTM Service Model Version 2.0* document for application across the pharmacy profession.

This service model is supported by the following organizations:

American Association of Colleges of Pharmacy

American College of Apothecaries

American College of Clinical Pharmacy

American Society of Consultant Pharmacists

American Society of Health-System Pharmacists

National Alliance of State Pharmacy Associations

National Community Pharmacists Association

Preface

Eleven national pharmacy organizations achieved consensus on a definition of medication therapy management (MTM) in July 2004 (Appendix A). Building on the consensus definition, the American Pharmacists Association and the National Association of Chain Drug Stores Foundation developed a model framework for implementing effective MTM services in a community pharmacy setting by publishing *Medication Therapy Management in Community Pharmacy Practice: Core Elements of an MTM Service Version 1.0.* The original version 1.0 document described the foundational or core elements of MTM services that could be provided by pharmacists across the spectrum of community pharmacy.[1]

Medication Therapy Management in Pharmacy Practice: Core Elements of an MTM Service Model Version 2.0 is an evolutionary document that focuses on the provision of MTM services in settings where patients* or their caregivers can be actively involved in managing their medications. This service model was developed with the input of an advisory panel of pharmacy leaders representing diverse pharmacy practice settings (listed in Addendum). While adoption of this model is voluntary, it is important to note that this model is crafted to maximize both effectiveness and efficiency of MTM service delivery across pharmacy practice settings in an effort to improve continuity of care and patient outcomes.

**In this document, the term patient refers to the patient, the caregiver, or other persons involved in the care of the patient.*

Introduction

Medication Therapy Management in Pharmacy Practice: Core Elements of an MTM Service Model Version 2.0 is designed to improve collaboration among pharmacists, physicians, and other healthcare professionals; enhance communication between patients and their healthcare team; and optimize medication use for improved patient outcomes. The medication therapy management (MTM) services described in this model empower patients to take an active role in managing their medications. The services are dependent upon pharmacists working collaboratively with physicians and other healthcare professionals to optimize medication use in accordance with evidence-based guidelines.[2,3]

MTM services,* as described in this model, are distinct from medication dispensing and focus on a patient-centered, rather than an individual product-centered, process of care.[4] MTM services encompass the assessment and evaluation of the patient's complete medication therapy regimen, rather than focusing on an individual medication product. This model framework describes core elements of MTM service delivery in pharmacy practice and does not represent a specific minimum or maximum level of all services that could be delivered by pharmacists.[5]

Medication-related problems are a significant public health issue within the healthcare system. Incidence estimates suggest that more than 1.5 million preventable medication-related adverse events occur each year in the United States, accounting for an excess of $177 billion in terms of medication-related morbidity and mortality.[6,7] The Institute of Medicine advocates that healthcare should be safe, effective, patient-centered, timely, efficient, and effective to meet patients' needs and that patients should be active participants in the healthcare process to prevent medication-related problems.[3,7]

MTM services, as described in this service model, may help address the urgent public health need for the prevention of medication-related morbidity and mortality.[3] MTM services may contribute to medication error prevention, result in improved reliability of healthcare delivery, and enable patients to take an active role in medication and healthcare self-management.[7] The MTM services outlined in this model are aligned with the Centers for Medicare & Medicaid Services' expectations, as stated in the Medicare Prescription Drug, Improvement, and Modernization Act of 2003, that MTM services will enhance patients' understanding of appropriate drug use, increase adherence to medication therapy, and improve detection of adverse drug events.[8]

MTM programs are demonstrating positive clinical, economic, and humanistic outcomes across diverse patient populations in various patient care settings.[9–15] MTM services are currently being delivered in both the public and private sectors. In the public sector, some state Medicaid and Medicare Part D plans have focused on a comprehensive medication therapy review as the foundation of their MTM programs. Pharmacists participating in these programs often provide patients with an initial comprehensive assessment and ongoing follow-up assessments to identify and resolve medication-related problems.[11, 16–20] In the private sector, MTM programs are beginning to emerge nationwide, offering MTM services to traditional insured groups, managed-care populations, self-insured employers, and self-paying individual patients.[9,10,12]

Any patient who uses prescription and nonprescription medications, herbal products, or other dietary supplements could potentially benefit from the MTM core elements outlined in this model. As part of the effort to effectively address the urgent public health issue of medication-related morbidity and mortality, MTM services should be considered for any patient with actual or potential medication-related problems, regardless of the number of medications they use, their specific disease states, or their health plan coverage. Although MTM program structure and the needs of individual patients may vary, the use of a consistent and recognizable framework for core MTM services, as described in this model, will enhance their efficient delivery and effective quality measurement. As new opportunities arise, pharmacists in all practice settings must share a common vision for patient-centered MTM services that improve medication therapy outcomes and provide value within our nation's healthcare system.

**MTM services are built upon the philosophy and process of pharmaceutical care that was first implemented in pharmacy practice in the early 1990s. As pharmacy education, training, and practice continue to evolve to a primarily clinical "patient-centered" focus, pharmacists are gaining recognition from other healthcare professionals and the public as "medication therapy experts." Recognizing the pharmacist's role as the medication therapy expert, the pharmacy profession has developed a consensus definition for medication therapy management and is increasingly using this term to describe the services provided by pharmacists to patients.*

Framework for Pharmacist-Provided MTM Services

This framework for MTM service delivery in pharmacy practice is designed to facilitate collaboration among the pharmacist, patient, physician, and other healthcare professionals to promote safe and effective medication use and achieve optimal patient outcomes. MTM services in all patient care settings should include structures supporting the establishment and maintenance of the patient–pharmacist relationship.

Providing MTM Services in Various Patient Care Settings

Patients with a potential need for MTM services can be identified by the pharmacist, the physician or other healthcare professionals, the health plan, or the patients themselves when medication-related problems are suspected. Appendix B provides considerations for identification of patients who may benefit from MTM services. Patients may be especially vulnerable to medication-related problems during transitions of care* such as when their healthcare setting changes, when they change physicians, or when their payer status changes. These transitions of care often result in medication therapy changes that may be due to changes in the patient's needs or resources, the patient's health status or condition, or formulary requirements. It is important that systems be established so that pharmacist-provided MTM services can focus on reconciling the patient's medications and ensuring the provision of appropriate medication management during transitions of care.

For ambulatory patients, MTM services typically are offered by appointment but may be provided on a walk-in basis. MTM services should be delivered in a private or semi-private area, as required by the Health Insurance Portability and Accountability Act, by a pharmacist whose time can be devoted to the patient during this service.[21] In other patient care settings (e.g., acute care, long-term care, home care, managed care), the environment in which MTM services are delivered may differ because of variability in structure and facilities design. Even so, to the extent MTM core elements are implemented, a consistent approach to their delivery should be maintained.

The Delivery of MTM Services by the Pharmacist

Within the MTM core elements service model, the patient receives an annual comprehensive medication therapy review and additional medication therapy reviews according to the patient's needs. The patient may require ongoing monitoring by the pharmacist to address new or recurring medication-related problems.

The total number of reviews required to successfully manage a patient's therapy will vary from patient to patient and will be ultimately determined by the complexity of the individual patient's medication-related problems. The extent of health plan benefits or other limitations imposed by the patient's payer may affect coverage for MTM services; however, this would not preclude additional services provided by the pharmacist for which the patient pays on a fee-for-service basis.

To perform the most comprehensive assessment of a patient, personal interaction with direct contact between a healthcare professional and a patient is optimal. A face-to-face interaction optimizes the pharmacist's ability to observe signs of and visual cues to the patient's health problems (e.g., adverse reactions to medications, lethargy, alopecia, extrapyramidal symptoms, jaundice, disorientation) and can enhance the patient–pharmacist relationship.[22] The pharmacist's observations may result in early detection of medication-related problems and thus have the potential to reduce inappropriate medication use, emergency department visits, and hospitalizations. It is recognized, however, that alternative methods of patient contact and interaction such as telephonic may be necessary for those patients for whom a face-to-face interaction is not possible or not desired (e.g., homebound patients) or in pharmacy practice settings in which the pharmacist serves in a consultative role on the healthcare team. Irrespective of whether the MTM service is provided by the pharmacist to the patient face-to-face or by alternative means, the service is intended to support the establishment and maintenance of the patient–pharmacist relationship.

**Examples of transitions of care may include but are not limited to changes in healthcare setting (e.g., hospital admission, hospital to home, hospital to long-term care facility, home to long-term care facility), changes in healthcare professionals and/or level of care (e.g., treatment by a specialist), or changes in payer status (e.g., change or loss of health plan benefits/insurance).*

Core Elements of an MTM Service Model in Pharmacy Practice

The MTM service model in pharmacy practice includes the following five core elements:

- Medication therapy review (MTR)
- Personal medication record (PMR)
- Medication-related action plan (MAP)
- Intervention and/or referral
- Documentation and follow-up

These five core elements form a framework for the delivery of MTM services in pharmacy practice. Every core element is integral to the provision of MTM; however, the sequence and delivery of the core elements may be modified to meet an individual patient's needs.

Medication Therapy Review: *The medication therapy review (MTR) is a systematic process of collecting patient-specific information, assessing medication therapies to identify medication-related problems, developing a prioritized list of medication-related problems, and creating a plan to resolve them.*

An MTR is conducted between the patient and the pharmacist. Pharmacist-provided MTR and consultation in various settings has resulted in reductions in physician visits, emergency department visits, hospital days, and overall healthcare costs.[9,10,12,14,20,23–25] In addition, pharmacists have been shown to obtain accurate and efficient medication-related information from patients.[10,26,27] The MTR is designed to improve patients' knowledge of their medications, address problems or concerns that patients may have, and empower patients to self-manage their medications and their health condition(s).

The MTR can be comprehensive or targeted to an actual or potential medication-related problem. Regardless of whether the MTR is comprehensive or targeted, patients may be identified as requiring this service in a variety of ways. Commonly, patients may be referred to a pharmacist by their health plan, another pharmacist, physician, or other healthcare professionals. Patients may also request an MTR independent of any referral. Additional opportunities for providing an MTR include when a patient is experiencing a transition of care, when actual or potential medication-related problems are identified, or if the patient is suspected to be at higher risk for medication-related problems.

In a comprehensive MTR, ideally the patient presents all current medications to the pharmacist, including all prescription and nonprescription medications, herbal products, and other dietary supplements. The pharmacist then assesses the patient's medications for the presence of any medication-related problems, including adherence, and works with the patient, the physician, or other healthcare professionals to determine appropriate options for resolving identified problems. In addition, the pharmacist supplies the patient with education and information to improve the patient's self-management of his or her medications.

Targeted MTRs are used to address an actual or potential medication-related problem. Ideally, targeted MTRs are performed for patients who have received a comprehensive MTR. Whether for a new problem or subsequent monitoring, the pharmacist assesses the specific therapy problem in the context of the patient's complete medical and medication history. Following assessment, the pharmacist intervenes and provides education and information to the patient, the physician or other healthcare professionals, or both, as appropriate. The MTR is tailored to the individual needs of the patient at each encounter.

Depending on its scope, the MTR may include the following:

- Interviewing the patient to gather data including demographic information, general health and activity status, medical history, medication history, immunization history, and patients' thoughts or feelings about their conditions and medication use[28]
- Assessing, on the basis of all relevant clinical information available to the pharmacist, the patient's physical and overall health status, including current and previous diseases or conditions
- Assessing the patient's values, preferences, quality of life, and goals of therapy
- Assessing cultural issues, education level, language barriers, literacy level, and other characteristics of the patient's communication abilities that could affect outcomes
- Evaluating the patient to detect symptoms that could be attributed to adverse events caused by any of his or her current medications
- Interpreting, monitoring, and assessing patient's laboratory results

- Assessing, identifying, and prioritizing medication-related problems related to
  - » The clinical appropriateness of each medication being taken by the patient, including benefit versus risk
  - » The appropriateness of the dose and dosing regimen of each medication, including consideration of indications, contraindications, potential adverse effects, and potential problems with concomitant medications
  - » Therapeutic duplication or other unnecessary medications
  - » Adherence to the therapy
  - » Untreated diseases or conditions
  - » Medication cost considerations
  - » Healthcare/medication access considerations
- Developing a plan for resolving each medication-related problem identified
- Providing education and training on the appropriate use of medications and monitoring devices and the importance of medication adherence and understanding treatment goals
- Coaching patients to be empowered to manage their medications
- Monitoring and evaluating the patient's response to therapy, including safety and effectiveness
- Communicating appropriate information to the physician or other healthcare professionals, including consultation on the selection of medications, suggestions to address identified medication problems, updates on the patient's progress, and recommended follow-up care[29]

In this service model, a patient would receive an annual comprehensive MTR and additional targeted MTRs to address new or ongoing medication-related problem(s). Significant events such as important changes in the patient's medication therapy, changes in the patient's needs or resources, changes in the patient's health status or condition, a hospital admission or discharge, an emergency department visit, or an admission or discharge from a long-term care or assisted-living facility could necessitate additional comprehensive MTRs.

Personal Medication Record: *The personal medication record (PMR) is a comprehensive record of the patient's medications (prescription and nonprescription medications, herbal products, and other dietary supplements).*

Within the MTM core elements service model, the patient receives a comprehensive record of his or her medications (prescription and nonprescription medications, herbal products, and other dietary supplements) that has been completed either by the patient with the assistance of the pharmacist or by the pharmacist, or the patient's existing PMR is updated. Ideally, the patient's PMR would be generated electronically, but it also may be produced manually. Whether the pharmacist provides the PMR manually or electronically, the information should be written at a literacy level that is appropriate for and easily understood by the patient. In institutional settings, the PMR may be created at discharge from the medication administration record or patient chart for use by the patient in the outpatient setting. The PMR contains information to assist the patient in his or her overall medication therapy self-management. A sample PMR is included in Appendix C.

The PMR, which is intended for use by the patient, may include the following information:[30]

- Patient name
- Patient birth date
- Patient phone number
- Emergency contact information (Name, relationship, phone number)
- Primary care physician (Name and phone number)
- Pharmacy/pharmacist (Name and phone number)
- Allergies (e.g., What allergies do I have? What happened when I had the allergy or reaction?)
- Other medication-related problems (e.g., What medication caused the problem? What was the problem I had?)
- Potential questions for patients to ask about their medications (e.g., When you are prescribed a new drug, ask your doctor or pharmacist...)
- Date last updated
- Date last reviewed by the pharmacist, physician, or other healthcare professional
- Patient's signature
- Healthcare provider's signature
- For each medication, inclusion of the following:
  - » Medication (e.g., drug name and dose)
  - » Indication (e.g., Take for...)
  - » Instructions for use (e.g., When do I take it?)
  - » Start date
  - » Stop date
  - » Ordering prescriber/contact information (e.g., doctor)
  - » Special instructions

The PMR is intended for patients to use in medication self-management. The maintenance of the PMR is a collaborative effort among the patient, pharmacist, physician, and other healthcare professionals. Patients should be encouraged to maintain and update this perpetual document. Patients should be educated to carry the PMR with them at all times and share it at all healthcare visits and at all admissions to or discharges from institutional settings to help ensure that all healthcare professionals are aware of their current medication regimen.

Each time the patient receives a new medication; has a current medication discontinued; has an instruction change; begins using a new prescription or nonprescription medication, herbal product, or other dietary supplement; or has any other changes to the medication regimen, the patient should update the PMR to help ensure a current and accurate record. Ideally, the pharmacist, physician, and other healthcare professionals can actively assist the patient with the PMR revision process.

Pharmacists may use the PMR to communicate and collaborate with physicians and other healthcare professionals to achieve optimal patient outcomes. Widespread use of the PMR will support uniformity of information provided to all healthcare professionals and enhance the continuity of care provided to patients while facilitating flexibility to account for pharmacy- or institution-specific variations.

Medication-Related Action Plan:
The medication-related action plan (MAP) is a patient-centric document containing a list of actions for the patient to use in tracking progress for self-management.

A care plan is the health professional's course of action for helping a patient achieve specific health goals.[31] The care plan is an important component of the documentation core element outlined in this service model. In addition to the care plan, which is developed by the pharmacist and used in the collaborative care of the patient, the patient receives an individualized MAP for use in medication self-management. Completion of the MAP is a collaborative effort between the patient and the pharmacist. The patient MAP includes only items that the patient can act on that are within the pharmacist's scope of practice or that have been agreed to by relevant members of the healthcare team. The MAP should not include outstanding action items that still require physician or other healthcare professional review or approval. The patient can use the MAP as a simple guide to track his or her progress. The Institute of Medicine has advocated the need for a patient-centered model of healthcare.[7] The patient MAP, coupled with education, is an essential element for incorporating the patient-centered approach into the MTM service model. The MAP reinforces a sense of patient empowerment and encourages the patient's active participation in his or her medication-adherence behavior and overall MTM. A sample MAP is included in Appendix D.

The MAP, which is intended for use by the patient, may include the following information:

- Patient name
- Primary care physician
  (Doctor's name and phone number)
- Pharmacy/pharmacist
  (Pharmacy name/pharmacist name and phone number)
- Date of MAP creation (Date prepared)
- Action steps for the patient: "What I need to do..."
- Notes for the patient: "What I did and when I did it..."
- Appointment information for follow-up with pharmacist, if applicable

Specific items that require intervention and that have been approved by other members of the healthcare team and any new items within the pharmacist's scope of practice should be included on a MAP distributed to the patient on a follow-up visit. In institutional settings the MAP could be established at the time the patient is discharged for use by the patient in medication self-management.

Intervention and/or Referral: *The pharmacist provides consultative services and intervenes to address medication-related problems; when necessary, the pharmacist refers the patient to a physician or other healthcare professional.*

During the course of an MTM encounter, medication-related problems may be identified that require the pharmacist to intervene on the patient's behalf. Interventions may include collaborating with physicians or other healthcare professionals to resolve existing or potential medication-related problems or working with the patient directly. The communication of appropriate information to the physician or other healthcare professional, including consultation on the selection of medications, suggestions to address medication problems, and recommended follow-up care, is integral to the intervention component of the MTM service model.[29]

The positive impact of pharmacist interventions on outcomes related to medication-related problems has been demonstrated in numerous studies.[32-37] Appropriate resolution of medication-related problems involves collaboration and communication between the patient, the pharmacist, and the patient's physician or other healthcare professionals.

Some patients' medical conditions or medication therapy may be highly specialized or complex and the patient's needs may extend beyond the core elements of MTM service delivery. In such cases, pharmacists may provide additional services according to their expertise or refer the patient to a physician, another pharmacist, or other healthcare professional.

Examples of circumstances that may require referral include the following:

- A patient may exhibit potential problems discovered during the MTR that may necessitate referral for evaluation and diagnosis
- A patient may require disease management education to help him or her manage chronic diseases such as diabetes
- A patient may require monitoring for high-risk medications (e.g., warfarin, phenytoin, methotrexate)

The intent of intervention and/or referral is to optimize medication use, enhance continuity of care, and encourage patients to avail themselves of healthcare services to prevent future adverse outcomes.

Documentation and Follow-up: *MTM services are documented in a consistent manner, and a follow-up MTM visit is scheduled based on the patient's medication-related needs, or the patient is transitioned from one care setting to another.*

Documentation is an essential element of the MTM service model. The pharmacist documents services and intervention(s) performed in a manner appropriate for evaluating patient progress and sufficient for billing purposes.

Proper documentation of MTM services may serve several purposes including, but not limited, to the following:

- Facilitating communication between the pharmacist and the patient's other healthcare professionals regarding recommendations intended to resolve or monitor actual or potential medication-related problems
- Improving patient care and outcomes
- Enhancing the continuity of patient care among providers and care settings
- Ensuring compliance with laws and regulations for the maintenance of patient records
- Protecting against professional liability
- Capturing services provided for justification of billing or reimbursement (e.g., payer audits)
- Demonstrating the value of pharmacist-provided MTM services
- Demonstrating clinical, economic, and humanistic outcomes

MTM documentation includes creating and maintaining an ongoing patient-specific record that contains, in chronological order, a record of all provided care in an established standard healthcare professional format (e.g., the SOAP [subjective observations, objective observations, assessment, and plan] note[38]).

Ideally, documentation will be completed electronically or alternatively on paper. The inclusion of resources such as a PMR, a MAP, and other practice-specific forms will assist the pharmacist in maintaining consistent professional documentation. The use of consistent documentation will help facilitate collaboration among members of the healthcare team while accommodating practitioner, facility, organizational, or regional variations.

Documentation elements for the patient record may include, but are not limited to, the following:[22,29,38–40]

Documentation category	Examples
Patient demographics	Basic information: address, phone, e-mail, gender, age, ethnicity, education status, patient's special needs, health plan benefit/insurance coverage
Subjective observations	Pertinent patient-reported information: previous medical history, family history, social history, chief complaints, allergies, previous adverse drug reactions
Objective observations	Known allergies, diseases, conditions, laboratory results, vital signs, diagnostic signs, physical exam results, review of systems
Assessment	Problem list, assessment of medication-related problems
Plan	A care plan is the healthcare professional's course of action for helping a patient achieve specific health goals
Education	Goal setting and instruction provided to the patient with verification of understanding
Collaboration	Communication with other healthcare professionals: recommendations, referrals, and correspondence with other professionals (cover letter, SOAP note)
PMR	A record of all medications, including prescription and nonprescription medications, herbal products, and other dietary supplements
MAP	Patient-centric document containing a list of actions to use in tracking progress for self-management
Follow-up	Transition plan or scheduling of next follow-up visit
Billing	Amount of time spent on patient care, level of complexity, amount charged

External Communication of MTM Documentation

Following documentation of the MTM encounter, appropriate external communication should be provided or sent to key audiences, including patients, physicians, and payers. Providing the patient with applicable documentation that he or she can easily understand is vital to facilitating active involvement in the care process. Documentation provided to the patient at the MTM encounter may include the PMR, MAP, and additional education materials. Documentation to physicians and other healthcare professionals may include a cover letter, the patient's PMR, the SOAP note, and care plan. Communicating with payers and providing appropriate billing information may also be necessary and could include the name of the pharmacist or pharmacy and appropriate identifier, services provided, time spent on patient care, and appropriate billing codes.

Follow-up

When a patient's care setting changes (e.g., hospital admission, hospital to home, hospital to long-term care facility, home to long-term care facility), the pharmacist transitions the patient to another pharmacist in the patient's new care setting to facilitate continued MTM services. In these situations, the initial pharmacist providing MTM services participates cooperatively with the patient's new pharmacist provider to facilitate the coordinated transition of the patient, including the transfer of relevant medication and other health-related information.

If the patient will be remaining in the same care setting, the pharmacist should arrange for consistent follow-up MTM services in accordance with the patient's unique medication-related needs. All follow-up evaluations and interactions with the patient and his or her other healthcare professional(s) should be included in MTM documentation.

Conclusion

The MTM core elements, as presented in this document, are intended to be applicable to patients in all care settings where the patients or their caregivers can be actively involved with managing their medication therapy, taking full advantage of the pharmacist's role as the "medication therapy expert." A flow chart of the core elements of an MTM service model contained in this document can be found in Appendix E. As the core elements service model continues to evolve to meet diverse patient needs, pharmacists are encouraged to make the most of the framework provided to improve patient outcomes and medication use.

References

1. American Pharmacists Association, National Association of Chain Drug Stores Foundation. Medication therapy management in community pharmacy practice: core elements of an MTM service (version 1.0). *J Am Pharm Assoc.* 2005;45:573-9.
2. Wagner EH. Chronic disease management: What will it take to improve care for chronic illness? *Effective Clinical Practice.* 1998;1(1):2-4.
3. Institute of Medicine. Cros*sing the Quality Chasm: A New Health System for the 21st Century.* Washington, DC: Institute of Medicine; 2001.
4. Cipolle RJ. Strand LM, Morley PC. *Pharmaceutical Care Practice: The Clinician's Guide.* New York: McGraw Hill; 2004.
5. McGivney MS, Meyer SM, Duncan-Hewitt W, et al. Medication therapy management: its relationship to patient counseling, disease management, and pharmaceutical care. *J Am Pharm Assoc.* 2007;45:620-8.
6. Ernst FR, Grizzle AJ. Drug-related morbidity and mortality: updating the cost-of-illness model. *J Am Pharm Assoc.* 2001;41:192-9.
7. Institute of Medicine. *Report Brief: Preventing Medication Errors.* Washington, DC: Institute of Medicine; July 2006. http://www.iom.edu/Object.File/Master/35/943/medication%20errors%20new.pdf. Accessed September 1, 2007.
8. Centers for Medicare & Medicaid Services. Medicare Prescription Drug Benefit Final Rule: 42 CFR Parts 400, 403, 411, 417, and 423 Medicare Program. *Federal Register*, vol. 70, no. 18. January 28, 2005. http://a257.g.akamaitech.net/7/257/2422/01jan20051800/edocket.access.gpo.gov/2005/pdf/05-1321.pdf. Accessed September 1, 2007.
9. Garrett D, Bluml B. Patient self-management program for diabetes: first-year clinical, humanistic, and economic outcomes. *J Am Pharm Assoc.* 2005;45:130-7.
10. Cranor CW, Bunting BA, Christensen DB. The Asheville Project: long-term clinical and economic outcomes of a community pharmacy diabetes care program. *J Am Pharm Assoc.* 2003;43:173-90.
11. Chrischilles EA, Carter BL, Lund BC, et al. Evaluation of the Iowa Medicaid pharmaceutical case management program. *J Am Pharm Assoc.* 2004;44:337-49.
12. Bunting BA, Cranor CW. The Asheville Project: long-term clinical, humanistic, and economic outcomes of a community-based medication therapy management program for asthma. *J Am Pharm Assoc.* 2003;46:133-47.
13. Jameson J, VanNoord G, Vanderwould K. The impact of a pharmacotherapy consultation on the cost and outcome of medical therapy. *J Fam Pract.* 1995;41(5):469-72.
14. Lipton HL, Bero LA, Bird JA, et al. The impact of clinical pharmacists' consultations on physicians' geriatric drug prescribing. *Med Care.* 1992;30:646-58.
15. Schumock GT, Butler MG, Meek PD, et al. Evidence of the economic benefit of clinical pharmacy services: 1996–2000. *Pharmacotherapy.* 2003;23:113-132.
16. Minnesota Department of Human Services. MHCP enrolled professionals: medication therapy management services. http://www.dhs.state.mn.us/main/idcplg?IdcService=GET_DYNAMIC_CONVERSION&RevisionSelectionMethod=LatestReleased&dDocName=id_055325#P116_7762. Accessed February 5, 2007.
17. Traynor K. Wyoming program brings pharmacist consultations home. *Am J Health Syst Pharm.* 2004;61:760.
18. North Carolina Department of Health and Human Services. *North Carolina Medicaid: Medication Therapy Management Program (MTMP).* August 2006. http://www.dhhs.state.nc.us/dma/Forms/mtmpinstructions.pdf. Accessed September 1, 2007.
19. Touchette DR, Burns AL, Bough MA, et al. Survey of medication therapy management programs under Medicare part D. *J Am Pharm Assoc.* 2006;46:683-91.
20. Galt KA. Cost avoidance, acceptance, and outcomes associated with a pharmacotherapy consult clinic in a Veterans Affairs medical center. *Pharmacotherapy.* 1998;18:1103-11.
21. Rovers J, Currie J, Hagel H, et al. Re-engineering the pharmacy layout. In: *A Practical Guide to Pharmaceutical Care.* 2nd ed. Washington, DC: American Pharmacists Association; 2003:261-6.
22. Rovers J, Currie J, Hagel H, et al. Patient data collection. In: *A Practical Guide to Pharmaceutical Care.* 2nd ed. Washington, DC: American Pharmacists Association; 2003:26-51.
23. Borgsdorf LR, Miano JS, Knapp KK. Pharmacist-managed medication review in a managed care system. *Am J Hosp Pharm.* 1994;51:772-7.
24. Bond CA, Raehl CL, Franke T. Clinical pharmacy services, pharmacy staffing, and the total cost of care in the United States hospitals. *Pharmacotherapy.* 2000;20:609-21.
25. Christensen D, Trygstad T, Sullivan R, et al. A pharmacy management intervention for optimizing drug therapy for nursing home patients. *Am J Geriatr Pharmacother.* 2004;2:248-56.
26. Gurwich EL. Comparison of medication histories acquired by pharmacists and physicians. *Am J Hosp Pharm.* 1983;40:1541-2.
27. Nester TM, Hale LS. Effectiveness of a pharmacist-acquired medication history in promoting patient safety. *Am J Health Syst Pharm.* 2003;3-14.
28. Rovers J, Currie J, Hagel H, et al. The case for pharmaceutical care. In: *A Practical Guide to Pharmaceutical Care.* 2nd ed. Washington, DC: American Pharmacists Association, 2003:3-4.
29. Berger BA. Interacting with physicians. In: *Communication Skills for Pharmacists.* 2nd ed. Washington, DC: American Pharmacists Association; 2005:131-9.
30. Executive summary of the American Society of Health System Pharmacists (ASHP) and ASHP Research and Education Foundation Continuity of Care in Medication Use Summit. *Am J Health Syst Pharm.* In press.
31. Rovers J, Currie J, Hagel H, et al. Patient care plan development. In: *A Practical Guide to Pharmaceutical Care.* 2nd ed. Washington, DC: American Pharmacists Association, 2003:69.
32. Rupp MT. Value of the community pharmacists' interventions to correct prescribing errors. *Ann Pharmacother.* 1992;26:1580-4.
33. McMullin ST, Hennenfent JA, Ritchie D, et al. A prospective randomized trial to assess the cost impact of pharmacist-initiated interventions. *Arch Intern Med.* 1999;159:2306-9.
34. Knapp KK, Katzman H, Hambright JS, et al. Community pharmacist intervention in a capitated pharmacy benefit contract. *Am J Health Syst Pharm.* 1998;55:1141-5.
35. Dobie RL, Rascati KL. Documenting the value of pharmacist interventions. *Am Pharm.* 1994;NS34(5):50-4.
36. Hepler CD, Strand LM. Opportunities and responsibilities in pharmaceutical care. *Am J Hosp Pharm.* 1990;47:533-43.
37. Bootman JL, Harrison DL, Cox E. The healthcare cost of drug-related morbidity and mortality in nursing facilities. *Arch Intern Med.* 1997;157:2089-96.
38. Zierler-Brown S, Brown TR, Chen D, et al. Clinical documentation for patient care: models, concepts, and liability considerations for pharmacists. *Am J Health Syst Pharm.* 2007;64:1851-8.
39. Currie JD, Doucette WR, Kuhle J, et al. Identification of essential elements in documentation of pharmacist-provided care. *J Am Pharm Assoc.* 2003;43:41-9.
40. Culhane N, Brooks A, Cohen V, et al. Medication therapy management services: Application of the core elements in ambulatory settings. American College of Clinical Pharmacy. March 14, 2007.

Appendix A. Definition of Medication Therapy Management (MTM)❖

Medication Therapy Management is a distinct service or group of services that optimize therapeutic outcomes for individual patients. Medication Therapy Management services are independent of, but can occur in conjunction with, the provision of a medication product.

Medication Therapy Management encompasses a broad range of professional activities and responsibilities within the licensed pharmacist's, or other qualified healthcare provider's, scope of practice. These services include but are not limited to the following, according to the individual needs of the patient:

a. Performing or obtaining necessary assessments of the patient's health status
b. Formulating a medication treatment plan
c. Selecting, initiating, modifying, or administering medication therapy
d. Monitoring and evaluating the patient's response to therapy, including safety and effectiveness
e. Performing a comprehensive medication review to identify, resolve, and prevent medication-related problems, including adverse drug events
f. Documenting the care delivered and communicating essential information to the patient's other primary care providers
g. Providing verbal education and training designed to enhance patient understanding and appropriate use of his/her medications
h. Providing information, support services, and resources designed to enhance patient adherence with his/her therapeutic regimens
i. Coordinating and integrating medication therapy management services within the broader healthcare management services being provided to the patient

A program that provides coverage for Medication Therapy Management services shall include:

a. Patient-specific and individualized services or sets of services provided directly by a pharmacist to the patient.* These services are distinct from formulary development and use, generalized patient education and information activities, and other population-focused quality-assurance measures for medication use
b. Face-to-face interaction between the patient* and the pharmacist as the preferred method of delivery. When patient-specific barriers to face-to-face communication exist, patients shall have equal access to appropriate alternative delivery methods. Medication Therapy Management programs shall include structures supporting the establishment and maintenance of the patient*–pharmacist relationship
c. Opportunities for pharmacists and other qualified healthcare providers to identify patients who should receive medication therapy management services
d. Payment for medication therapy management services consistent with contemporary provider payment rates that are based on the time, clinical intensity, and resources required to provide services (e.g., Medicare Part A and/or Part B for CPT and RBRVS)
e. Processes to improve continuity of care, outcomes, and outcome measures

Approved July 27, 2004, by the Academy of Managed Care Pharmacy, the American Association of Colleges of Pharmacy, the American College of Apothecaries, the American College of Clinical Pharmacy, the American Society of Consultant Pharmacists, the American Pharmacists Association, the American Society of Health-System Pharmacists, the National Association of Boards of Pharmacy,** the National Association of Chain Drug Stores, the National Community Pharmacists Association, and the National Council of State Pharmacy Association Executives.

* *In some situations, medication therapy management services may be provided to the caregiver or other persons involved in the care of the patient.*

** *Organization policy does not allow NABP to take a position on payment issues.*

❖ *Bluml BM. Definition of medication therapy management: development of profession wide consensus. J Am Pharm Assoc. 2005;45:566–72.*

Appendix B. Considerations for Identification of Patients Who May Benefit From MTM Services

Any patients using prescription and nonprescription medications, herbal products, and other dietary supplements could potentially benefit from the medication therapy management (MTM) services described in the core elements outlined in this service model, especially if medication-related problems or issues are discovered or suspected. Patients may be evaluated for MTM services regardless of the number of medications they use, their specific disease state(s), or their health plan coverage.

Opportunities for the identification of patients targeted for MTM services may result from many sources including, but not limited to, pharmacist identification, physician referral, patient self-referral, and health plan or other payer referral. Pharmacists may wish to notify physicians or other healthcare professionals in their community or physicians within their facility, if applicable, of their MTM services, so that physicians may refer patients for MTM services.

To provide assistance in prioritizing who may benefit most from MTM services, pharmacists, health plans, physicians, other healthcare professionals, and health systems may consider using one or more of the following factors to target patients who are likely to benefit most from MTM services:

- Patient has experienced a transition of care, and his or her regimen has changed
- Patient is receiving care from more than one prescriber
- Patient is taking five or more chronic medications (including prescription and nonprescription medications, herbal products, and other dietary supplements)
- Patient has at least one chronic disease or chronic health condition (e.g., heart failure, diabetes, hypertension, hyperlipidemia, asthma, osteoporosis, depression, osteoarthritis, chronic obstructive pulmonary disease)
- Patient has laboratory values outside the normal range that could be caused by or may be improved with medication therapy
- Patient has demonstrated nonadherence (including underuse and overuse) to a medication regimen
- Patient has limited health literacy or cultural differences, requiring special communication strategies to optimize care
- Patient wants or needs to reduce out-of-pocket medication costs
- Patient has experienced a loss or significant change in health plan benefit or insurance coverage
- Patient has recently experienced an adverse event (medication or non-medication-related) while receiving care
- Patient is taking high-risk medication(s), including narrow therapeutic index drugs (e.g., warfarin, phenytoin, methotrexate)
- Patient self-identifies and presents with perceived need for MTM services

Appendix C. Sample Personal Medication Record

Patients, professionals, payers, and health information technology system vendors are encouraged to develop a format that meets individual needs, collecting elements such as those in the sample personal medication record (PMR).

(Note: Sample PMR is two pages or one page front and back)

MY MEDICATION RECORD

side 1

Name:____________________ **Birth date:** ____________ LOGO

Include all of your medications on this reord: prescription medications, nonprescription medications, herbal products, and other dietary supplements.
Always carry your medication record with you and show it to all your doctors, pharmacists and other healthcare providers.

Drug		Take for...	When do I take it?				Start Date	Stop Date	Doctor	Special Instructions
Name	Dose		Morning	Noon	Evening	Bedtime				
Glyburide	5mg	Diabetes	1		1		1/15/08		Johnson (000-0000)	Take with food

08-029

This sample Personal Medical Record (PMR) is provided only for general informational purposes and does not constitute professional health care advice or treatment. The patient (or other user) should not, under any circumstances, solely rely on, or act on the basis of, the PMR or the information therein. If he or she does so, then he or she does so at his or her own risk. While intended to serve as a communication aid between patient (or other user) and health care provider, the PMR is not a substitute for obtaining professional healthcare advice or treatment. This PMR may not be appropriate for all patients (or other users). The National Association of Chain Drug Stores Foundation and the American Pharmacists Association assume no responsibility for the accuracy, currentness, or completeness of any information provided or recorded herein.

MY MEDICATION RECORD

side 2

Name: ______________ **Birth date:** __________ **Phone:** __________

Always carry your medication record with you and show it to all your doctors, pharmacists and other healthcare providers.

Emergency Contact Information
Name
Relationship
Phone Number
Primary Care Physician
Name
Phone Number
Pharmacy/Pharmacist
Name
Phone Number

Allergies	
What allergies do I have? (Medicines, food, other)	What happened when I had the allergy or reaction?

Other Medicine Problems	
Name of medicine that caused problem	What was the problem I had with the medicine?

When you are prescribed a new drug, ask your doctor or pharmacist:
• What am I taking?
• What is it for?
• When do I take it?
• Are there any side effects?
• Are there any special instructions?
• What if I miss a dose?

Notes:

Patient's Signature	Healthcare Provider's Signature	Date last updated	
		Date last reviewed by healthcare provider	

APhA and the NACDS Foundation encourage the use of this document in a manner and form that serves the individual needs of practitioners. All reproductions, including modified forms, should include the following statement: "This form is based on forms developed by the American Pharmacists Association and the National Association of Chain Drug Stores Foundation. Reproduced with permission from APhA and NACDS Foundation."

16

Appendix D. Sample Medication-Related Action Plan (for the Patient)

Patients, healthcare professionals, payers, and health information technology system vendors are encouraged to develop a format that meets individual and customer needs, collecting elements such as those included on the sample medication-related action plan (MAP) below.

MY MEDICATION-RELATED ACTION PLAN

Patient:	
Doctor (Phone):	
Pharmacy/Pharmacist (Phone):	
Date Prepared:	

The list below has important Action Steps to help you get the most from your medications. Follow the checklist to help you work with your pharmacist and doctor to manage your medications AND make notes of your actions next to each item on your list.

Action Steps ➡ What I need to do...	Notes ➡ What I did and when I did it...
☐	
☐	
☐	
☐	

My Next Appointment with My Pharmacist is on:______________(date) at ________ ☐ AM ☐ PM

APhA and the NACDS Foundation encourage the use of this document in a manner and form that serves the individual needs of practitioners. All reproductions, including modified forms, should include the following statement: "This form is based on forms developed by the American Pharmacists Association and the National Association of Chain Drug Stores Foundation. Reproduced with permission from APhA and NACDS Foundation."

Appendix E. Flow Chart of a Medication Therapy Management Service Model

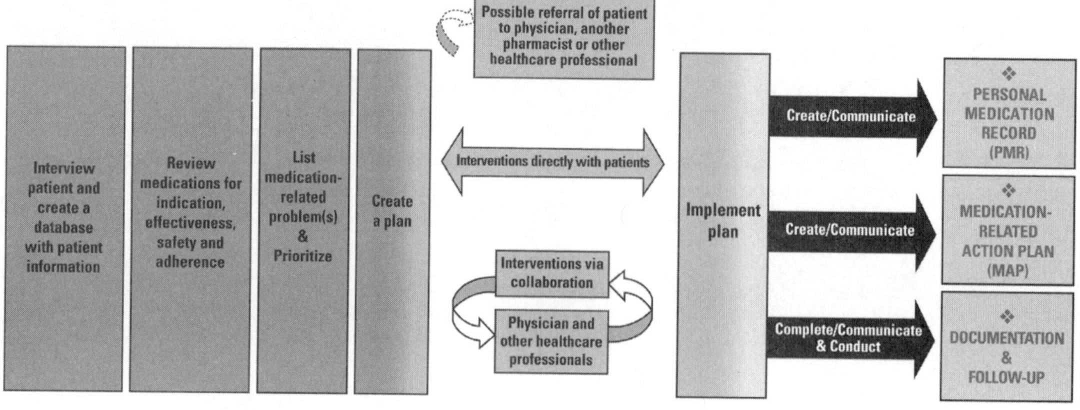

18

Addendum

Medication Therapy Management in Pharmacy Practice: Core Elements of an MTM Service Model Version 2.0 was developed with the input of an advisory panel of pharmacy leaders representing diverse pharmacy practice settings. The pharmacy practice setting areas represented by members of the advisory panel included ambulatory care, community, government technical support services, hospital, long-term care, managed care health systems, managed care organization plan administration, and outpatient clinics.

MTM Core Elements Service Model Version 2.0 Advisory Panel Members

Marialice S. Bennett, RPh, FAPhA
The Ohio State University

Rebecca W. Chater, RPh, MPH, FAPhA
Kerr Drug, Inc.

Kimberly Sasser Croley, PharmD, CGP, FASCP
Knox County Hospital

Rachael Deck, PharmD
Walgreen Co.

Jeffrey C. Delafuente, MS, FCCP, FASCP
Virginia Commonwealth University School of Pharmacy

Susan L. Downard, RPh
Kaiser Permanente of the Mid-Atlantic States, Inc

Margherita Giuliano, RPh
Connecticut Pharmacists Association

Zandra Glenn, PharmD
HRSA Pharmacy Services Support Center

Melinda C. Joyce, PharmD, FAPhA, FACHE
The Medical Center

Sandra Leal, PharmD, CDE
El Rio Community Health Center

Macary Weck Marciniak, PharmD, BCPS
Albany College of Pharmacy

Randy P. McDonough, PharmD, MS, CGP, BCPS
Towncrest and Medical Plaza Pharmacies

Melissa Somma McGivney, PharmD, CDE
University of Pittsburgh School of Pharmacy

Rick Mohall, PharmD
Rite Aid Corporation

Anthony Provenzano, PharmD, CDE
SUPERVALU Pharmacies, Inc.

Michael Sherry, RPh
CVS Caremark

Steven T. Simenson, RPh, FAPhA
Goodrich Pharmacies

Donna S. Wall, RPh, PharmD, BCPS, FASHP
Clarian Healthcare Partners, Indiana University Hospital

Winston Wong, PharmD
CareFirst BCBS

Staff

Ben Bluml, RPh
American Pharmacists Association Foundation

Anne Burns, RPh
American Pharmacists Association

Ronna Hauser, PharmD
National Association of Chain Drug Stores

Crystal Lennartz, PharmD, MBA
National Association of Chain Drug Stores

James Owen, PharmD
American Pharmacists Association

Afton Yurkon, PharmD
National Association of Chain Drug Stores

Medication Therapy Management in Pharmacy Practice: Core Elements of an MTM Service Model Version 2.0 advisory panel members provided expert advice. The content of this document does not necessarily represent all of their opinions or those of their affiliated organizations.

Resource A

Medication Therapy Management in Pharmacy Practice

Core Elements of an MTM Service Model

Version 2.0

07-515

Medication Therapy Management Services: A Critical Review

Executive Summary Report

Prepared For:

American Pharmacists Association

May 17, 2005

Medication Therapy Management Services: A Critical Review

Final Report

Prepared for:

American Pharmacists Association

Prepared by:

Joan DaVanzo, Ph.D., M.S.W.
Allen Dobson, Ph.D.
Lane Koenig, Ph.D.
Robert Book, Ph.D.

May 17, 2005

Resource B

The Lewin Group would like to acknowledge the cooperation of the various providers, plans and administrators who agreed to be interviewed for this report and for the various individuals, committees and organizations who reviewed the report content, particularly the American College of Clinical Pharmacy, the American Society of Health-System Pharmacists, and the National Council of State Pharmacy Association Executives.

MEDICATION THERAPY MANAGEMENT SERVICES: A CRITICAL REVIEW FACT SHEET

It has been demonstrated that Medication Therapy Management Services (MTMS) currently being delivered at both local and regional levels can lead to a reduction in overall health care expenditures by optimizing therapeutic outcomes. The American Pharmacists Association (APhA) commissioned The Lewin Group to identify existing MTMS standards of practice and to develop an illustrative model for payers to consider in evaluating the compensation of pharmacists for MTMS. This report is intended to serve as a resource for individuals charged with designing and implementing a Medicare Medication Therapy Management (MTM) program under the Medicare Modernization Act of 2003 (MMA) as well as for those interested in expanding MTMS in both the public and private sectors.

In the final rule implementing the MMA, the Centers for Medicare and Medicaid Services (CMS) said that MTMS must "evolve and become a cornerstone of the Medicare Prescription Drug Benefit."

The type of payment is a critical feature of the business model for MTMS in that different forms of compensation create varying incentives for providers. As Medicare Advantage-Prescription Drug Plan (MA-PD) and Prescription Drug Plan (PDP) sponsors contemplate developing MTM programs, including fee structures for MTMS under the MMA, they likely will find that a significant body of evidence in the literature exists as well as a number of different payment models currently in use.

Today, the majority of MTMS payment systems are variants of fee-for-service (FFS). Although we observed some variation in the unit of payment for MTMS, the majority of programs paid based on services provided (e.g., for an assessment or a visit). Most programs varied payments by type or intensity of service to reflect differences in the amount of resources required to deliver it.

KEY FINDINGS:

- Interview findings and the literature review suggest that cost reduction and improved health outcomes can occur when MTMS are provided, especially to elderly patients.
- Adjustments will be needed regarding both the scope of services and provider incentives under Medicare if CMS is to achieve the legislation's intended outcome of improving medication use and patient-care quality.
- The MMA might be too limited in its definition of the population required to receive MTMS under Medicare. Future amendments to the MMA might expand the MTMS-eligible population to test the hypothesis that **preventing** high-severity cases could be cost-effective.
- Important, practical differences exist between the dispensing and MTM roles of pharmacists. These differences are intrinsic to the economics of the pharmacy industry. MTMS unlikely will be provided if these differences are not recognized, encouraged, and ultimately rewarded financially.
- Interview respondents noted that patients are generally thought to be highly supportive of MTMS; the fact that MTMS are sometimes self-paid supports this contention. Many

The Lewin Group
378848

patients find that pharmacists are approachable and better prepared to spend time answering such basic questions as "How can I better manage my diabetes and the medications I am taking to control it?"

- Interview respondents reported that many physicians are realizing that MTMS can leverage them, in that pharmacists can field many patient questions in a timely fashion. Physicians also are learning that in the case of patient wellness, MTMS activities could improve patient health outcomes and perhaps lessen the need for additional medications, ensure that appropriate medications are taken correctly, or both. The acceptance of physicians' use of "incident to" payment structures in some states is evidence that physicians are willing to view the pharmacist as a partner in patient care.
- MTMS can reduce the use of physician and hospital services by reducing adverse health events. MTMS might increase or decrease drug costs, but evidence suggests that MTMS can reduce per-member per-month (PMPM) total health costs.
- MA-PD plans can immediately benefit from MTMS if they can internalize resulting savings. Because PDPs presumably will attempt to minimize drug costs, however, it is difficult to see how MTM programs that might increase drug costs would be viewed by PDPs as beneficial or in their interest. Without incentives for PDPs, such as bonus payments for certain MTMS thought to decrease overall PMPM health expenditures, they will have little incentive to pay for MTMS that increase drug costs.
- To ensure beneficiary access to medically necessary, high-quality care while creating incentives for provider efficiency, payment system components should include unit of payment, patient or risk classification, relative value payment, payment adjustments, and a payment update factor.
- Although a full array of MTMS that could improve health and reduce total health care costs is available, the law requires services to be provided only to a select few Medicare beneficiaries. The incentive structure is likely to restrict 22 million beneficiaries from receiving comprehensive MTMS (especially those that might increase drug costs).
- A payment system must provide unit payments adequate to cover at least pharmacist labor costs (approximately $1.00 to $2.00 per minute, according to industry estimates) or, to be sustainable, total costs (approximately $2.00 to $3.00 per minute, according to industry estimates). The pricing system must also provide adequate aggregate payments to sustain and provide for growth in number of providers.
- Current fee schedules often fail to reflect the above-referenced unit payments. This omission likely is because MTMS concepts have been developed in public programs (which often fail to provide for adequate payments), and the private sector is just now beginning to explore MTMS. As new rates are introduced, they likely will be more sustainable, as both private- and public-sector programs utilizing rates that provide insufficient compensation will probably prove unsustainable in the marketplace over the long run.
- In an illustrative payment model developed by The Lewin Group, the PMPM provider fee was calculated to be $1.56 for a hypothetical plan. This hypothetical plan would deliver Medication Therapy Review (MTR) to 10% of enrollees and MTM to the 3% of enrollees identified by the review as needing services.

The Lewin Group
378848

EXECUTIVE SUMMARY

Pharmacists' value to the healthcare delivery team is evidenced throughout the literature by the wide variety of innovative Medication Therapy Management Services (MTMS) currently being delivered at both local and regional levels. It has been demonstrated that MTMS, appropriately employed, can lead to a reduction in overall health care expenditures through optimizing therapeutic outcomes, especially in elderly patients. Better health outcomes result in a reduction of adverse medication events along with their attendant emergency room visits and hospital stays. The current state of pharmacy practice is characterized by diverse MTMS offerings of varying levels of complexity and intensity. The American Pharmacists Association (APhA) commissioned The Lewin Group to develop a report presenting the range of current Medication Therapy Management (MTM) programs and practices and how they are paid. In addition, The Lewin Group was charged with developing a methodology for evaluating payments that could provide a sound economic base for the continued development of MTMS.

The purpose of this report is to identify existing MTMS standards of practice and compensation models and to develop from them a model for payers to use in compensating pharmacists for MTMS. This report is intended to serve as a resource for individuals charged with designing and implementing a Medicare MTM program under the Medicare Modernization Act of 2003 (MMA) as well as for those interested in expanding MTMS in both the public and private sectors.

In recognition of the potential value of MTMS for Medicare beneficiaries, the MMA opened the door for Medicare Advantage-Prescription Drug Plans (MA-PD) and Prescription Drug Plans (PDP) to work with existing prototypes and move MTMS to the next stage of their development. In the final rule implementing the MMA, the Centers for Medicare and Medicaid Services (CMS) said that MTMS must "evolve and become a cornerstone of the Medicare Prescription Drug Benefit." It is hoped that this report can serve as a starting point for identifying the best practices that might evolve into industry standards for both delivering MTMS and paying for them.

Methods

We used a three-part research approach to collect, analyze, and synthesize a wide range of qualitative information. First, we reviewed the published literature on MTMS provided through public- and private-sector programs. Our review included systematic evaluations and peer reviewed journal articles describing the results programs were able to achieve. Concurrent with the literature review, we conducted a series of key opinion leader interviews to discuss additional programs for which few published studies exist, such as those currently being provided by independent, chain and supermarket pharmacies. A broad cross section of stakeholder groups was interviewed. Potential respondents were selected from a list of contacts provided by APhA. A total of thirty-two 45-minute interviews were conducted among representatives of six major groups. In addition, during the month of January after the release of the final rule implementing the new Medicare Part D (prescription drug benefit), we held informal discussions with potential PDP sponsors and health plans as well as with CMS officials regarding the content and intent of the MMA legislation.

Defining MTMS

The way in which PDPs implement MTMS is of paramount importance for Medicare beneficiaries. Neither the legislation nor the final rule provide MA-PDs or PDPs with guidance in designing or reimbursing MTMS except to say that programs will be "patient focused services aimed at improving therapeutic outcomes" that are developed in conjunction with practicing pharmacists and paid out of the plan's administrative fee.

The MMA fails to explicitly define the services comprising MTMS, but it specifies that services are for Medicare beneficiaries with multiple chronic diseases, who are taking multiple medications and who are expected to incur prescription drug expenses of at least $4,000.00 in 2006. Because these beneficiaries are at high risk for adverse medication events, they stand to gain the most when medications are used appropriately.

In 2004, APhA hosted the Pharmacy Stakeholders Conference on Medication Therapy Management Services, which included representatives from eleven different national pharmacy associations. Program criteria as well as a description of medication therapy management services were developed at the consensus-building conference. The new criteria define MTM as "a distinct service or group of services that optimizes therapeutic outcomes for individual patients. MTMS are independent of, but can occur in conjunction with, the provision of a medication product."

Other criteria from the Pharmacy Stakeholders Conference on Medication Therapy Management Services are that services should be individualized and patient specific as well as be provided in face-to-face interaction with the patient as the preferred method of delivery (per the definition). Programs shall include structures supporting the establishment and maintenance of the patient-pharmacist-prescriber relationship. Pharmacists should be able to identify "targeted" beneficiaries who should receive MTMS and participate in processes to improve continuity of care and outcomes. Finally, payment should be consistent with current provider payment in that it is based on time, clinical intensity, and the resources required to provide services.

MTMS Business Model: Essential Components

Our overall understanding of how MTM programs could be developed is embodied in the business model presented in ***Figure ES-1***. The components included represent the essential elements comprising an MTM program. For example, in deciding who will be eligible for MTMS, the MA-PD/PDP might consider all enrollees to be eligible in an attempt to improve health outcomes and reduce per-member per-month (PMPM) costs for the enrollee population as a whole. On the other hand, the MA-PD/PDP might limit eligibility to only enrollees with high health care costs because these enrollees are the most vulnerable and the plan might achieve better return on investment by targeting eligibility in this way. The MA-PD/PDP might limit eligibility to only enrollees for whom the expected cost savings exceed the cost of the MTMS intervention.

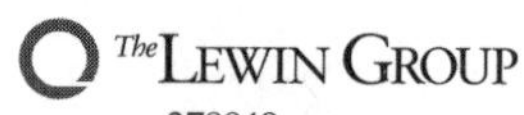

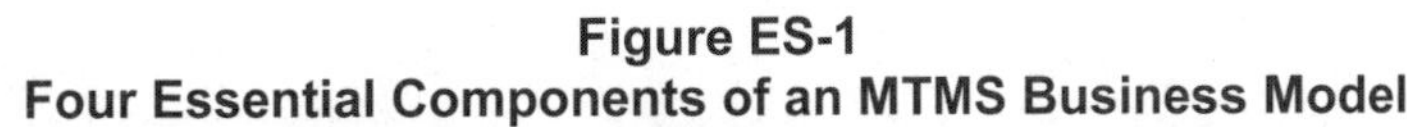

Figure ES-1
Four Essential Components of an MTMS Business Model

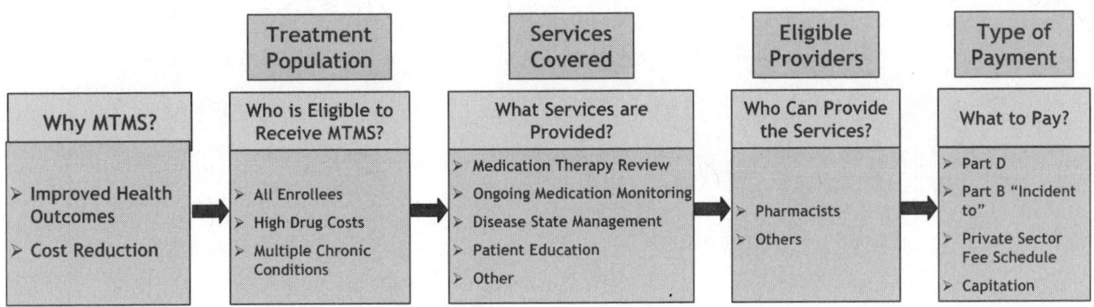

In terms of services covered, the MA-PD/PDP might offer MTMS of different intensities to different groups of enrollees, depending on enrollee need, expected uptake, and projected savings for the group. Pharmacist-provided services can include many different activities, ranging from a review of current medications to patient education on the appropriate use of medications to ongoing disease management.

Pharmacists are the only health care providers specifically mentioned in the MMA as being able to deliver MTMS. However, important differences exist between the dispensing function and the MTM function, and to truly "optimize therapeutic outcomes," there must be pharmacists specifically dedicated to and compensated for providing direct patient care.

The type of payment is a critical feature of the business model for MTMS in that different forms of compensation create varying incentives for providers. As MA-PDs and PDPs contemplate developing MTM programs, including fee structures for MTMS under the MMA, they likely will find that a significant body of evidence in the literature exists as well as a number of different payment models currently in use. The majority of MTMS payment systems today are variants of fee-for-service (FFS). Although we observed some variation in the unit of payment for MTMS, the majority of programs paid based on services provided (e.g., for an assessment or a visit). Most programs varied payments by type or intensity of service to reflect differences in the amount of resources required to deliver it.

Why MTMS?

Both our interview findings and the results of our review of the literature suggest that improved health outcomes and cost reduction can occur when MTMS are provided, especially to elderly patients. Although a rigorous review of the evidence was out of the scope of this study, we did find support for both cost reduction and improved health outcomes in the literature we reviewed as well as in our interviews.

It is well known that pharmaceuticals are a leading driver of health care expenditures and inflation. For instance, between 1998 and 2002, pharmaceutical expenditures rose from $86.73

billion to $179.18 billion, or by 106% over the 5-year period.[1] The literature suggests that for every dollar spent on pharmaceuticals, another dollar of spending results from "drug misadventures."[2, 3] The literature contains several studies in which the positive impact of pharmacists in improving medication adherence by patients and improving prescribing by physicians was examined.[4, 5] A recent review of the literature using the Cochrane Database found that pharmacist intervention can change patient behavior and adherence to medication regimens.[6]

Who is Eligible to Receive MTMS?

The major program distinction in terms of eligible recipients of MTMS is whether the plan offers services to **all** of its enrollees or whether there are specific groups of targeted recipients, such as those having particular diseases or chronic conditions or those taking particular medications or having a minimum threshold level of spending for drugs. Health plans tend to focus on their enrollee population as a whole, while clinical programs tend to focus on individual patients.

The MMA requires Medicare MTMS to be provided to "targeted beneficiaries," limiting the service requirement to patients who "(I) have multiple chronic diseases . . . (II) are taking multiple covered part D drugs; and (III) are identified as likely to incur annual costs that exceed $4,000." These individuals presumably require a different set of MTMS than those requiring wellness services to prevent them from falling into the targeted categories. Thus, of the full array of MTMS that might improve health and reduce total health care costs, only a selected few would be required of PDPs in the proposed Medicare Part D program. The MMA might be too limited in its definition of the population required to receive MTMS under Medicare. Perhaps future amendments to the MMA might expand the MTMS-eligible population to test the hypothesis that preventing high-severity cases could be highly cost-effective.

What Services Are Provided?

A key topic of the interviews was the types of MTMS that are currently being provided. We heard throughout our interviews that services are on a continuum, ranging from a 2-minute conversation with a patient at the counter to an hour-long consultation with a patient concerning his or her drug regimen held in a private area. At one end of the continuum is the drug use review (DUR) that accompanies dispensing a prescription and is mandated by the Omnibus Reconciliation Act of 1990 (OBRA-90). On the other end are intensive disease-specific direct patient care activities, often delivered in an outpatient clinic.

In the final rule implementing the MMA, CMS stated that insufficient standards and performance measures for MTMS exist at this time to support further government specification

---

1 The Lewin Group analysis using data from Centers for Medicare and Medicaid Services: Office of the Actuary.

2 Manasse HR. (1989). Medication use in an imperfect world: Drug misadventuring as an issue of public policy. Part 1. Am J Hosp Pharm, 46: 929–944.

3 Brooks JM, McDonough RP, Doucette W. (June 2000). Pharmacist reimbursement for pharmaceutical care services: Why insurers may flinch. Drug Benefit Trends, 45–62.

4 Lipton HL, Byrns PJ, Soumerai SB et al. (1995). Pharmacists as agents of change for rational drug therapy. Int J Technol Assess Health Care, 11: 485–508.

5 Indritz ME, Artz MB. (1999). Value added to health by pharmacists. Soc Sci Med, 48: 647–660.

6 Beney J, Bero LA, Bond C. (2000). Expanding the roles of outpatient pharmacists: Effects on health services, utilization, costs, and outcomes. In: The Cochrane Library, issue 3. Oxford, UK.

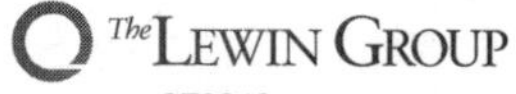

concerning MTMS and service-level requirements. MTM, as currently practiced, takes many forms and represents an evolving clinical discipline. We summarized the most prevalent MTM-related activities being provided by pharmacists into the following four main categories:

- Medication therapy management/polypharmacy
- Disease management
- Lab testing/screening
- Wellness programs/immunizations

Respondents generally indicated a distinction between MTM of high-risk, high-drug use individuals versus disease management, or more broadly managing all individuals in a group who have a specific disease. MTMS can be delivered at multiple levels of complexity, with licensed pharmacists delivering first-line medication management and more highly trained pharmacists, more highly credentialed pharmacists, or both delivering the more complex services (e.g., disease management). Additionally, pharmacists often collaborate with physicians to achieve the best therapeutic outcome for the patient by recommending alternative drugs or formulations or therapeutic substitution. Pharmacists work across a variety of settings including community, hospital, long term care, ambulatory care clinics, and physician practices to provide clinical services directly to patients.

Who Can Provide Services?

Three major questions are inherent in the issue of who can provide MTMS.

- *First, are the dispensing function and the MTM function totally separate, or can they be combined such that the same pharmacist can provide both?*

Important practical differences exist between pharmacists' dispensing and MTM roles. The dispensing function depends on the volume of prescriptions being filled, whereas the MTM function is patient focused, with the metric being improved health outcomes, avoidance of medication related problems for an individual patient, or both. Although in principle, any licensed pharmacist can perform MTMS, in practice, the dispensing and MTM roles are different. For MTMS, the focus is on the patient, while in dispensing, the pharmacist focuses on processing prescription orders. In interviews, we heard examples of pharmacists providing MTMS as part of dispensing as well as within specific patient care services. The level of MTMS provided was influenced by dispensing demands, staffing levels, and other administrative functions.

- *Second, can health care providers other than pharmacists provide MTMS?*

Pharmacists are the only health care providers specifically mentioned in the MMA. Although the proposed MMA rule indicated that pharmacists would be the primary providers of MTMS, in the final rule CMS indicated that MA-PD and PDP plans would have to decide who would provide MTMS within the overall context of their program design. CMS went on to say that face-to-face consultation was but one component of a successful MTM program. The accessibility of pharmacists to patients, and their in-depth training focused on MTM, support pharmacists being the primary provider of MTM services.

- *Third, how well are pharmacists accepted as health care providers by patients, physicians, and health plans?*

Patients

Interview respondents noted that patients are generally thought to be highly supportive of MTMS. The fact that MTMS are sometimes self-paid supports this contention. Many patients find that pharmacists are easy to approach and better prepared to spend the time answering questions related to medication therapy.[7] In addition, the increasing publicity about the dangers of certain medications might increase beneficiary acceptance of additional sources of independent information on appropriate medications and their use.

Physicians

Interview respondents reported that physicians can be skeptical of MTMS at first. In the past, pharmacists represented a possible source of competition. In practice, however, many physicians have come to realize that MTMS can represent a source of leverage for them in that the pharmacist can field many patient questions in a timely fashion. Physicians also are learning that in the case of patient wellness, MTMS activities can improve patient health outcomes and, perhaps, lessen the need for additional medications, and ensure that the appropriate medications are taken correctly.

Physicians' use of "incident to" payment structures and collaborative practice arrangements in some states are evidence that physicians are willing to view the pharmacist as a partner in patient care. This fact is particularly true of clinics or closed settings like Kaiser Permanente. A beneficial relationship of FFS physicians to pharmacists is built and maintained with education and ongoing experience with MTMS.

Health Plans

Fully capitated plans could be the natural beneficiary of MTMS. If MTMS reduce overall PMPM total healthcare expenditures, as is suggested in the literature and by interview respondents, they would be extremely valuable to MA-PD plans. The market experience seems to be that integrated plans (e.g., Kaiser Permanente) find MTMS to be highly advantageous.

Because PDPs will not be at risk for overall health costs, they might find MTMS less financially rewarding. PDPs will be paid risk-adjusted PMPM payments based on expected drug costs. MTMS are designed to ensure that medications are used appropriately and to optimize therapeutic outcomes. Because PDPs presumably will attempt to minimize drug costs, it is difficult to see how MTM programs that might increase drug costs would be viewed by PDPs as being in their interest. Any savings on PMPM total health care costs are external to PDPs under Part D. CMS could provide some explicit direction for PDPs in terms of taking into account the resources and time associated with pharmacists' provision of MTMS when developing payment. For instance, PDPs could be given bonus payments for certain MTMS services that

---

[7] JAPhA (1999); 39:127-135.

have demonstrated a relationship to improved health outcomes, decreased overall PMPM health care expenditures, or both.

The fact that MTMS must be paid out of administrative costs could work against this positive incentive though, even for MA-PDs, if adequate funds are unavailable. In practice, the application for MA-PDs requires plans to specify the number of targeted beneficiaries in their population, the number expected to take up services, and the fees that will be paid for the services. Section V on Worksheet 1 of the bid pricing tool that plans will use in developing their bids contains the PMPM non-pharmacy expenses, such as marketing and sales, crossover fees, uncollected beneficiary premiums, direct and indirect administrative expenses, and MTMS. Additionally, plans are required to report to CMS on their MTM programs, including about the fees that are paid.

What Type of Payment?

Successful payment systems offer incentives to providers to deliver high-quality care. Each existing payment model, however, has its strengths and weaknesses. The findings presented in this section offer the Medicare program and others a starting point for establishing standards for paying for MTMS. By developing a payment system or a set of "guiding principles," CMS can help encourage MA-PDs and PDPs to ensure that Medicare beneficiaries get access to MTMS. Moreover, payment systems used by CMS frequently offer a model for private payers.

Table ES-1 summarizes the payment methods we found in our review of current practices. In most cases, the organization or pharmacy is paid, as in the physician practice model, although we did find instances in which the individually employed pharmacist is paid directly. In cases of self-employed pharmacists, they are usually paid directly for professional services.

Examining Payment for MTMS under MMA

As payers contemplate setting prices for MTMS under MMA, they have a considerable body of evidence from which to draw. The majority of payment systems today are variants of FFS. In some settings, pharmacists are providing clinical services and billing "incident to" the physician.

Table ES-1 provides a range of payment amounts provided by interview respondents. Many of these amounts do not amount to the $2.00 to $3.00 per minute "rule of thumb" suggested by several interview respondents likely because MTMS concepts have been developed in public programs (which often fail to provide for adequate payments).

Crosswalking Payment Rates for MTMS to Existing Physician Fee Schedules

Many payers use Current Procedural Terminology (CPT) evaluation and management (E&M) codes. At this time, the Pharmacist Services Technical Advisory Coalition (PSTAC) has submitted a Coding Change Request to the American Medical Association CPT Committee for MTMS codes for health professional reimbursement.

Table ES-1
Sample Payment Rates as Provided in the Interviews

Payment Rates
1. Private MTMS Program Provider
$30.00 for Comprehensive Medication Review $20.00 for prescriber consultation to resolve a drug therapy problem ($20.00 per problem) $15.00 for patient consultation to resolve a compliance-related drug therapy problem $10.00 for patient E&M (per medication)
2. Independent Pharmacy
$1.00 to $2.00 per minute Initial visits - $75.00 to $120.00 Follow-up visits - $35.00 to $60.00
3. Independent Retail Pharmacy Franchiser
$7.00 - lowest cost avoidance items $30.00 for more complex reviews or $100.00 per person per year offset by savings
4. Supermarket Pharmacy
$40.00 for initial visit or consult $20.00 for reviews $10.00 per administration of immunizations
5. Iowa Medicaid Program
$75.00 for initial assessment $40.00 for new problem or problem follow-up assessment $25.00 for preventive follow-up assessment
6. Mississippi Medicaid
Mississippi Medicaid: initial payment of $20.00 per visit with a twelve-visits-per-year cap
7. Pharmacy Benefit Manager
Working on a payment system - $125.00 for initial visit or $25.00 per month for monitoring Attempted to pay $20.00 per service to pharmacists who called physicians, but pharmacists did not accept this rate
8. Independent Retail Pharmacy Franchiser
Wisconsin Medicaid pays $40.11 "per encounter" for monitoring patient compliance. Some HMOs pay per event (i.e., $10.00 for detect and correct and $20.00 for blood glucose education).
9. Chain Pharmacy
Charges - $2.50 to $3.00 per minute $75.00 for limited assessment $40.00 for follow-up $40.00 for new problem $20.00 for mandatory follow-up visit at 6 months
10. Ambulatory Care Clinic
Bill "incident to" for Level 4 E&M for established patients
11. Otherwise Mentioned
$500.00 per year for four to five 30-minute appointments $140.00 flat fee for three visits at 20 minutes each $250.00 to enroll a patient with CHF in MTMS for 1 year with bonus for improved test scores $7.00 for counseling claim (less than the cost of administration) Many private pay situations do not pay at all. Employers need to see value in MTMS

Using $2.00 to $3.00 per minute suggested by several interview respondents as an estimate of the average cost to pharmacies of providing MTMS, we test the feasibility of this approach.[8] *Table ES-2* presents sample CPT E&M codes for collaborative drug-therapy management services for established patients that reflect time in minutes and intensity of work effort

[8] Although several respondents mentioned this level of payment, none reported having conducted a full cost analysis.

comparable to MTMS.[9] The conversion factor (cf), or the dollar amount that converts relative values into payments for the 2005 Medicare Fee Schedule (MFS), is $37.90. This amount tracks with the 2005 non-facility relative value (rv) amount to produce the following results. In ***Table ES-2***, we take the 2005 MFS cf of $37.90 and multiply it by the MFS 2005 non-facility relative value (rv) for each CPT code. For 99211, $37.90 times 0.57 equals $21.60. We then multiply this amount by 0.8, which is the factor often used to reduce MFS physician payment amounts to an amount appropriate for payment to non-physicians. The resultant amounts on the far right column of ***Table ES-2*** we then call "MFS MTMS Payment" (e.g., $17.28 for code 99211). These payments are within the range of the values contained in ***Table ES-1*** for comparable services.

Table ES-2
Translation of the MFS CPT Codes into MTMS Payment Amounts

CPT Code	2005 cf	2005 rv	Total Payment	Non-physician Share	MFS MTMS Payment
99211	$37.90	.57	$21.60	0.8	$17.28
99212	$37.90	1.02	$38.66	0.8	$30.92
99213	$37.90	1.39	$52.68	0.8	$42.14
99214	$37.90	2.18	$82.62	0.8	$66.09
99215	$37.90	3.17	$120.14	0.8	$96.00

In ***Table ES-3,*** we show how this calculation was accomplished. We used the number of minutes reflected in the CPT code description and multiplied by $2.00 and by $3.00 to obtain a low and high expected payment. ***Table ES-3*** results indicate that in most cases, the MFS payment lies between the $2.00-per-minute expected payment and the $3.00-per-minute expected payment. As problem severity increases, however, the MFS payment is compressed, which is consistent with other prospective payment systems (e.g., Diagnostic Related Grouping [DRG] weights).

Table ES-3
Comparison of CPT Values of $2.00 and $3.00 per Minute to MFS

CPT Code	Minutes	Problem Severity	Low per-Minute Payment	Expected Payment	High per-Minute Payment	Expected Payment	MFS Payment
99211	5	minimal	$2.00	$10.00	$3.00	$15.00	$17.28
99212	10	minor to moderate	$2.00	$20.00	$3.00	$30.00	$30.92
99213	15	minor to moderate	$2.00	$30.00	$3.00	$45.00	$42.14
99214	25	moderate to high	$2.00	$50.00	$3.00	$75.00	$66.09
99215	40	moderate to high	$2.00	$80.00	$3.00	$120.00	$96.00

Although the MMA specified that the time and resources necessary to implement MTM programs must be taken into account when PDP sponsors establish fees, it failed to specify how

9 Kuo GM, Buckley TE, Fitsimmons DS, Steinbauer JR. (2004). Collaborative drug therapy management services and reimbursement in a family medicine clinic. Amer J Health Syst Pharm 61(4), 2004.

these fees should be paid. CMS considers fees for MTM programs separate and distinct from dispensing fees, and fees for MTMS are to be included in a plan's administrative costs. ***Table ES-4*** contains a hypothetical situation in which a plan develops an MTM program for its 1,000 covered lives, showing the calculation of the PMPM expense that would be included in the plan's bid for provider services as a PDP.

Table ES-4
Illustrative PMPM Payment Calculation for a Sample MTMS Package [a/]

	Description	Estimated Cost	Persons Eligible	Total Costs
Pharmacist-Provided Medication Review	One 15-minute visit @ $42.14	$42.14	293 [b/]	**$12,347.02**
Comprehensive Medication Therapy Review and Follow-up	One 40-minute comprehensive medication therapy review @ $96.00 Three 15-minute targeted follow-up visits @ $42.14	$222.42 [c/]	29 [d/]	**$6,450.18**
Total Annual Cost				**$18,797.20**
Number of Enrollees				**1,000**
Cost per Enrollee				**$18.80**
PMPM Provider Fee Cost				**$1.56**

a/ Assumes the plan has 1,000 enrollees and offers two levels of MTMS. Illustrative eligibility requirements are as follows: Pharmacist-provided Medication Review: Enrollees must have at least $4,000.00 in drug costs for a given year; Comprehensive Medication Therapy Review: Presence of several identified medical conditions and the taking of a specific number or type of medications each month.
b/ Assumes 29.3% of the enrollee population (of 1,000) would be eligible for the basic Medication Review benefit per The Lewin Group actuarial estimate.
c/ Assumes one comprehensive medication therapy review (MTR) and three targeted follow-up visits for each eligible enrollee.
d/ Assumes about 10% of persons eligible for Medication Review (or 3% of all enrollees) would qualify for the Comprehensive Medication Therapy Review and targeted follow-up visits.

Source: The Lewin Group illustration.

In the example shown in ***Table ES-4***, the plan has two potential levels of MTM service: a basic benefit which consists of a 15-minute Medication Review by a pharmacist, for which 29.3% of plan members are eligible.[10] The more complex benefit, the Comprehensive Medication Therapy Review (MTR), is restricted to the 3% of members who have several specifically identified medical conditions and who are taking a specified number or type of medications each month. (These individuals have been identified among the recipients of the plan's basic Medication Review benefit and comprise about 10% of Medication Review recipients). The total annual cost for the service offerings is allocated across the entire membership.

The resultant PMPM provider fee amount of $1.56 is considerably higher than the $0.45 PMPM for MTMS provided as an example in Section V on Worksheet 1 of the bid pricing tool on the CMS Website. This variation poses a dilemma for plans in providing clinically meaningful MTMS, even for a small subset of enrollees as shown in the illustrative calculation above.

10 The Lewin Group actuarial estimate found that 30.8% of all Medicare beneficiaries are expected to hit the $4,000.00 threshold in drug spending in 2006. For the 65+ Medicare population, the proportion is 29.3%, adjusting for under-reporting of drug expenditures in the Medicare Expenditures Panel Survey (MEPS), induced use, netted against drug discounts and other cost management tools that Part D plans are expected to use, and predicted adverse selection.

378848

Recommendations

The MMA represents an opportunity for providers of MTMS to demonstrate the value of these services for Medicare beneficiaries. Practicing pharmacists, physicians, and MA-PDs/PDPs will work together to determine the best service offerings for MTMS, such that meaningful therapies can be provided to targeted individuals within the MMA limits. Other payers can use the "lessons learned" from the Medicare MTMS implementation as well as documented experiences others have had in providing MTMS to develop a service package and business model that improve therapeutic outcomes for their enrollees. CMS must provide guidance on how best to fulfill the intent of Congress concerning MTMS. CMS also must realistically evaluate the relative value of mixes of MTMS to determine best value. We offer the following recommendations:

Pharmacists:

- Standardize and package MTM service offerings of varying levels of intensity.
- Determine work values for MTMS CPT codes (eg, benchmark from existing E&M codes).
- Use standards for billing and service delivery as developed by the pharmacy profession.
- Build supply capacity to meet demand for MTMS from plans (e.g., possibly creating training modules or recognition programs). Practical differences exist between the dispensing and MTM roles of pharmacists. MTM unlikely will be provided if these differences are not recognized, encouraged, and ultimately rewarded financially.
- Cultivate widespread patient support of pharmacist-provided MTMS. Patients are generally thought to be highly supportive of MTMS; the fact that MTMS are often self paid supports this contention. Many patients find that pharmacists are more approachable and better prepared to spend time answering such basic questions as "How can I better manage my diabetes and the medications I am taking to control it?"
- Increase physician awareness that pharmacist-provided MTMS can help leverage their time to higher value/priority activities. The acceptance of physicians' use of "incident to" payment structures in some states is evidence that physicians are willing to view the pharmacist as a partner in patient care.
- Conduct systematic evidence-based review of the literature concerning current MTMS practices and outcomes.

Health Plans and PDP Sponsors:

- Determine target number of eligibles; determine likely MTMS take-up rate.
- Work with practicing pharmacists, both internally and externally, to develop MTM service offerings (e.g., balance between basic MTMS for many or all enrollees versus more complex MTMS for targeted ones).
- Price service offerings on PMPM basis for bid submission as "non-pharmacy expense" on Worksheet 1.

- Develop mechanisms to measure the impact of MTMS on overall health costs. MTMS can reduce the use of physician and hospital services by improving health outcomes and reducing adverse health events. MTMS might increase or decrease drug costs; however, PMPM total health costs can be reduced by MTMS.
- Develop payment systems that provide unit payments adequate to cover at least pharmacist labor costs (approximately $1.00 to $2.00 per minute according to industry estimates) or total costs ($2.00 to $3.00 per minute according to industry estimates). The pricing system must also provide adequate aggregate payments to sustain and provide for growth in number of providers.

NPI Fact Sheet

For Healthcare Providers Who Are Individuals

January 2006

Are you drowning in a sea of provider numbers? Do you have to keep track of many different identi ers, provider numbers, and provider identi cation numbers? Do you forget which number to use with which payer? If so, help is on the way!

In authority delegated by the Secretary of Health and Human Services, the Centers for Medicare & Medicaid Services (CMS) is pleased to announce the availability of the standard unique health identi er for health care providers. This new identi er, the National Provider Identi er (NPI), is a single health care provider identi er that will replace the provider identi er(s) you currently use in the standard transactions that you conduct with each health plan with which you do business. The NPI was adopted by the Secretary in accordance with the requirement of the Health Insurance Portability and Accountability Act of 1996 (HIPAA) that the Secretary adopt a standard unique health identi er for health care providers. This identi er must be used by all HIPAA covered entities, which are health plans, health care clearinghouses, and those health care providers who transmit any health data in connection with a transaction for which the Secretary has adopted a standard (known as standard transactions). All HIPAA covered entities must accept and use NPIs in standard transactions by May 23, 2007 (small health plans have until May 23, 2008). After those compliance dates, covered health care providers will use only their NPIs to identify themselves in standard transactions where a health care provider identi er is required.

CMS now has a web page dedicated to the NPI: *http://www.cms.hhs.gov/NationalProvIdentStand/.* This site contains links to a wealth of general NPI information. Check this site often for updates. From this site, you can:

- Read the CMS NPI "Dear Provider" letter from CMS Administrator, Dr. Mark B. McClellan;
- Link to the latest NPI information, including Medlearn Matters articles;
- Learn how to apply for your NPI;
- Use the NPI Viewlet, an instructional web tool for completing the paper NPI application;
- Familiarize yourself with Medicare's timeline for NPI implementation;
- View statistics from the National Plan and Provider Enumeration System (NPPES);
- Discover educational material, including the NPI Final Rule and Frequently Asked Questions;
- Learn more about HIPAA and HIPAA's Administrative Simpli cations; and
- Much more, all in one convenient location.

Get enumerated. You may apply for your NPI using an easy web-based application process by going to the NPPES web site: *https://nppes.cms.hhs.gov/NPPES/Welcome.do.* This site also contains a link to the downloadable paper application (if you prefer to use the paper form to apply) and contact information if you have questions. An employer or other organization with whom you are af liated may obtain an NPI for you, with your permission, through the electronic le interchange (EFI) (bulk enumeration) process.

Important NPI Note: A sole proprietor/sole proprietorship is an Individual and is eligible for a single NPI. The sole proprietor must apply for the NPI using his or her own SSN, not an EIN even if he/she has an EIN. Because a sole proprietor/sole proprietorship is an Individual, he/she cannot be a subpart and cannot designate subparts.

Information Required to Obtain Your NPI

For providers who are Individuals:

Provider Name	Provider Date of Birth
Country of Birth	State of Birth (if Country of Birth is U.S.)
Provider Gender	SSN or other proof of identity
Mailing Address	Practice Location Address and Phone Number
Taxonomy (Provider Type)	State License Information *
Contact Person Name	Contact Person Phone Number and E-mail

* *(required for certain taxonomies only)*

Note: Taxonomy codes describe provider type/classi cation/specialization of Individual and Organization health care providers. A complete list of taxonomy codes is available from the Washington Publishing Company and can be found at *http://www.wpc-edi.com/codes/taxonomy.*

Important Advice Concerning Your National Provider Identifier (NPI):

- **Take control of your NPI.** If you are a billing provider, your NPI will be your billing number. Your NPI does not belong to your employer or to any health plan, even if your employer or a health plan obtained it for you by bulk enumeration. It is the one number that identi es you as a health care provider in standard transactions with other health care providers, health plans, and health care clearinghouses.
- **Use your NPI.** After May 23, 2007, the NPI will be the only health care provider identi er that you or health plans will use to identify you as a health care provider in standard transactions, such as claims and encounter information transactions, coordination of bene ts transactions, claims status inquiries/responses, eligibility inquiries/responses, payment and remittance advices, enrollment/disenrollment in health plans, and referrals. Your NPI will be used by all health plans, including Medicare, Medicaid, and all other private and public payers, to identify you as a health care provider.
- **Protect your NPI.** As an Individual you are eligible for only one NPI regardless of the number of different places you furnish health care or the number of different contracts you may have with health plans and other health care providers. Your NPI is yours for life and will never expire or be recycled and assigned to a different health care provider. Only in rare and unique circumstances, such as fraudulent use of your NPI by another, will you be able to contact the NPI Enumerator in order to obtain a new NPI to replace the one that was initially assigned to you.
- **Take care of your NPI.** You are responsible for updating NPI-related information with NPPES, the National Plan and Provider Enumeration System. If you are a covered health care provider, you must report any changes to any of the information that was furnished to obtain your NPI within 30 days of the change.
- **Share your NPI as needed.** There are certain covered entities and others who will need to know your NPI in order to conduct standard transactions. These may include, but may not be limited to, your employer, hospitals where you have privileges, and health care providers to whom you refer patients. These health care providers cannot be reimbursed unless they know your NPI so that they can use it in the standard claims transactions that they conduct. Also, health plans in which you are enrolled and to whom you submit claims need to know your NPI; they need to associate it with your enrollment information in order to ensure you receive proper payment for services rendered.

This fact sheet was prepared as a service to the public and is not intended to grant rights or impose obligations. This fact sheet may contain references or links to statutes, regulations, or other policy materials. The information provided is only intended to be a general summary. It is not intended to take the place of either the written law or regulations. We encourage readers to review the speci c statutes, regulations and other interpretive materials for a full and accurate statement of their contents.

NPI Fact Sheet

DEPARTMENT OF HEALTH AND HUMAN SERVICES
CENTERS FOR MEDICARE & MEDICAID SERVICES

Form Approved
OMB No. 0938-0931

NATIONAL PROVIDER IDENTIFIER (NPI) APPLICATION/UPDATE FORM

Please PRINT or TYPE all information so it is legible. Use only blue or black ink. Do not use pencil. Failure to provide complete and accurate information may cause your application to be returned and delay processing of your application. In addition, you may experience problems being recognized by insurers if the records in their systems do not match the information you have furnished on this form. Information submitted on this application (except for Social Security Number, IRS Individual Taxpayer Identification Number, and Date of Birth) may be made available on the internet.

SECTION 1 – BASIC INFORMATION

A. Reason For Submittal Of This Form (Check the appropriate box)

1. ❑ Initial Application
2. ❑ Change of Information (See instructions)
   NPI: ______________________
   ❑ Add Information
   ❑ Replace Information
3. ❑ Deactivation (See Instructions)
   NPI: ______________________
   Reason (Check one of the following)
   ❑ Death ❑ Business Dissolved
   ❑ Other, Specify: (See Instructions) ______________________
4. ❑ Reactivation (See Instructions)
   NPI: ______________________
   Reason: ______________________

B. Entity Type (Check only one box)

1. ❑ An individual who renders health care. **(Complete Sections 2A, 3, 4A and 5 only)**
   - Is the individual a sole proprietor? (See Instructions) ❑ Yes ❑ No
2. ❑ An organization that renders health care. **(Complete Sections 2B, 3, 4B and 5 only)**
   - Is the organization a subpart? (See Instructions) ❑ Yes ❑ No
   - If yes, enter the Legal Business Name (LBN) and Taxpayer Identification Number (TIN) of the "parent" organization health care provider:
     Parent Organization LBN: ______________________
     Parent Organization TIN: ______________________

SECTION 2 – IDENTIFYING INFORMATION

A. Individuals

1. Prefix (e.g.,Major, Mrs.)	2. First	3. Middle	4. Last
5. Suffix (e.g., Jr., Sr.)		6. Credential (e.g., M.D., D.O.)	

Other Name Information (If applicable. Use additional sheets of paper if necessary)

7. Prefix (e.g.,Major, Mrs.)	8. First	9. Middle	10. Last
11. Suffix (e.g., Jr., Sr.)		12. Credential (e.g., M.D., D.O.)	

13. Type of other Name
❑ Former Name ❑ Professional Name ❑ Other, specify: ______________________

14. Date of Birth (mm/dd/yyyy)	15. State of Birth (U.S. only)	16. Country of Birth (If other than U.S.)

17. Gender
❑ Male ❑ Female

18. Social Security Number (SSN)	19. IRS Individual Taxpayer Identification Number (ITIN) (See Instructions)

B. Organizations (includes Groups)

1. Name (Legal Business Name)	2. Employer Identification Number (EIN)

3. Other Name (Use additional sheets of paper if necessary)

4. Type of Other Name
❑ Former Legal Business Name ❑ D/B/A Name ❑ Other (Describe) ______________________

Form CMS-10114 (05-07) EF (06-07)

SECTION 3 – BUSINESS ADDRESSES AND OTHER INFORMATION

A. Business Mailing Address Information

1. Business Mailing Address Line 1 (Street Number and Name or P.O. Box)

2. Business Mailing Address Line 2 (Address Information; e.g., Suite Number)

3. Business City	4. Business State	5. ZIP+4 or Foreign Postal Code

6. Business Country Name (if outside U.S.)

7. Business Telephone Number (Include Area Code & Extension)	8. Business Fax Number (Include Area Code)

B. Business Practice Location Information

1. Business Primary Practice Location Address Line 1 (Street Number and Name – P.O. Boxes Not Acceptable)

2. Business Primary Practice Location Address Line 2 (Address Information; e.g., Suite Number)

3. Business City	4. Business State	5. ZIP+4 or Foreign Postal Code

6. Business Country Name (if outside U.S.)

7. Business Telephone Number (Include Area Code & Extension) (Required)	8. Business Fax Number (Include Area Code)

C. Other Provider Identification Numbers *(Use additional sheets of paper if necessary) Do not include SSN or ITIN in this section.*

Issuer	Number	State *(If applicable)*	*Issuer (For Other Number Type Only)*
Medicare UPIN	______	______	
Medicare OSCAR/Certification	______	______	
Medicare PIN	______	______	
Medicare NSC	______	______	
Medicaid	______	______ (State is required if Medicaid number is furnished.)	
Other, Specify:	______	______	______
	______	______	______

D. Provider Taxonomy Code *(Provider Type/Specialty. Enter one or more codes)* and License Number Information

Information on provider taxonomy codes is available at *www.wpc-edi.com/taxonomy*. Please see instructions if you plan to submit more than one taxonomy code for a Type 2 (organization) entity.

1. **Primary** Provider Taxonomy Code or describe your specialty or provider type (e.g., chiropractor, pediatric hospital)

☐☐☐☐☐☐☐☐☐☐

2. License Number (See Instructions)	3. State where issued

4. Provider Taxonomy Code or describe your specialty or provider type (e.g., chiropractor, pediatric hospital)

☐☐☐☐☐☐☐☐☐☐

5. License Number (See Instructions)	6. State where issued

7. Provider Taxonomy Code or describe your specialty or provider type (e.g., chiropractor, pediatric hospital)

☐☐☐☐☐☐☐☐☐☐

8. License Number (See Instructions)	9. State where issued

Form CMS-10114 (05-07) EF (06-07) 2

PENALTIES FOR FALSIFYING INFORMATION ON THE NATIONAL PROVIDER IDENTIFIER (NPI) APPLICATION/UPDATE FORM

18 U.S.C. 1001 authorizes criminal penalties against an individual who in any matter within the jurisdiction of any department or agency of the United States knowingly and willfully falsifies, conceals or covers up by any trick, scheme or device a material fact, or makes any false, fictitious or fraudulent statements or representations, or makes any false writing or document knowing the same to contain any false, fictitious or fraudulent statement or entry. Individual offenders are subject to fines of up to $250,000 and imprisonment for up to 5 years. Offenders that are organizations are subject to fines of up to $500,000. 18 U.S.C. 3571(d) also authorizes fines of up to twice the gross gain derived by the offender if it is greater than the amount specifically authorized by the sentencing statute.

SECTION 4 – CERTIFICATION STATEMENT

I, the undersigned, certify to the following:

- This form is being completed by, or on behalf of, a health care provider as defined at 45 CFR 160.103.
- I have read the contents of the application and the information contained herein is true, correct and complete. If I become aware that any information in this application is not true, correct, or complete, I agree to notify the NPI Enumerator of this fact immediately.
- I authorize the NPI Enumerator to verify the information contained herein. I agree to notify the NPI Enumerator of any changes in this form within 30 days of the effective date of the change.
- I have read and understand the Penalties for Falsifying Information on the NPI Application/Update Form as printed in this application. I am aware that falsifying information will result in fines and/or imprisonment.
- I have read and understand the Privacy Act Statement.

A. Individual Practitioner's Signature

1. Applicant's Signature (First, Middle, Last, Jr., Sr., M.D., D.O., etc.)	2. Date (mm/dd/yyyy)

B. Authorized Official's Information and Signature for the Organization

1. Prefix (e.g.,Major, Mrs.)	2. First	3. Middle	4. Last
5. Suffix (e.g., Jr., Sr.)		6. Credential (e.g., M.D., D.O.)	
7. Title/Position			8. Telephone Number (Area Code & Extension)
9. Authorized Official's Signature (First, Middle, Last, Jr., Sr., M.D., D.O., etc.)			10. Date (mm/dd/yyyy)

SECTION 5 – CONTACT PERSON

A. Contact Person's Information

❑ Check here if you are the same person identified in 2A or 4B.
If you checked the box, complete only items 8 and 9 in this section (Section 5).

1. Prefix (e.g.,Major, Mrs.)	2. First	3. Middle	4. Last
5. Suffix (e.g., Jr., Sr.)		6. Credential (e.g., M.D., D.O.)	
7. Title/Position	8. E-Mail Address		9. Telephone Number

For the most efficient and fast receipt of your NPI, please use the web-based NPI process at the following address: *https://nppes.cms.hhs.gov.* NPI web is a quick and easy way for you to get your NPI.

Or send the completed signed application to:

NPI Enumerator
P.O. Box 6059
Fargo, ND 58108-6059

According to the Paperwork Reduction Act of 1995, no persons are required to respond to a collection of information unless it displays a valid OMB control number. The valid OMB control number for this information collection is 0938-0931. The time required to complete this information collection is estimated to average 20 minutes per response for new applications and 10 minutes for changes, including the time to review instructions, search existing data resources, gather the data needed, and complete and review the information collection. If you have any comments concerning the accuracy of the time estimate or suggestions for improving this form, please write to: CMS, Attn: Reports Clearance Officer, 7500 Security Boulevard, Baltimore, Maryland 21244-1850. **Do not send the applications to this address.**

Form CMS-10114 (05-07) EF (06-07) 3

PRIVACY ACT STATEMENT

Section 1173 of the Social Security Act authorizes the adoption of a standard unique health identifier for all health care providers who conduct electronically any standard transaction adopted under 45 CFR 162. The purpose of collecting this information is to assign a standard unique health identifier, the National Provider Identifier (NPI), to each health care provider for use on standard transactions. The NPI will simplify the administrative processing of certain health information. Further, it will improve the efficiency and effectiveness of standard transactions in the Medicare and Medicaid programs and other Federal health programs and private health programs. The information collected will be entered into a new system of records called the National Provider System (NPS), HHS/HCFA/OIS No. 09-70-0008. Institutional providers' data are protected by section 1106 of the Social Security Act and the Freedom of Information Act, while individually identifiable providers' data are protected by the Privacy Act of 1974.

Failure to provide complete and accurate information may cause the application to be returned and delay processing. In addition, you may experience problems being recognized by insurers if the records in their systems do not match the information you furnished on the form. (See the instructions for completing the NPI application/update form to find the information that is voluntary or mandatory.)

Information may be disclosed under specific circumstances to:

1. The entity that contracts with HHS to perform the enumeration functions, and its agents, and the NPS for the purpose of uniquely identifying and assigning NPIs to providers.
2. Entities implementing or maintaining systems and data files necessary for compliance with standards promulgated to comply with title XI, part C, of the Social Security Act.
3. A congressional office, from the record of an individual, in response to an inquiry from the congressional office made at the request of that individual.
4. Another Federal agency for use in processing research and statistical data directly related to the administration of its programs.
5. The Department of Justice, to a court or other tribunal, or to another party before such tribunal, when
   (a) HHS, or any component thereof, or
   (b) Any HHS employee in his or her official capacity; or
   (c) Any HHS employee in his or her individual capacity, where the Department of Justice (or HHS, where it is authorized to do so) has agreed to represent the employee; or
   (d) The United States or any agency thereof where HHS determines that the litigation is likely to affect HHS or any of its components

   is party to litigation or has an interest in such litigation, and HHS determines that the use of such records by the Department of Justice, the tribunal, or the other party is relevant and necessary to the litigation and would help in the effective representation of the governmental party or interest, provided, however, that in each case HHS determines that such disclosure is compatible with the purpose for which the records were collected.
6. An individual or organization for a research, demonstration, evaluation, or epidemiological project related to the prevention of disease or disability, the restoration or maintenance of health, or for the purposes of determining, evaluating and/or assessing cost, effectiveness, and/or the quality of health care services provided.
7. An Agency contractor for the purpose of collating, analyzing, aggregating or otherwise refining or processing records in this system, or for developing, modifying and/or manipulating automated data processing (ADP) software. Data would also be disclosed to contractors incidental to consultation, programming, operation, user assistance, or maintenance for ADP or telecommunications systems containing or supporting records in the system.
8. An agency of a State Government, or established by State law, for purposes of determining, evaluating and/or assessing cost, effectiveness, and/or quality of health care services provided in the State.
9. Another Federal or State agency
   (a) As necessary to enable such agency to fulfill a requirement of a Federal statute or regulation, or a State statute or regulation that implements a program funded in whole or in part with Federal funds.
   (b) For the purpose of identifying health care providers for debt collection under the provisions of the Debt Collection Information Act of 1996 and the Balanced Budget Act.

Form CMS-10114 (05-07) EF (06-07) 4

INSTRUCTIONS FOR COMPLETING THE NATIONAL PROVIDER IDENTIFIER (NPI) APPLICATION/UPDATE FORM

Please PRINT or TYPE all information so it is legible. Use only blue or black ink. Do not use pencil. Failure to provide complete and accurate information may cause your application to be returned and delay processing of your application. In addition, you may experience problems being recognized by insurers if the records in their systems do not match the information you have furnished on this form. **Please note: Social Security Number (SSN) or IRS Individual Taxpayer Identification Number (ITIN) information should only be listed in block 18 or block 19 of this form. DO NOT report SSN or ITIN information in any other section of this application form.**

This application is to be completed by, or on behalf of, a health care provider or a subpart seeking to obtain an NPI. (See 45 CFR 162.408 and 162.410 (a) (1).

SECTION 1 – BASIC INFORMATION

This section is to identify the reason for submittal of this form and the type of entity seeking to obtain an NPI.

A. Reason for Submittal of this Form

This section identifies the reason the health care provider is submitting this form. *(Required)*

1. **Initial Application**
   If applying for a NPI for the first time check box #1, and complete appropriate sections as indicated in Section 1B for your entity type.
2. **Change of Information**
   If changing information, check box #2, write your NPI in the space provided, and provide the add/replace information within the appropriate section. If you are adding information, please check the 'Add Information' box and fill out the appropriate section(s) with the information you are adding. If you are replacing information, please check the 'Replace Information' box and fill out the appropriate section(s) with the replaced information. See the instructions in Section 4, then sign and date the certification statement in Section 4A or 4B. All changes must be reported to the NPI Enumerator within 30 days of the change. It is not necessary to complete sections that are not being changed; however, please ensure that your NPI is legible and correct. Complete Section 5 so that we may contact you in the event of problems processing this form.
3. **Deactivation**
   If you are deactivating the NPI, check box #3. Record the NPI you want to deactivate, indicate the reason for deactivation, and complete Section 2. Sign and date the certification statement in Section 4A or 4B, as appropriate. See instructions for Section 4. Use additional sheets of paper if necessary.
4. **Reactivation**
   If you are reactivating the NPI, check box #4. Record the NPI you want to reactivate, provide the reason for reactivation, and complete Section 2. Sign and date the certification statement in Section 4A or 4B, as appropriate. See instructions for Section 4. Use additional sheets of paper if necessary.

B. Entity Type

Check only one box (Required for initial applications)

Entity Type 1: Individuals who render health care or furnish health care to patients; e.g., physicians, dentists, nurses, chiropractors, pharmacists, physical therapists. Note that incorporated individuals may obtain NPIs for themselves if they are health care providers and may obtain NPIs for their corporations (EntityType 2 Organizations). A sole proprietor is an Entity Type 1. (A sole proprietorship is a form of business in which one person owns all the assets of the business and is solely liable for all the debts of the business in an individual capacity. Therefore, sole proprietorships are not organization health care providers.) Note that sole proprietors may obtain only one NPI. Sole proprietors must report their SSNs (not EINs even if they have EINs).

Entity Type 2: Organizations that render health care or furnish health care supplies to patients; e.g., hospitals, home health agencies, ambulance companies, group practices, health maintenance organizations, durable medical equipment suppliers, pharmacies. If the organization is a subpart, check yes and furnish the Legal Business Name (LBN) and Taxpayer Identification Number (TIN) of the "parent" organization health care provider. (A subpart is a component of an organization health care provider. A subpart may be a different location or may furnish a different type of health care than the organization health care provider.For ease of reference, we refer to that organization health care provider as the "parent".)

SECTION 2 – IDENTIFYING INFORMATION

A. Individual

NOTE: An individual may obtain only one NPI, regardless of the number of taxonomies (specialties), licenses, or business practice locations he/she may possess. SSN or ITIN information should only be listed in block 18 or block 19 of this form. DO NOT report SSN and ITIN information in any other section of this application form.

A sole proprietor is an individual.

Name Information

1–6. Provide your full legal name. (Required first and last name) Do not use initials or abbreviations. If you furnish your social security number in block 18, this name must match the name on file with the Social Security Administration (SSA). In addition, the date of birth must match that on file with SSA. You may include multiple credentials. Use additional sheets of paper for multiple credentials if necessary.

Other name information *(Use additional sheets of paper if necessary)*

7-12. If you have used another name, including a maiden name, supply that "Other Name" in this area. (Optional) You may include multiple credentials. Use additional sheets of paper for multiple credentials if necessary.

13. Mark the check box to indicate the type of "Other Name" you used. (Required if 7-12 are completed)

14-16. Provide the date *(Required)*, State *(Required)*, and country *(Required, if other than U.S.)* of your birth. Do not use abbreviations other than United States (U.S.).

17. Indicate your gender. *(Required)*

18. Furnish your Social Security Number (SSN) for purposes of unique identification. *(Optional)* If you furnish your SSN, this name must match the name and date of birth on file with the Social Security Administration (SSA). If you do not furnish your SSN, processing of your application may be delayed because of the difficulty of verifying your identity via other means; you may also have difficulty establishing your proper identity with insurers from which you receive payments. If you are not eligible for an SSN, see item #19. **If you do not furnish your SSN, you must furnish 2 proofs of identity with this application form: passport, birth certificate, a photocopy of your driver's license, State issued identification, or information requested in item #19.**

19. If you do not qualify for an SSN, furnish your IRS Individual Taxpayer Identification Number (ITIN) along with a photocopy of your driver's license, State issued ID, birth certificate or passport. **You may not use an ITIN if you have an SSN. Do not enter an Employer Identification Number (EIN) in the ITIN field. Note: Your passport, birth certificate, photocopy of the driver's license or State issued identification must accompany your ITIN. If you do not furnish the information requested in blocks 18 or 19, you must furnish 2 proofs of identity with this application form: passport, birth certificate, a photocopy of your driver's license or State issued identification.** Examples of individuals who need ITINs include:
    - Non-resident alien filing a U.S. tax return and not eligible for an SSN;
    - U.S. resident alien *(based on days present in the United States)* filing a U.S. tax return and not eligible for an SSN;
    - Dependent or spouse of a U.S. citizen/resident alien; and
    - Dependent or spouse of a non-resident alien visa holder.

B. Organizations and Groups

1-2. Provide your organization's or group's name *(legal business name used to file tax returns with the IRS)* and Employer Identification Number *(assigned by the IRS) (Required)*

3. If your organiza tion or group uses or previously used another name, supply that "Other Name" in this area. *(Optional)* Use additional sheets of paper if necessary.

4. Mark the check box to indicate the type of "Other Name" used by your organization. *(D/B/A Name=Doing Business As Name.) (Required if 3 is completed.)*

SECTION 3 – ADDRESSES AND OTHER INFORMATION

A. Business Mailing Address Information*(Required)*

This information will assist us in contacting you with any questions we may have regarding your application for an NPI or with other information regarding NPI. You must provide an address and telephone number where we can contact you directly to resolve any issues that may arise during our review of your application.

B. Business Practice Location Information*(Required)*

Provide information on the address of your primary practice location. If you have more than one practice location, select one as the "primary" location. Do not furnish information about additional locations on additional sheets of paper.

C. Other Provider Identification Numbers*(Optional)*

To assist health plans in matching your NPI to your existing health plan assigned identification number(s), you may wish to list the provider identification number(s) you currently use that were assigned to you by health plans. If you do not have such numbers, you are not required to obtain them in order to be assigned an NPI. Organizations should only furnish other provider identification numbers that belong to the organization; do not list identification numbers that belong to health care providers who are individuals who work for the Organizations. NOTE: Information provided may be disclosed under specific circumstances (See PrivacyStatement on Page 4). DO NOT report SSN or ITIN information in this section of the application form.

D. Provider Taxonomy Code*(Provider Type/Specialty) (Required)*

Provide your 10-digit taxonomy code. You must select a primary taxonomy code in order to facilitate aggregate reporting of providers byclassification/specialization. If you need additional taxonomy codes to describe your type/classification/specialization, you may select additional codes. Information on taxonomy codes is available at www.wpc-edi.com/taxonomy.

Furnish the provider's health care license, registration, or certificate number(s) (if applicable). If issued by a State, show the State that issued the license/certificate. The following individual practitioners are required to submit a license number *(If you are one of the following and do not have a license or certificate, you must enclose a letter to the Enumerator explaining why not)*:

- Certified Registered Nurse Anesthetist
- Chiropractor
- Clinical Nurse Specialist
- Clinical Psychologist
- Dentist
- Licensed Nurse
- Nurse Practitioner
- Optometrist
- Pharmacist
- Physician/Osteopath
- Podiatrist
- Registered Nurse

You may use the same license, registration, or certification number for multiple taxonomies; e.g., if you are a physician with several different specialties.

NOTE: A health care provider that is an organization, such as a hospital, may obtain an NPI for itself and for any subparts that it determines need to be assigned NPIs. In some cases, the subparts have Provider Taxonomy Codes that may be different from that of the hospital and of each other, and each subpart may require separate licensing by the State (e.g., General Acute Care Hospital and Psychiatric Unit). If the organization provider chooses to include these multiple Provider Taxonomy Codes in a request for a single NPI, and later determines that the subparts should have been assigned their own NPIs with their associated Provider Taxonomy Codes, the organization provider must delete from its NPPES record any Provider Taxonomy Codes that belong to the subparts who will be obtaining their own NPIs. The organization provider must do this by initiating the Change of Information option on this form.

SECTION 4 – CERTIFICATION STATEMENT *(Required)*

This section is intended for the applicant to attest that he/she is aware of the requirements that must be met and maintained in order to obtain and retain an NPI. This section also requires the signature and date of signature of the "Individual" who is the type 1 provider, or the "Authorized Official" of the type 2 organization who can legally bind the provider to the laws and regulations relating to the NPI. See below to determine who within the provider qualifies as an Authorized Official. Review these requirements carefully.

Authorized Official's Information and Signature for the Organization

By his/her signature, the authorized official binds the provider/supplier to all of the requirements listed in the Certification Statement and acknowledges that the provider may be denied a National Provider Identifier if any requirements are not met. This section is intended for organizations; not health care providers who are individuals. All signatures must be original. Stamps, faxed or photocopied signatures are unacceptable. You may include multiple credentials. Use additional sheets of paper for multiple credentials if necessary.

An authorized official is an appointed official with the legal authority to make changes and/or updates to the provider's status (e.g., change of address, etc.) and to commit the provider to fully abide by the laws and regulations relating to the National Provider Identifier. The authorized official must be a general partner, chairman of the board, chief financial officer, chief executive officer, direct owner of 5 percent or more of the provider being enumerated, or must hold a position of similar status and authority within the provider.

Only the authorized official(s) has the authority to sign the application on behalf of the provider.

By signing this application for the National Provider Identifier, the authorized official agrees to immediately notify the NPI Enumerator if any information in the application is not true, correct, or complete. In addition, the authorized official, by his/her signature, agrees to notify the NPI Enumerator of any changes to the information contained in this form within 30 days of the effective date of the change.

SECTION 5 – CONTACT PERSON *(If the contact person is the same person identified in 2A or 4B, complete items 8 & 9 in this section.) (Required)*

To assist in the timely processing of the NPI application, provide the name and telephone number of an individual who can be reached to answer questions regarding the information furnished in this application. The contact person can be the health care provider. The contact person will recieve the NPI notification once the health care provider has been assigned an NPI. Please note that if a contact person is not provided, all questions about this application will be directed to the health care provider named in Section 2 or the authorized official named in Section 4, as appropriate. You may include multiple credentials. Use additional sheets of paper for multiple credentials if necessary.

Form CMS-10114 (05-07) EF (06-07) 6

ASHP Guidelines on Documenting Pharmaceutical Care in Patient Medical Records

Purpose

The professional actions of pharmacists that are intended to ensure safe and effective use of drugs and that may affect patient outcomes should be documented in the patient medical record (PMR). These guidelines describe the kinds of information pharmacists should document in the PMR, how that information should be documented, methods for obtaining authorization for pharmacist documentation, and the important role of training and continuous quality improvement (CQI) in documentation.

Background

Pharmaceutical care is the direct, responsible provision of medication-related care for the purpose of achieving definite outcomes that improve a patient's quality of life.[1] A core principle of pharmaceutical care is that the pharmacist accepts professional responsibility for patient outcomes.[2] Integrating pharmaceutical care into a patient's overall health care plan requires effective and efficient communication among health care professionals. As an integral member of the health care team, the pharmacist must document the care provided. Such documentation is vital to a patient's continuity of care and demonstrates both the accountability of the pharmacist and the value of the pharmacist's services. Moreover, because clinical services (e.g., those incident to a physician's services) are generally considered reimbursable only when they are necessary for the medical management of a patient and when the service provided and the patient's response are carefully documented, thorough documentation may increase the likelihood of reimbursement. Early implementation of such documentation practices may help health-system pharmacies cope with documentation requirements in the event pharmacists' clinical services become reimbursable.

The PMR's primary purpose is to convey information for use in patient care; it serves as a tool for communication among health care professionals. Information in the PMR may also be used in legal proceedings (e.g., as evidence), education (e.g., for training students), research (e.g., for evaluating clinical drug use), and quality assurance evaluations (e.g., to ascertain adherence to practice standards).[3]

Clinical recommendations made by a pharmacist on behalf of the patient, as well as actions taken in accordance with these recommendations, should be documented in a permanent manner that makes the information available to all the health care professionals caring for the patient. ASHP believes that, to ensure proper coordination of patients' medication therapies, health care systems must be designed to enable, foster, and facilitate communication and collaboration among health care providers.[2] Health care systems must not erect barriers to that communication or to the exercise of the professional judgment of health care providers.

Although telephone calls and other oral communication may be necessary for immediate interventions, they do not allow for the dissemination of information to care providers who are not a part of the conversation. Such interventions should be documented in the PMR as soon as possible after the acute situation has settled. For less urgent and routine recommendations, timely documentation is also preferred, because delays in response to telephone calls or pager messages may lead to miscommunicated or undocumented recommendations. Unofficial, temporary, or removable notes placed in the PMR do not provide a standard of acceptable communication or documentation and therefore are discouraged. Documentation that is not a part of the PMR (e.g., documentation in pharmacy records) may provide a degree of risk reduction; however, such documentation does not provide important information to other care providers and can interrupt continuity of care when the patient is discharged or transferred.

Documenting Pharmaceutical Care

Pharmacists should be authorized and encouraged to make notations in the PMR for the purpose of documenting their findings, assessments, conclusions, and recommendations.[2] ASHP believes that all significant clinical recommendations and resulting actions should be documented in the appropriate section of the PMR. The pharmacy department should establish policies and procedures for documenting information in the PMR. Such policies and procedures will help pharmacists exercise good judgment in determining what information to document in the PMR and how to present it.

Examples of information a pharmacist may need to document in the PMR include, but are not limited to, the following:

1. A summary of the patient's medication history on admission, including medication allergies and their manifestations.
2. Oral and written consultations provided to other health care professionals regarding the patient's drug therapy selection and management.
3. Physicians' oral orders received directly by the pharmacist.
4. Clarification of drug orders.
5. Adjustments made to drug dosage, dosage frequency, dosage form, or route of administration.
6. Drugs, including investigational drugs, administered.
7. Actual and potential drug-related problems that warrant surveillance.
8. Drug therapy-monitoring findings, including
   - a. The therapeutic appropriateness of the patient's drug regimen, including the route and method of administration.
   - b. Therapeutic duplication in the patient's drug regimen.
   - c. The degree of patient compliance with the prescribed drug regimen.
   - d. Actual and potential drug–drug, drug–food, drug–laboratory test, and drug–disease interactions.
   - e. Clinical and pharmacokinetic laboratory data pertinent to the drug regimen.
   - f. Actual and potential drug toxicity and adverse effects.
   - g. Physical signs and clinical symptoms relevant to the patient's drug therapy.

9. Drug-related patient education and counseling provided.

Documentation by pharmacists should meet established criteria for legibility, clarity, lack of judgmental language, completeness, need for inclusion in the PMR (versus an alternative form of communication), appropriate use of a standard format (e.g., SOAP [subjective, objective, assessment, and plan] or TITRS [title, introduction, text, recommendation, and signature]), and how to contact the pharmacist (e.g., a telephone or pager number).[4]

The authority to document pharmaceutical care in the PMR comes with a responsibility to ensure that patient privacy and confidentiality are safeguarded and the communication is concise and accurate. Local, state, and federal guidelines and laws (including the Health Insurance Portability and Accountability Act of 1996 [HIPAA]) and risk management sensitivities should be considered. Nonjudgmental language should be used, with care taken to avoid words that imply blame (e.g., *error, mistake, misadventure,* and *inadvertent*) or substandard care (e.g., *bad, defective, inadequate, inappropriate, incorrect, insufficient, poor, problem,* and *unsatisfactory*).[3] Facts should be documented accurately, concisely, and objectively; such documentation should reflect the goals established by the medical team.

Documentation of a formal consultation solicited by a physician or other health care provider may include direct recommendations or suggestions as appropriate. However, unsolicited informal consultations, clinical impressions, findings, suggestions, and recommendations should generally be documented more subtly, with indirect recommendations presented in a way that allows the provider to decline the suggestion without incurring a liability. For example, the phrase "may want to consider" creates an opportunity for the suggestion to be acted upon or not, depending on presenting clinical factors.

Obtaining Authorization to Document Pharmaceutical Care

The authority to document pharmaceutical care in the PMR is granted by the health care organization in accordance with organizational and medical staff policies. Although documenting pharmaceutical care in the PMR is a pharmacist's professional responsibility, physicians and other health care professionals may not be accustomed to or open to this practice.

The following steps are recommended for obtaining authorization to document pharmaceutical care in the PMR:

1. Determine the existing organizational and medical staff policies regarding authority for documentation in the PMR. These policies may provide specific guidance on how to proceed.
2. Ascertain whether other nonphysician and nonnurse providers in the organization or affiliated organizations have been granted authority to document patient care activities in the PMR. If so, consult them regarding the process used to establish the authority.
3. Identify physicians in the organization who are willing to support documentation of pharmaceutical care in the PMR.
4. Identify the committees in the organization whose recommendations or decisions will be required to establish authority for pharmacists to document pharmaceutical care in the PMR. Determine the necessary sequence of these approvals. Committees typically involved include the pharmacy and therapeutics (P&T) committee, the executive committee of the medical staff, a quality-assurance committee (e.g., the CQI committee), and the medical records committee.
5. Determine the accepted method and format for submitting a proposal requesting authority to document pharmaceutical care in the PMR. In some organizations, a written proposal may be required. If so, determine the desired format (length, style, and necessary justification) and deadlines for proposal submission. An oral presentation to the deciding bodies may be required. If so, determine in advance the desired presentation format and supporting materials desired by these bodies.
6. Draft a written plan describing
   a. Examples of information to be documented in the PMR. It may be helpful to describe how this important information may be lost or miscommunicated if it is not documented in the PMR.
   b. The locations within the PMR where documentation will be made and any special format or forms proposed. New forms will have to comply with HIPAA regulations and will require review and approval by specific organizational or medical staff committees. To achieve the goal of effective communication among all the members of the health care team, compartmentalization of the PMR should be avoided.
   c. The persons who will be documenting pharmaceutical care in the PMR (i.e., pharmacists, residents, or students). If pharmacy residents or students will be making notations in the PMR, procedures regarding authority and cosignatures will also have to be described.
7. Review the draft plan with the chair of the P&T committee, the director of nursing, the director of medical records, and other appropriate administrative personnel, such as the organization's risk management officer and legal counsel.
8. Seek the endorsement and recommendation of the P&T committee.
9. In appropriate sequence, seek the endorsement or decision of any other committees necessary for ultimate approval. Monitor the proposal's course through the various committees and provide assistance, clarification, or additional data as necessary.
10. When the final approving body grants PMR documentation authority, participate in the required policy development and the communication of the new policy to the individuals or departments in the organization that will be affected by the change (e.g., nurses, the medical staff, the quality-assurance staff, and the medical records department).

Training and CQI

Pharmacist documentation in the PMR is a skill that requires ongoing training and evaluation.[4] A temporary committee may be formed to manage the initial training required to implement pharmacist documentation in the PMR. That committee may consider offering presentations by physicians or other members of the health care team to provide their perspective on how to effectively communicate using the PMR. The information in those presentations may be reinforced by workshops on documentation skills. Presentation and workshop topics may include the choice of communication method (i.e., when documentation in the PMR is preferred to other means of communication), the documentation format (e.g., SOAP or TITRS), documentation etiquette, and legal requirements.[4] Documentation skills should be demonstrated before a pharmacist is allowed to make notations in the PMR.[4] The ASHP Clinical Skills Program is another tool for training pharmacists to use the PMR.[3]

Documentation of pharmaceutical care should also be one of the many functions addressed in CQI efforts. Pharmacy department CQI efforts should include the development of quality indicators that can be used to evaluate pharmacist documentation in the PMR.[4] Other CQI efforts might analyze and improve systemwide policies and procedures for documenting medication use.[5] Periodic review of organizational policies and procedures will allow for their revision in response to changes in health care and advances in technology, including the availability of an electronic PMR.[6,7]

References

1. Hepler CD, Strand LM. Opportunities and responsibilities in pharmaceutical care. *Am J Hosp Pharm.* 1990; 47:533–43.
2. American Society of Hospital Pharmacists. ASHP statement on pharmaceutical care. *Am J Hosp Pharm.* 1993; 50:1720–3.
3. Shepherd MF. Professional conduct and use of patient medical records. In: ASHP Clinical Skills Program, module 1: reviewing patient medical charts. Bethesda, MD: American Society of Hospital Pharmacists; 1992:38–41.
4. Lacy CF, Saya FG, Shane RR. Quality of pharmacists' documentations in patients' medical records. *Am J Health-Syst Pharm.* 1996; 53:2171–5.
5. Matuschka P. Improving documentation of preoperative antimicrobial prophylaxis. *Am J Health-Syst Pharm.* 1998; 55:993–4.
6. Lau A, Balen RM, Lam R, et al. Using a personal digital assistant to document clinical pharmacy services in an intensive care unit. *Am J Health-Syst Pharm.* 2001; 58:1229–32.
7. Gordon W, Malyuk D, Taki J. Use of health-record abstracting to document pharmaceutical care activities. *Can J Hosp Pharm.* 2000; 53:199–205.

Approved by the ASHP Board of Directors, February 20, 2003. Revised by the ASHP Council on Professional Affairs. Supercedes the ASHP Guidelines for Obtaining Authorization for Documenting Pharmaceutical Care in Patient Medical Records dated November 16, 1988.

The bibliographic citation for this document is as follows: American Society of Health-System Pharmacists. ASHP guidelines on documenting pharmaceutical care in patient medical records. *Am J Health-Syst Pharm.* 2003; 60:705–7.

1500

HEALTH INSURANCE CLAIM FORM

APPROVED BY NATIONAL UNIFORM CLAIM COMMITTEE 08/05

PICA | PICA

CARRIER

PATIENT AND INSURED INFORMATION

1. MEDICARE (Medicare #) | MEDICAID (Medicaid #) | TRICARE CHAMPUS (Sponsor's SSN) | CHAMPVA (Member ID#) | GROUP HEALTH PLAN (SSN or ID) | FECA BLK LUNG (SSN) | OTHER (ID)

1a. INSURED'S I.D. NUMBER (For Program in Item 1)

2. PATIENT'S NAME (Last Name, First Name, Middle Initial)

3. PATIENT'S BIRTH DATE MM DD YY SEX M F

4. INSURED'S NAME (Last Name, First Name, Middle Initial)

5. PATIENT'S ADDRESS (No., Street)

6. PATIENT RELATIONSHIP TO INSURED Self Spouse Child Other

7. INSURED'S ADDRESS (No., Street)

CITY STATE

8. PATIENT STATUS Single Married Other

CITY STATE

ZIP CODE TELEPHONE (Include Area Code) ( )

Employed Full-Time Student Part-Time Student

ZIP CODE TELEPHONE (Include Area Code) ( )

9. OTHER INSURED'S NAME (Last Name, First Name, Middle Initial)

10. IS PATIENT'S CONDITION RELATED TO:

11. INSURED'S POLICY GROUP OR FECA NUMBER

a. OTHER INSURED'S POLICY OR GROUP NUMBER

a. EMPLOYMENT? (Current or Previous) YES NO

a. INSURED'S DATE OF BIRTH MM DD YY SEX M F

b. OTHER INSURED'S DATE OF BIRTH MM DD YY SEX M F

b. AUTO ACCIDENT? YES NO PLACE (State)

b. EMPLOYER'S NAME OR SCHOOL NAME

c. EMPLOYER'S NAME OR SCHOOL NAME

c. OTHER ACCIDENT? YES NO

c. INSURANCE PLAN NAME OR PROGRAM NAME

d. INSURANCE PLAN NAME OR PROGRAM NAME

10d. RESERVED FOR LOCAL USE

d. IS THERE ANOTHER HEALTH BENEFIT PLAN? YES NO *If yes,* return to and complete item 9 a-d.

READ BACK OF FORM BEFORE COMPLETING & SIGNING THIS FORM.

12. PATIENT'S OR AUTHORIZED PERSON'S SIGNATURE I authorize the release of any medical or other information necessary to process this claim. I also request payment of government benefits either to myself or to the party who accepts assignment below.

SIGNED ______ DATE ______

13. INSURED'S OR AUTHORIZED PERSON'S SIGNATURE I authorize payment of medical benefits to the undersigned physician or supplier for services described below.

SIGNED ______

PHYSICIAN OR SUPPLIER INFORMATION

14. DATE OF CURRENT: MM DD YY ILLNESS (First symptom) OR INJURY (Accident) OR PREGNANCY(LMP)

15. IF PATIENT HAS HAD SAME OR SIMILAR ILLNESS. GIVE FIRST DATE MM DD YY

16. DATES PATIENT UNABLE TO WORK IN CURRENT OCCUPATION FROM MM DD YY TO MM DD YY

17. NAME OF REFERRING PROVIDER OR OTHER SOURCE

17a.

17b. NPI

18. HOSPITALIZATION DATES RELATED TO CURRENT SERVICES FROM MM DD YY TO MM DD YY

19. RESERVED FOR LOCAL USE

20. OUTSIDE LAB? YES NO $ CHARGES

21. DIAGNOSIS OR NATURE OF ILLNESS OR INJURY (Relate Items 1, 2, 3 or 4 to Item 24E by Line)

1. ___ . ___

2. ___ . ___

3. ___ . ___

4. ___ . ___

22. MEDICAID RESUBMISSION CODE ORIGINAL REF. NO.

23. PRIOR AUTHORIZATION NUMBER

24. A. DATE(S) OF SERVICE From MM DD YY	To MM DD YY	B. PLACE OF SERVICE	C. EMG	D. PROCEDURES, SERVICES, OR SUPPLIES (Explain Unusual Circumstances) CPT/HCPCS	MODIFIER	E. DIAGNOSIS POINTER	F. $ CHARGES	G. DAYS OR UNITS	H. EPSDT Family Plan	I. ID. QUAL.	J. RENDERING PROVIDER ID. #
1										NPI	
2										NPI	
3										NPI	
4										NPI	
5										NPI	
6										NPI	

25. FEDERAL TAX I.D. NUMBER SSN EIN

26. PATIENT'S ACCOUNT NO.

27. ACCEPT ASSIGNMENT? (For govt. claims, see back) YES NO

28. TOTAL CHARGE $

29. AMOUNT PAID $

30. BALANCE DUE $

31. SIGNATURE OF PHYSICIAN OR SUPPLIER INCLUDING DEGREES OR CREDENTIALS (I certify that the statements on the reverse apply to this bill and are made a part thereof.)

SIGNED DATE

32. SERVICE FACILITY LOCATION INFORMATION

a. NPI b.

33. BILLING PROVIDER INFO & PH # ( )

a. NPI b.

NUCC Instruction Manual available at: www.nucc.org

APPROVED OMB-0938-0999 FORM CMS-1500 (08/05)

BECAUSE THIS FORM IS USED BY VARIOUS GOVERNMENT AND PRIVATE HEALTH PROGRAMS, SEE SEPARATE INSTRUCTIONS ISSUED BY APPLICABLE PROGRAMS.

NOTICE: Any person who knowingly files a statement of claim containing any misrepresentation or any false, incomplete or misleading information may be guilty of a criminal act punishable under law and may be subject to civil penalties.

REFERS TO GOVERNMENT PROGRAMS ONLY

MEDICARE AND CHAMPUS PAYMENTS: A patient's signature requests that payment be made and authorizes release of any information necessary to process the claim and certifies that the information provided in Blocks 1 through 12 is true, accurate and complete. In the case of a Medicare claim, the patient's signature authorizes any entity to release to Medicare medical and nonmedical information, including employment status, and whether the person has employer group health insurance, liability, no-fault, worker's compensation or other insurance which is responsible to pay for the services for which the Medicare claim is made. See 42 CFR 411.24(a). If item 9 is completed, the patient's signature authorizes release of the information to the health plan or agency shown. In Medicare assigned or CHAMPUS participation cases, the physician agrees to accept the charge determination of the Medicare carrier or CHAMPUS fiscal intermediary as the full charge, and the patient is responsible only for the deductible, coinsurance and noncovered services. Coinsurance and the deductible are based upon the charge determination of the Medicare carrier or CHAMPUS fiscal intermediary if this is less than the charge submitted. CHAMPUS is not a health insurance program but makes payment for health benefits provided through certain affiliations with the Uniformed Services. Information on the patient's sponsor should be provided in those items captioned in "Insured"; i.e., items 1a, 4, 6, 7, 9, and 11.

BLACK LUNG AND FECA CLAIMS

The provider agrees to accept the amount paid by the Government as payment in full. See Black Lung and FECA instructions regarding required procedure and diagnosis coding systems.

SIGNATURE OF PHYSICIAN OR SUPPLIER (MEDICARE, CHAMPUS, FECA AND BLACK LUNG)

I certify that the services shown on this form were medically indicated and necessary for the health of the patient and were personally furnished by me or were furnished incident to my professional service by my employee under my immediate personal supervision, except as otherwise expressly permitted by Medicare or CHAMPUS regulations.

For services to be considered as "incident" to a physician's professional service, 1) they must be rendered under the physician's immediate personal supervision by his/her employee, 2) they must be an integral, although incidental part of a covered physician's service, 3) they must be of kinds commonly furnished in physician's offices, and 4) the services of nonphysicians must be included on the physician's bills.

For CHAMPUS claims, I further certify that I (or any employee) who rendered services am not an active duty member of the Uniformed Services or a civilian employee of the United States Government or a contract employee of the United States Government, either civilian or military (refer to 5 USC 5536). For Black-Lung claims, I further certify that the services performed were for a Black Lung-related disorder.

No Part B Medicare benefits may be paid unless this form is received as required by existing law and regulations (42 CFR 424.32).

NOTICE: Any one who misrepresents or falsifies essential information to receive payment from Federal funds requested by this form may upon conviction be subject to fine and imprisonment under applicable Federal laws.

NOTICE TO PATIENT ABOUT THE COLLECTION AND USE OF MEDICARE, CHAMPUS, FECA, AND BLACK LUNG INFORMATION
(PRIVACY ACT STATEMENT)

We are authorized by CMS, CHAMPUS and OWCP to ask you for information needed in the administration of the Medicare, CHAMPUS, FECA, and Black Lung programs. Authority to collect information is in section 205(a), 1862, 1872 and 1874 of the Social Security Act as amended, 42 CFR 411.24(a) and 424.5(a) (6), and 44 USC 3101;41 CFR 101 et seq and 10 USC 1079 and 1086; 5 USC 8101 et seq; and 30 USC 901 et seq; 38 USC 613; E.O. 9397.

The information we obtain to complete claims under these programs is used to identify you and to determine your eligibility. It is also used to decide if the services and supplies you received are covered by these programs and to insure that proper payment is made.

The information may also be given to other providers of services, carriers, intermediaries, medical review boards, health plans, and other organizations or Federal agencies, for the effective administration of Federal provisions that require other third parties payers to pay primary to Federal program, and as otherwise necessary to administer these programs. For example, it may be necessary to disclose information about the benefits you have used to a hospital or doctor. Additional disclosures are made through routine uses for information contained in systems of records.

FOR MEDICARE CLAIMS: See the notice modifying system No. 09-70-0501, titled, 'Carrier Medicare Claims Record,' published in the Federal Register, Vol. 55 No. 177, page 37549, Wed. Sept. 12, 1990, or as updated and republished.

FOR OWCP CLAIMS: Department of Labor, Privacy Act of 1974, "Republication of Notice of Systems of Records," Federal Register Vol. 55 No. 40, Wed Feb. 28, 1990, See ESA-5, ESA-6, ESA-12, ESA-13, ESA-30, or as updated and republished.

FOR CHAMPUS CLAIMS: PRINCIPLE PURPOSE(S): To evaluate eligibility for medical care provided by civilian sources and to issue payment upon establishment of eligibility and determination that the services/supplies received are authorized by law.

ROUTINE USE(S): Information from claims and related documents may be given to the Dept. of Veterans Affairs, the Dept. of Health and Human Services and/or the Dept. of Transportation consistent with their statutory administrative responsibilities under CHAMPUS/CHAMPVA; to the Dept. of Justice for representation of the Secretary of Defense in civil actions; to the Internal Revenue Service, private collection agencies, and consumer reporting agencies in connection with recoupment claims; and to Congressional Offices in response to inquiries made at the request of the person to whom a record pertains. Appropriate disclosures may be made to other federal, state, local, foreign government agencies, private business entities, and individual providers of care, on matters relating to entitlement, claims adjudication, fraud, program abuse, utilization review, quality assurance, peer review, program integrity, third-party liability, coordination of benefits, and civil and criminal litigation related to the operation of CHAMPUS.

DISCLOSURES: Voluntary; however, failure to provide information will result in delay in payment or may result in denial of claim. With the one exception discussed below, there are no penalties under these programs for refusing to supply information. However, failure to furnish information regarding the medical services rendered or the amount charged would prevent payment of claims under these programs. Failure to furnish any other information, such as name or claim number, would delay payment of the claim. Failure to provide medical information under FECA could be deemed an obstruction.

It is mandatory that you tell us if you know that another party is responsible for paying for your treatment. Section 1128B of the Social Security Act and 31 USC 3801-3812 provide penalties for withholding this information.

You should be aware that P.L. 100-503, the "Computer Matching and Privacy Protection Act of 1988", permits the government to verify information by way of computer matches.

MEDICAID PAYMENTS (PROVIDER CERTIFICATION)

I hereby agree to keep such records as are necessary to disclose fully the extent of services provided to individuals under the State's Title XIX plan and to furnish information regarding any payments claimed for providing such services as the State Agency or Dept. of Health and Human Services may request.

I further agree to accept, as payment in full, the amount paid by the Medicaid program for those claims submitted for payment under that program, with the exception of authorized deductible, coinsurance, co-payment or similar cost-sharing charge.

SIGNATURE OF PHYSICIAN (OR SUPPLIER): I certify that the services listed above were medically indicated and necessary to the health of this patient and were personally furnished by me or my employee under my personal direction.

NOTICE: This is to certify that the foregoing information is true, accurate and complete. I understand that payment and satisfaction of this claim will be from Federal and State funds, and that any false claims, statements, or documents, or concealment of a material fact, may be prosecuted under applicable Federal or State laws.

According to the Paperwork Reduction Act of 1995, no persons are required to respond to a collection of information unless it displays a valid OMB control number. The valid OMB control number for this information collection is 0938-0999. The time required to complete this information collection is estimated to average 10 minutes per response, including the time to review instructions, search existing data resources, gather the data needed, and complete and review the information collection. If you have any comments concerning the accuracy of the time estimate(s) or suggestions for improving this form, please write to: CMS, Attn: PRA Reports Clearance Officer, 7500 Security Boulevard, Baltimore, Maryland 21244-1850. This address is for comments and/or suggestions only. DO NOT MAIL COMPLETED CLAIM FORMS TO THIS ADDRESS.

Sample Superbill for Clinical Pharmacy Services[a,b]

Pharmacists' Services
123 Main Street
Birmingham, AL 12345
123-456-7890 (P) 987-654-3210 (F)

Date of service:			Insurance:	
Patient name:			Cardholder name:	Previous balance:
Address:			Group #:	Today's charge:
Phone:			ID #:	Today's payment:
DOB:	Age:	Sex:	Provider name:	Balance due:

Description	*CPT Code*	*Billable Units*	*Description*	*CPT Code*	*Billable Units*	*Description*	*CPT Code*	*Billable Units*
Medication Therapy Management (MTM) Service			**Laboratory Services/Procedures**			**Immunization Services**		
New patient	99605		POC blood glucose	W82962		Influenza >3 yr old	90658 + G008	
Established pt.	99606		POC A1c	W85018		Influenza intranasal		
Additional 15 min	99607		POC INR	W85610		HPV	90649	
Full MTM review (check)			POC TC/HDL			Varicella (chickenpox)	90716	
Follow-up MTM review (check)			POC lipid panel	QW8006 1		VZV	90736	
MTM for diabetes self-management education			POC ALT	W84460		MMR	90707	
Initial	G0108		Other blood test			Immune globulin		
Established pt. level 1	G0108		Urine drug screen	80100/ 80101		PPV	90732 + G0009	
Established pt. level 2	G0108		Bone densitometry			Hepatitis A	90632	
Group education	G0109		Spirometry	94010		Hepatitis A/B combined	90636	
Group education, nondiabetes	$XX		Other			Hepatitis B	90746	
Smoking cessation consultation (individual)	$XX		Drug administration (nonvaccine)	90772		Tdap	90715	
Self-care consultation	$XX		International travel consult.	$XX		Td	90718	
						IPV	90713	

Known diagnosis (ICD-9 codes)							
		Incident to billing in a physician's office or clinic					
		New patient			Established patient		
			99201			99211	
			99202			99212	
			99203			99213	
			99204			99214	
			99205			99215	

Next patient visit:	
Referral to:	Provider signature: ______________________________
Instructions:	NPI #: __________________

You have agreed to the services provided above. We will make every attempt to collect from your insurance company, if applicable, any amount due above your copayment. You will be responsible for any services not covered by your insurance company.

[a]Used to document for patients and third-party payers the types of medication therapy management services provided.

[b]CPT = Current Procedural Terminology; POC = point of care; INR = international normalized ratio; TC/HDL = total cholesterol/high-density lipoprotein; ALT = alanine aminotransferase; HPV = human papillomavirus; VZV = varicella zoster vaccine; MMR = measles, mumps, rubella; PPV = pneumococcal polysaccharide vaccine; Tdap = tetanus–diphtheria–acellular pertussis vaccine; Td = tetanus–diphtheria vaccine; IPV = inactivated polio vaccine; ICD-9 = International Classification of Diseases, 9th edition.

Organizations Marketing Pharmacist-Provided Medication Therapy Management Services (MTMS) and Systems for Documenting MTMS

American Pharmacists Association Foundation
Washington, D.C.
www.aphafoundation.org/pharmacists___other_providers/HealthMapRx/
HealthMapRx partners local medication therapy management networks with employers and provides documentation system.

excelleRx, Inc.
Philadelphia, Pennsylvania
www.excellerx.com/excelleRx/index.asp
Provides MTMS and Xeris documentation system.

Medication Management Systems, Inc.
Minneapolis, Minnesota
www.medsmanagement.com/index.html
Provides Assurance system for documentation.

Mirixa Corporation
Alexandria, Virginia
www.mirixa.com/
Provides medication therapy management network administration and MirixaPro documentation system.

Outcomes Pharmaceutical Healthcare
Des Moines, Iowa
www.getoutcomes.com/
Provides medication therapy management network administration and documentation system.

PharmMD Solutions, LLC
Brentwood, Tennessee
www.pharmmd.com/
Provides medication therapy management, network administration, and documentation system.

Additional Information Sources

In addition to the professional resources identified in Chapter 5, pharmacists may find the following resources of value.

For the CPT coding manual and information about CPT codes:
American Medical Association
www.ama-assn.org/ama/pub/category/3113.html
800-621-8335

To purchase this or other textbooks related to practice development and medication therapy management services (MTMS):
American Pharmacists Association
www.pharmacist.com
800-237-2742

To learn of state-based opportunities in MTMS, contact your state pharmacy association, or:
National Alliance of State Pharmacy Associations
www.naspa.us/
804-285-4431

To find ICD-9 and ICD-10 diagnosis codes free of charge (online only):
MediLexicon
www.medilexicon.com/icd9codes.php

To find Health Care Procedural Coding System (HCPCS) codes free of charge (online only):
Centers for Medicare and Medicaid Services
www.cms.hhs.gov/HCPCSReleaseCodeSets/ANHCPCS/list.asp

An excellent continuing-education resource on developing marketing strategies for your MTMS:
American Pharmacists Association
www.pharmacist.com/AM/Template.cfm?Section=Pharmacist_Practitioners&TEMPLATE=/CM/ContentDisplay.cfm&CONTENTID=14637

For a discussion of documentation of MTMS that goes beyond the overview provided in Chapter 7:
www.pharmacist.com/AM/Template.cfm?Section=Pharmacist_Practitioners&TEMPLATE=/CM/ContentDisplay.cfm&CONTENTID=14639

Index

Note: Italic *f* indicates material in figures; italic *t* indicates material in tables.

Index

D

Index

Index

T

U

V

W